Praise for Sonia Sotomayor's

MY BELOVED WORLD

"In her own often straightforward, occasionally soaring writing style, Sotomayor succeeds in *My Beloved World* in crafting an often old-fashioned tale of overcoming obstacles." —*Los Angeles Times*

"By turns supernatural and amusing, tragic, sensuous and pragmatic. . . . She is not only a Supreme Court justice; Sonia Sotomayor is a fine writer." —*San Francisco Chronicle*

"*My Beloved World* is primarily a story of a child's astonishing resilience and determination in the face of formidable circumstances. . . . Sotomayor's steely resolve and sharp memory . . . attest not only to the truth of her story but to its usefulness as a primer on how to succeed in life." —*The Plain Dealer*

"[*My Beloved World*] stands very much on its own—not unlike Barack Obama's first book, *Dreams From My Father*— as a compelling and powerfully written memoir about identity and coming of age. . . . If the outlines of Justice Sotomayor's life are well known by now, her searching and emotionally intimate memoir, *My Beloved World*, nonetheless has the power to surprise and move the reader." —*The New York Times*

"[A] solitary journey, and it ends with Sotomayor donning one set of black robes, soon to be followed by others. An individual achievement that stands as a landmark in the much larger, collective civic awakening of the Latino U.S."
—*Richmond Times Dispatch*

"Perhaps the most rewarding takeaway is the self-assuredness one gleans from the pages of Sotomayor's memoir. For it is a personal embrace of the qualities we all strive to hold on to: a strong sense of family, a connection to traditions, and a solid understanding of one's roots. . . . They are part of an identity that Sotomayor has never rejected. Indeed, she has used it to shape her ability to overcome weaknesses by gaining new strengths."
—*Indian Country Today*

"You'll see in Sotomayor a surprising wealth of candor, wit, and affection. No topic is off limits, not her diabetes, her father's death, her divorce, or her cousin's death from AIDS. Put the kettle on, reader, it's time for some real talk with Titi Sonia. . . . The author shines in her passages on childhood, family, and self-discovery. Her magical portraits of loved ones bring to mind Sandra Cisneros's *The House on Mango Street*; both authors bring a sense of childlike wonder and empathy to a world rarely seen in books, a Latin-American and womancentric world."
—*The Christian Science Monitor*

"Amazingly candid. . . . [A]n intimate and honest look at her extraordinary life and the support and blessings that propelled her forward."
—*Booklist* (starred review)

"The book delivers on its promise of intimacy in its depictions of Sotomayor's family, the corner of Puerto Rican immigrant New York where she was raised, and the link she feels to the island where she spent childhood summers. . . . This is a woman who knows where she comes from and has the force to bring you there. Sotomayor does this by being clear-eyed about the flaws of the adults who raised her—she lets them be complicated. . . . 'I've spent my whole life learning how to do things that were hard for me,' Sotomayor tells an acquaintance when he asks whether becoming a judge will be difficult for her. Yes, she has. And by the time you close *My Beloved World*, you understand how she has mastered judging, too."

—*The New York Times Book Review*

"With buoyant humor and thoughtful candor, she recounts her rise from a crime-infested neighborhood in the South Bronx to the nation's highest court. 'I will be judged as a human being by what readers find here,' Sotomayor writes. We, the jury in this case, find her irresistible."

—*Washingtonian*

"*My Beloved World* is filled with inspiring, and surprisingly candid, stories about how the Supreme Court's first Hispanic justice overcame a troubled childhood to attend Princeton and Yale Law School, eventually earning a seat on the nation's highest court."   —*The Wall Street Journal*

"Remarkable. . . . A portrait of a genuinely interesting person."   —*Daily Beast*

"In a refreshing conversational style, Sotomayor tells her fascinating life story with the hope of providing 'comfort, perhaps even inspiration' to others, particularly children, who face hard times. 'People who live in difficult circumstances,' Sotomayor writes in her preface, 'need to know that happy endings are possible.'"

—*The Boston Globe*

"Classic Sotomayor: intelligent, gregarious and at times disarmingly personal. . . . A portrait of an underprivileged but brilliant young woman who makes her way into the American elite and does her best to reform it from the inside. . . . I certainly hope *My Beloved World* inspires readers to chase their dreams." —Jason Farago, NPR

"Vital, loving, and incisive. . . . In this revealing memoir, Supreme Court Justice Sotomayor candidly and gracefully recounts her formative years. Her memoir shows both her continued self-reliance and her passion for community."

—*Library Journal* (starred review)

"Justice Sotomayor recounts numerous obstacles and remarkable achievements in this personal and inspiring autobiography. . . . Readers across the board will be moved by this intimate look at the life of a justice."

—*Publishers Weekly*

Sonia Sotomayor

MY BELOVED WORLD

Sonia Sotomayor graduated summa cum laude from Princeton in 1976 and from Yale Law School in 1979. She worked as assistant district attorney in New York County and then at the law firm of Pavia & Harcourt. From 1992 to 1998, she served as a judge of the U.S. District Court, Southern District of New York, and from 1998 to 2009 on the United States Court of Appeals for the Second Circuit. In May 2009, President Barack Obama nominated her as an Associate Justice of the Supreme Court; she assumed this role on August 8, 2009.

MY
BELOVED
WORLD

MY
BELOVED
WORLD

Sonia Sotomayor

VINTAGE BOOKS

A DIVISION OF RANDOM HOUSE LLC

NEW YORK

The Library of Congress has cataloged the Knopf edition as follows:
Sotomayor, Sonia.
My beloved world / Sonia Sotomayor.
p. cm.
1. Sotomayor, Sonia, 1954–
2. Hispanic American judges—Biography.
3. Hispanic American women—Biography.
4. Women judges—Biography. 5. Judges—United States—Biography.
6. United States. Supreme Court—Officials and employees—Biography.
I. Title.
KF8745.S67A3 2013
347.73'2634092—dc23
[B] 2012031797

Vintage ISBN: 978-0-345-80483-9

Book design by Cassandra J. Pappas

www.vintagebooks.com

Perdonadle al desterrado
ese dulce frenesí:
vuelvo a mi mundo adorado,
y yo estoy enamorado
de la tierra en que nací.

. . .

Forgive the exile
this sweet frenzy:
I return to my beloved world,
in love with the land where I was born.

—*from "To Puerto Rico (I Return),"*
by José Gautier Benítez

Preface

Since my appointment to the Supreme Court, I have spoken to a wide variety of groups in different settings, answering all sorts of questions. Many people, predictably, have asked about the law, the Court, and my journey as a judge. But many more, to my surprise, have asked about my personal story, curious to know how I had managed and been shaped by various circumstances in my early life, especially the ones that didn't naturally promise success.

At a conference on juvenile diabetes, a six-year-old asked plaintively if living with the disease ever gets easier. Elsewhere, a child who had recently lost a parent asked how I had coped with losing my father at an early age. Minority students have asked what it is like to live between two worlds: How do I stay connected to my community? Have I ever experienced discrimination? Many young lawyers, men as well as women, have asked how I balance my personal life with the demands of career. Most perplexing of all was the question that inspired this book: How much did I owe to having had a happy childhood? I struggled with that one; until this book I have not spoken publicly about some of my darker experiences growing up, and I would not have considered myself unqualifiedly happy as a child. Ultimately, though, I realized I did have sources of deep happiness, and these bred in me an optimism that proved stronger than any adversity.

Underlying all these questions was a sense that my life's story touches people because it resonates with their own circumstances. The challenges I have faced—among them material poverty, chronic illness, and being raised by a single mother—are not uncommon, but neither have they kept me from uncommon achievements. For many it is a source of hope to see someone realize her dreams while bearing such burdens. Having caught people's attention in this way, I've thought long and hard about what lessons my life might hold for others, young people especially. How is it that adversity has spurred me on instead of knocking me down? What are the sources of my own hope and optimism? Most essentially, my purpose in writing is to make my hopeful example accessible. People who live in difficult circumstances need to know that happy endings are possible.

A student recently posed another question that gave me pause: "Given that there are only nine Supreme Court Justices, each with life tenure, can anyone realistically aspire to such a goal? How do we hold on to dreams that, statistically, are almost impossible?" As I tell in these pages, the dream I first followed was to become a judge, which itself seemed far-fetched until it actually happened. The idea of my becoming a Supreme Court Justice—which, indeed, as a goal would inevitably elude the vast majority of aspirants—never occurred to me except as the remotest of fantasies. But experience has taught me that you cannot value dreams according to the odds of their coming true. Their real value is in stirring within us the will to aspire. That will, wherever it finally leads, does at least move you forward. And after a time you may recognize that the proper measure of success is not how much you've closed the distance to some far-off goal but the quality of what you've done today.

I have ventured to write more intimately about my personal life than is customary for a member of the Supreme Court, and with that candor comes a measure of vulnerability. I will be judged as a human being by what readers find here. There are hazards to openness, but they seem minor compared with the possibility that some readers may find comfort, perhaps even inspiration, from a close examination of how an ordinary person, with strengths and weaknesses like anyone else, has managed an extraordinary journey.

My law clerks will no doubt be aghast to see how often I've broken my own very strict rules about formal writing, which include injunctions against the use of contractions and split infinitives. Every rule, however, is bound by context, and a personal memoir requires a different style than a legal opinion.

Neither is a memoir the same as a biography, which aims for the most objective, factual account of a life. A memoir, as I understand it, makes no pretense of denying its subjectivity. Its matter is one person's memory, and memory by nature is selective and colored by emotion. Others who participated in the events I describe will no doubt remember some details differently, though I hope we would agree on the essential truths. I have taken no liberties with the past as I remember it, used no fictional devices beyond reconstructing conversations from memory. I have not blended characters, or bent chronology to convenience. And yet I have tried to tell a good story. If particular friends or family members find themselves not mentioned, or are disappointed to see their roles rendered as less prominent than they might have expected, I hope they will understand that the needs of a clear and focused telling must outweigh even an abundance of feeling.

Some readers may be disappointed that I have chosen to end this story twenty years ago, when I first became a judge. I've made this choice because of the personal nature of what I wish to tell. For though I believe my personal growth has continued since that time, it was by then that the person I remain was essentially formed. On the other hand, I have no such perspective or sense of completion regarding my judicial career. Each stage of it—first on the district court, then on the court of appeals, and now on the Supreme Court—has been unique; and I can't say with any certainty how any part will inform what I may yet accomplish as a Justice. In the meanwhile, it seems inappropriate to reflect on a course still taking shape, let alone on the political drama attending my nomination to the High Court, however curious some may be about that.

A final, more private, motive for writing this book bears mention. This new phase of my career has brought with it a profoundly disconcerting shift in my life. The experience of living in the public eye was impossible to anticipate fully and has, at times, been overwhelming. The psychological hazards of such a life are notorious, and it seems wise to pause and reflect on the path that has brought me to this juncture and to count the blessings that have made me who I am, taking care not to lose sight of them, or of my best self, as I move forward.

MY
BELOVED
WORLD

Prologue

I WAS BARELY AWAKE, and my mother was already screaming. I knew Papi would start yelling in a second. That much was routine, but the substance of their argument was new, and it etched that morning into my memory.

"You have to learn how to give it to her, Juli. I can't be here all the time!"

"I'm afraid to hurt her. My hands are trembling." It was true. When my father made his first attempt at giving me the insulin shot the day before, his hands were shaking so much I was afraid he would miss my arm entirely and stab me in the face. He had to jab hard just to steady his aim.

"Whose fault is it your hands tremble?"

Uh-oh, here we go.

"You're the nurse, Celina! You know how to do these things."

Actually, when Mami gave me the shot my first morning home from the hospital, she was so nervous that she jabbed me even harder, and hurt me even worse, than Papi would the next day.

"That's right, I'm the nurse. I have to work and help support this family. I have to do everything! But I can't be here all the time, Juli, and she's going to need this for the rest of her life. So you better figure it out."

The needles hurt, but the screaming was worse. It made me feel tired, carrying around the weight of their sadness. It was bad enough when they were fighting about the milk, or the housework, or the money, or the drinking. The last thing I wanted was for them to fight about me.

"I swear, Juli, you'll kill that child if you don't learn how to do this!"

As usual, she walked away and slammed the door behind her, so she had to scream even louder to continue the fight.

If my parents couldn't pick up the syringe without panicking, an even darker prospect loomed: my grandmother wouldn't be up to the job either. That would be the end of my weekly sleepovers at her apartment and my only escape from the gloom at home. It then dawned on me: if I needed to have these shots every day for the rest of my life, the only way I'd survive was to do it myself.

The first step, I knew, was to sterilize the needle and syringe. Not yet eight years old, I was barely tall enough to see the top of the stove, and I wasn't sure how to perform the tricky maneuver with match and gas to light the burner. So I dragged a chair the couple of feet from table to stove—the kitchen was tiny—and climbed up to figure it out. The two small pots for Mami's *café con leche* were sitting there, getting cold while they fought, the coffee staining its little cloth sack in one pot, *la nata* forming a wrinkled skin on top of the milk in the other.

"Sonia! What are you doing? You'll burn the building down, *nena*!"

"I'm going to give myself the shot, Mami." That silenced her for a moment.

"Do you know how?" She looked at me levelly, seriously.

"I think so. At the hospital they had me practice on an orange."

My mother showed me how to hold the match while turning the dial, to make the flame whoosh to life in a blue ring. Together we filled the pot with water, enough to cover the syringe and needle and some extra in case it boiled down. She directed me to wait for the bubbles and only then to start counting five minutes by the clock. I had learned how to tell time the year before, in first grade. After the water had boiled long enough, she said, I would still need to wait for the syringe to cool. I watched the pot and the invisibly slow creep of the clock's hand until tiny, delicate chains of bubbles rose from the glass syringe and the needle, my mind racing through a hundred other things as I marked the time.

Watching water boil would try the patience of any child, but I was as physically restless as I was mentally and had well earned the family nickname Ají—hot pepper—for my eagerness to jump headlong into any mischief impelled by equal parts curiosity and rambunctiousness. But believing that my life now depended on this morning ritual, I would soon figure out how to manage the time efficiently: to get dressed, brush my teeth, and get ready for school in the intervals while the pot boiled or cooled. I probably learned more self-discipline from living with diabetes than I ever did from the Sisters of Charity.

Fainting in church was how it all started. We had just stood up to sing, and I felt as if I were suffocating. The singing seemed far away, and then the light from the stained-glass windows turned yellow. Everything turned yellow, and then it went black.

When I opened my eyes, all I could see was the principal, Sister Marita Joseph, and Sister Elizabeth Regina, their worried faces upside down and pale inside their black bonnets. I was lying on the tile floor in the sacristy, shivering cold from the water splashed all over my face. And scared. So they called my mother.

Although I went to Mass every Sunday, which was obligatory for students at Blessed Sacrament School, my parents never did. When my mother arrived, the Sisters made a big fuss. Had this ever happened before? Come to think of it, there was the time I'd fallen off the slide, the sudden dizziness as I stepped over the top of the ladder before the ground came rushing up to me in a long moment of panic . . . She had to take me to the doctor, the nuns insisted.

Dr. Fisher was already firmly established as a family hero. All of our relatives were under his care at one time or another, and his house calls did as much to ease fears and panics as they did aches and pains. A German immigrant, he was an old-fashioned country doctor who just happened to be practicing in the Bronx. Dr. Fisher asked a lot of questions, and Mami told him I was losing weight and always thirsty and that I had started wetting the bed, which was so mortifying that I would try not to fall asleep.

Dr. Fisher sent us to the lab at Prospect Hospital, where my mother worked. I didn't see trouble coming, because I perceived Mr. Rivera in the lab to be a friend of mine. I thought I could trust him, unlike Mrs. Gibbs, my mother's supervisor, who had tried to hide the needle behind her back when I'd had my tonsils out. But when he tied a rubber tube around my arm, I realized this was no ordinary shot. The syringe looked almost as big as my arm, and as he got closer, I could see that the needle was sliced off at an angle with the hole gaping like a little mouth at the end of it.

As he approached, I screamed, "No!" Knocking the chair back, I ran across the hall and right out the front door. It seemed as if half the hospital were running right behind me, shouting "Catch her!" but I didn't turn around to look. I just dove under a parked car.

I could see their shoes. One of them bent down and stuck his nose into the shadow of the undercarriage. Shoes all around now, and hands reaching under the car. But I scrunched up like a turtle, until someone caught me by the foot. I was hollering so loud as they dragged me back to the lab that I couldn't have hollered any louder when the needle went in.

When we went back to Dr. Fisher after they took my blood, it was the first time I'd ever seen my mother cry. I was outside in the waiting room, but his office door was open a crack. I could hear her voice break and see her shoulders quaking. The nurse closed the door when she noticed I was watching, but I'd seen enough to understand that something was seriously wrong. Then Dr. Fisher opened the door and called me in. He explained that there was sugar in my blood, that it's called diabetes, and that I would have to change the way I ate. He reassured me that the bed-wetting would end when we had things under control: it was just the body's way of getting rid of excess blood sugar. He even told me that he also had diabetes, although I understood later that he had the more common type 2, while I had the rarer juvenile diabetes, or type 1, in which the pancreas stops producing insulin, making daily injections of insulin necessary.

Then he took a bottle of soda from the cupboard behind him and popped the top off. "Taste it. It's called No-Cal. Just like soda but without sugar."

I took a sip. "I don't really think so." Poor Dr. Fisher. My mother insisted that we always be polite even if that meant softening a strong opinion, a lesson that stuck with me. Perhaps my eventual enjoyment of being a litigator owes something to the license it gave me to disagree more openly with people.

"Well, there are lots of other flavors. Even chocolate."

I thought to myself: This doesn't add up. He's making it sound as if it's no big deal. Just skip dessert and drink a different soda. Why is my mother so upset?

We went straight from Dr. Fisher's office to my grandmother's home. Abuelita tucked me into her bed, even though it was the middle of the afternoon and I had long outgrown naps. She closed the curtains, and I lay there in the half dark listening as the front door kept opening and voices filled the living room. I could hear my father's sisters, Titi Carmen and Titi Gloria. My cousin Charlie was there too, and Gallego, my step-grandfather. Abuelita sounded terribly upset. She was talking about my mother as if she weren't there, and since I didn't hear Mami's voice at all, it was clear that she had left.

"It runs in families, *como una maldición.*"

"This curse is from Celina's side, for sure, not ours."

There was speculation about whether Mami's own mother had died of this terrible affliction and talk of a special herb that might cure it. Abuelita knew all about healing with herbs. The least sniffle or stomachache had her brewing noxious potions that would leave me with a lifelong aversion to tea of any sort. Now she was scheming with my aunts to get word to her brother in Puerto Rico. She would tell him where to find the plant, which he was to pick at dawn before boarding a flight from San Juan the same day so she could prepare it at the peak of potency. He actually pulled it off, but sadly Abuelita's herbal remedy would prove ineffective, and this failure of her skill in a case so close to her heart would disturb her deeply.

Abuelita's obvious anxiety that afternoon, and the talk of my other grandmother's death, did achieve one thing: it made me realize how serious this situation was. Now my mother's crying made sense to me, and I was shaken. I was even more shaken when I learned that I had to be hospitalized to stabilize my blood sugar levels, which was routine in those days.

IN 1962, when I was first diagnosed, the treatment of juvenile diabetes was primitive by today's standards, and life expectancy was much shorter. Nevertheless, Dr. Fisher had managed to locate the best care for the disease in New York City, and possibly in the entire country. He discovered that the Albert Einstein College of Medicine, a leader in juvenile diabetes research, ran a clinic at Jacobi Medical Center, a public hospital, which by luck happened to be located in the Bronx. The vastness of Jacobi Medical Center awed me. It made Prospect Hospital seem like a dollhouse.

Every morning, starting at eight o'clock, they would draw my blood repeatedly for testing. Hourly, they used the thick needle with the rubber tube on my arm, and every half hour they would slice my finger with a lance for a smaller sample. It continued until noon, and the next day they did the same thing over again. This went on for an entire week and part of the next. I didn't holler and I didn't run, but I have never forgotten the pain.

Other things they did, though less painful, seemed strange. They attached electrodes to my head. They brought me to a classroom in the hospital where I sat facing rows of young doctors who stared at me as an older doctor lectured about diabetes, about the tests they had done and more they still had to do. He rattled off terms like "ketones," "acidosis," "hypo-this and hyper-that," and much else that I didn't understand, all the while feeling very much the guinea pig and terrified.

BUT EVEN MORE THAN the clinical procedures, it was my absence from school for so long that set off my inner alarm. I knew I had to be seriously sick for my mother to allow it. School was just as important as work, she insisted, and she never once stayed home from work. Equally worrying, she brought me a present almost every day I was in the hospital: a coloring book, a puzzle, once even a comic book, which meant she was thinking hard about what I would like instead of what she wanted me to have.

My very last day at the hospital started again at eight o'clock with the big needle and the lances. My arm was aching, and my fingers were burning right from the very beginning. I made it through the first two hours, but just as they were lining up their instruments for the ten o'clock torture, something inside me broke. After all those days of being brave and holding it in, I started crying. And once I started, I couldn't stop. My mother must have heard me because she burst in, and I flew sobbing into her arms. "Enough!" she said, fiercer than I'd ever seen her. Fiercer even than when she fought with my father. "We stop now. She's done." She said it in a way that nobody—not the lab technician standing there with the syringe in his hand, not any doctor in Jacobi Medical Center—was going to argue with her.

———————

"DO YOU KNOW how much to give, Sonia?"

"Up to this line here."

"That's right. But do it carefully. You can't give too little and you can't give too much. And you have to be careful, Sonia, not to let any bubbles get into the needle. That's dangerous."

"I know how to do this part. But it doesn't make sense to say I'm *giving* it, Mami. I'm the one who's *getting* the shot."

"Whatever you say, Sonia."

"I'm doing both."

And I did. I held my breath, and I gave myself the shot.

One

I WAS NOT YET eight years old when I was diagnosed with diabetes. To my family, the disease was a deadly curse. To me, it was more a threat to the already fragile world of my childhood, a state of constant tension punctuated by explosive discord, all of it caused by my father's alcoholism and my mother's response to it, whether family fight or emotional flight. But the disease also inspired in me a kind of precocious self-reliance that is not uncommon in children who feel the adults around them to be unreliable.

There are uses to adversity, and they don't reveal themselves until tested. Whether it's serious illness, financial hardship, or the simple constraint of parents who speak limited English, difficulty can tap unsuspected strengths. It doesn't always, of course: I've seen life beat people down until they can't get up. But I have never had to face anything that could overwhelm the native optimism and stubborn perseverance I was blessed with.

At the same time, I would never claim to be self-made—quite the contrary: at every stage of my life, I have always felt that the support I've drawn from those closest to me has made the decisive difference between success and failure.

And this was true from the beginning. Whatever their limitations and frailties, those who raised me loved me and did the best they knew how. Of that I am sure.

The world that I was born into was a tiny microcosm of Hispanic New York City. A tight few blocks in the South Bronx bounded the lives of my extended family: my grandmother, matriarch of the tribe, and her second husband, Gallego, her daughters and sons. My playmates were my cousins. We spoke Spanish at home, and many in my family spoke virtually no English. My parents had both come to New York from Puerto Rico in 1944, my mother in the Women's Army Corps, my father with his family in search of work as part of a huge migration from the island, driven by economic hardship.

My brother, now Juan Luis Sotomayor Jr., M.D., but to me forever Junior, was born three years after I was. I found him a nuisance as only a little brother can be, following me everywhere, mimicking my every gesture, eavesdropping on every conversation. In retrospect, he was actually a quiet child who made few demands on anyone's attention. My mother always said that compared with me, caring for Junior was like taking a vacation. Once, when he was still tiny and I wasn't much bigger, my exasperation with him inspired me to lead him into the hallway outside the apartment and shut the door. I don't know how much later it was that my mother found him, sitting right where I'd left him, sucking his thumb. But I do know I got walloped that day.

But that was just domestic politics. On the playground, or once he started school at Blessed Sacrament with me, I watched out for him, and any bully thinking of messing with him would have to mix it up with me first. If I got beat up on

Junior's account, I would settle things with him later, but no one was going to lay a hand on him except me.

Around the time that Junior was born, we moved to a newly constructed public housing project in Soundview, just a ten-minute drive from our old neighborhood. The Bronxdale Houses sprawled over three large city blocks: twenty-eight buildings, each seven stories tall with eight apartments to a floor. My mother saw the projects as a safer, cleaner, brighter alternative to the decaying tenement where we had lived. My grandmother Abuelita, however, saw this move as a venture into far and alien territory, *el jurutungo viejo* for all practical purposes. My mother should never have made us move, she said, because in the old neighborhood there was life on the streets and family nearby; in the projects we were isolated.

I knew well enough that we were isolated, but that condition had more to do with my father's drinking and the shame attached to it. It constrained our lives as far back as my memory reaches. We almost never had visitors. My cousins never spent the night at our home as I did at theirs. Even Ana, my mother's best friend, never came over, though she lived in the projects too, in the building kitty-corner from ours, and took care of my brother, Junior, and me after school. We always went to her place, never the other way around.

The only exception to this rule was Alfred. Alfred was my first cousin—the son of my mother's sister, Titi Aurora. And just as Titi Aurora was much older than Mami, and more of a mother to her than a sister, Alfred, being sixteen years older than I, acted more as an uncle to me than a cousin. Sometimes my father would ask Alfred to bring him a bottle from the liquor store. We counted on Alfred a lot, in part because my father avoided driving. This annoyed me, as it clearly contributed to our isolation—and what's the point of having a car if you never drive it? I didn't understand until I was older that his drinking was probably the reason.

My father would cook dinner when he got home from work; he was an excellent cook and could re-create from memory any new dish he encountered as well as the Puerto Rican standards he no doubt picked up in Abuelita's kitchen. I loved every dish he made without exception, even his liver and onions, which Junior hated and shoveled over to me when Papi's back was turned. But as soon as dinner was over, the dishes still piled in the sink, he would shut himself in the bedroom. We wouldn't see him again until he came out to tell us to get ready for bed. It was just Junior and I every night, doing homework and not much else. Junior wasn't much of a conversationalist yet. Eventually, we got a television, which helped to fill the silence.

My mother's way of coping was to avoid being at home with my father. She worked the night shift as a practical nurse at Prospect Hospital and often on weekends too. When she wasn't working, she would drop us off at Abuelita's or sometimes at her sister Aurora's apartment and then disappear for hours with another of my aunts. Even though my mother and I shared the same bed every night (Junior slept in the other room with Papi), she might as well have been a log, lying there with her back to me. My father's neglect made me sad, but I intuitively understood that he could not help himself; my mother's neglect made me angry at her. She was beautiful, always elegantly dressed, seemingly strong and decisive. She was the one who moved us to the projects. Unlike my aunts, she chose to work. She was the one who insisted we go to Catholic school. Unfairly perhaps, because

I knew nothing then of my mother's own story, I expected more from her.

However much was said at home, and loudly, much also went unsaid, and in that atmosphere I was a watchful child constantly scanning the adults for cues and listening in on their conversations. My sense of security depended on what information I could glean, any clue dropped inadvertently when they didn't realize a child was paying attention. My aunts and my mother would gather in Abuelita's kitchen, drinking coffee and gossiping. "*¡No me molestes!* Go play in the other room now," an aunt would say, shooing me away, but I overheard much regardless: how my father had broken the lock on Titi Gloria's liquor cabinet, ruining her favorite piece of furniture; how whenever Junior and I slept over with our cousins, my father would phone every fifteen minutes all night long, asking, "Did you feed them? Did you give them a bath?" I knew well enough that my aunts and my grandmother were all prone to exaggeration. It wasn't really every fifteen minutes, but Papi did call a lot, as I gathered from my aunts' exasperated and mechanically reassuring side of the conversations.

The gossip would then take a familiar turn, my grandmother saying something like "Maybe if Celina ever came home, he wouldn't be drinking every night. If those kids had a mother who ever cooked a meal, Juli wouldn't be worrying about them all night." As much as I adored Abuelita—and no one resented my mother's absence more than I did—I couldn't bear this constant blaming. Abuelita was unconditionally loyal to blood kin. Her sons' wives were not outside the ambit of her protection, but they didn't enjoy the same immunity from prosecution. And often my mother's efforts to please Abuelita—whether a generously chosen gift or her ready services as a nurse—went dimly acknowledged. Even being Abuelita's favorite, I felt exposed and unmoored when she criticized my mother, whom I struggled to understand and forgive myself. In fact, she and I wouldn't achieve a final reconciliation before working on it for many years.

My surveillance activities became family legend the Christmas that Little Miss Echo arrived. I had seen the doll with its concealed tape recorder advertised on television and begged for it. It was the hottest gift of the season, and Titi Aurora had searched far and wide for a store that still had one in stock. I sent my cousin Miriam into the kitchen with the doll to bug the adults' conversation, knowing that I would have been immediately suspect. But before anything could be recorded, Miriam cracked and gave me up at the first question, and I got walloped anyway.

One overheard conversation had a lasting effect, though I now remember it only dimly. My father was sick: he had passed out, and Mami took him to the hospital. Tío Vitín and Tío Benny came to get Junior and me, and they were talking in the elevator about how our home was a pigsty, with dishes in the sink and no toilet paper. They spoke as if we weren't there. When I realized what they were saying, my stomach lurched with shame. After that I washed the dishes every night, even the pots and pans, as soon as we finished dinner. I also dusted the living room once a week. Even though no one ever came over, the house was always clean. And when I went shopping with Papi on Fridays, I made sure we bought toilet paper. And milk. More than enough milk.

The biggest fight my parents ever had was because of the milk. At dinnertime, Papi was pouring a glass for me, and his hands were shaking so badly the milk spilled all over the table. I cleaned up the mess, and he tried again with the same result. "Papi, please don't!" I kept repeating. It was all I could do to keep myself from crying; I was utterly powerless to stop him. "Papi, I don't want any milk!" But he didn't stop until the carton was empty. When my mother got home from work later and there was no milk for her coffee, all hell broke loose. Papi was the one who had spilled the milk, but I was the one who felt guilty.

Two

ABUELITA WAS GOING to cook for a party, and she wanted me to come with her to buy the chickens. I was the only one who ever went with her to the *vivero*. I loved Abuelita, totally and without reservation, and her apartment on Southern Boulevard was a safe haven from my parents' storms at home. Since those years, I have come to believe that in order to thrive, a child must have at least one adult in her life who shows her unconditional love, respect, and confidence. For me it was Abuelita. I was determined to grow up to be just like her, to age with the same ungraying, exuberant grace. Not that we looked much alike: she had very dark eyes, darker than mine, and a long face with a pointed nose, framed by long straight hair—nothing like my pudgy nose and short, curly mop. But otherwise we recognized in each other a twin spirit and enjoyed a bond beyond explanation, a deep emotional resonance that sometimes seemed telepathic. We were so much alike, in fact, that people called me Mercedita—little Mercedes—which was a source of great pride for me.

Nelson, who among my many cousins was closest to me in age as well as my inseparable coconspirator in every adventure, also had a special connection with Abuelita. But even Nelson never wanted to go with Abuelita to the *vivero* on Saturday mornings because of the smell. It wasn't just the chickens that smelled. They had baby goats in pens and pigeons and ducks and rabbits in cages stacked up against a long wall. The cages were stacked so high that Abuelita would climb up a ladder on wheels to see into the top rows. The birds would all be squawking and clucking and flapping and screeching. There were feathers in the air and sticking to the wet floor, which was slippery when they hosed it down, and there were turkeys with mean eyes watching you. Abuelita inspected all the chickens to find a plump and lively one.

"*Mira*, Sonia, see that one in the corner just sitting there with droopy eyes?"

"He looks like he's falling asleep."

"That's a bad sign. But this one, see how he's ready to fight the others when they come close? He's feisty and fat, and I promise you he's tasty."

After Abuelita picked out the very best chicken, it was my job to watch them butcher it while she waited in line for eggs. In a room all closed up in glass, a man stood breaking necks, one after another, and a machine plucked the feathers. Another man cleaned the birds, and another weighed each one and wrapped it up in paper. It was a fast-moving line, as in a factory. I had to watch carefully to make sure that the chicken we'd chosen was the one we got in the end. I was supposed to tell Abuelita if they mixed them up, but it never happened.

We would walk back under the crisscrossed shadows of the train tracks overhead, up Westchester Avenue toward Southern Boulevard and home—which is what Abuelita's house felt like to me. Of course Abuelita's house wasn't a real house like the one her daughter Titi Gloria lived in, in the far northern part of the Bronx, with a front porch and rosebushes. Abuelita lived in a five-story tenement, three apartments to a floor, with a fire escape that zigzagged up the front, like our old building on Kelly Street, where we lived before moving to the projects.

As we walked back, Abuelita would stop to choose vegetables from the crates that were lined up on the sidewalk. For almost every meal she fried *tostones,* so we'd buy green plantains, and also peppers, some green ones and some little sweet ones, and onions, tomatoes, *recao,* and garlic to make *sofrito.* She would always haggle, and though she made it sound as if she were complaining about the quality and how expensive everything was, by the end she'd be laughing with the *vendedor.* All these years later, an open market still stirs in me the urge to haggle the way I learned from Abuelita.

"*¿Sonia, quieres una china?*"

Abuelita loved oranges, but they were expensive most of the year, so we would buy just one to share as a treat, and she'd ask me to choose. My father taught me how to choose fruit—how to make sure it's ripe by smelling its sweetness. My father had shown me how to choose good meat too, with enough fat for flavor, and how to recognize if it's not fresh. I went grocery shopping with Papi on Fridays, which was payday. Those shopping trips were the best times of the week for me, not counting my days at Abuelita's. Papi and I would walk to the new Pathmark that was built on the empty lot near our projects and come home with our cart filled. I'd pull the cart while Papi toted the extra bags that didn't fit.

I could tell we were almost back at Abuelita's when I saw the marquee across the street, though we never went to see movies there because of the prostitutes standing around.

When my cousin Miriam—Nelson's sister and Titi Carmen's daughter—asked me what "prostitute" meant, I wasn't sure either, but I knew it was bad and that they wore very short skirts and very high heels and lots of makeup. We would figure out more of what the occupation entailed by the time the look came into fashion in the late 1960s, distressing our mothers deeply. When Titi Gloria did take us to the movies, it was at a different theater, farther down Southern Boulevard, and usually to see Cantinflas, the brilliant Mexican comic actor whose humor was as deft verbally as Charlie Chaplin's was physically.

Our shopping trip would conclude with a final stop to pick up bread and milk at the bodega a few doors down from Abuelita's. The bodega, a tiny grocery store, is the heart of every Hispanic neighborhood and a lifeline in areas with no supermarkets in walking distance. In those days, the bread they sold was so fresh that its warm smell filled the store. Abuelita would give me *la tetita,* the crunchy end, even though she liked it too, I knew. The bodega was always crowded with the same guys having their daily party. They sat in the corner, reading *El Diario* and arguing about the news. Sometimes one of them would read the *Daily News* and explain to the others in Spanish what it said. I could tell when he was improvising or embellishing the story; I knew what news sounded like in English. Usually, they only read the *Daily News* for the horse-racing results, although they didn't actually follow the horses. The last three digits of the total bets taken at the track became the winning number for the illegal lottery they played.

Before Abuelita moved, when she still lived on Kelly Street, there was a bodega right downstairs from her apartment. Sometimes she would send me downstairs by myself with a dollar bill wrapped up in a napkin that had numbers written on it. I had to tell the man whether she wanted to play them straight or in combination, or fifty cents each way. My grandmother counted extraordinary luck among her many gifts. Sometimes she saw the winning numbers in her dreams. I've never dreamed of numbers, but I've inherited more than my share of luck at games of chance, winning many a stuffed animal, and I'm even better at games like poker, where skill mediates luck. Sometimes Abuelita would see bad luck coming too, and that brought fear to my family. Too often in the past she had been right.

The stairs up to the third-floor apartment were narrow and dark, and Abuelita didn't have an elevator to rely on as we did. But in the projects, the elevator was more than a convenience: Junior and I were absolutely forbidden to take the stairs, where my mother had once been mugged and where addicts regularly shot up, littering the scene with needles and other paraphernalia. I can still hear Mami's warning that we should never, but never, touch those needles or take that junk: if we did, we would surely die.

Mami and my aunts would often be at Abuelita's when we got back, crowded into the kitchen for coffee and gossip. Abuelita would join them while I joined Nelson and my other cousins at the bedroom window to make faces at the passengers zipping by on the elevated train that ran just at the height of Abuelita's apartment. Gallego, my step-grandfather, would be busy with his own preparations for the party, choosing the dance music. His hands trembled slightly with Parkinson's disease, still in its early stages then, as he lined up the record albums.

Once a month, my mother and aunts would help Abuelita make *sofrito,* the Puerto Rican vegetable and spice base that enhances the flavors in any dish. Abuelita's kitchen would turn into a factory, with all of the women cleaning and peeling, slicing and chopping. They would fill up jars and jars of the stuff, enough for a month's worth of dinners in each of their homes, and enough for the Saturday parties too. On the table, waiting for their turn in the blender, were big piles of chopped peppers, onions, tomatoes: my target.

"Sonia, get your hands out of there!"

"Give me that! *¡Te vas a enfermar!* You'll get sick; you can't eat it raw!" Oh yes I can. I inherited adventurous taste buds from Papi and Abuelita, and I'll still happily eat many things more timid palates won't venture.

WHEN WE WENT to Abuelita's for the parties that happened most Saturdays, Mami made the hopeless effort to have me get dressed up. My dress would get wrinkled or stained almost immediately, and ribbons never stayed put in my hair, which Abuelita blamed on the electrodes the doctors had applied to my head. It's true that my curls disappeared about that time, but my hair had always been too thin for ribbons. Miriam by contrast always looked like a princess doll in a glass case, no matter the occasion. It would take me most of my life to feel remotely put together, and it's still an effort.

As soon as the door opened, I would catapult into Abuelita's arms. Wherever in the apartment she was, I would find her first.

"Sonia, careful!" Mami would say to me. "We just got here and already you're a mess." And then, to Abuelita, "Too much energy, too much talking, too much running around. I'm sorry, Mercedes, I don't know what to do with her."

"*Para,* Celina. Let the child be. There's nothing wrong with her except too much energy." Abuelita was on my side, always, and Mami was always apologizing to Abuelita. Sometimes even I wanted to say "*¡Para, Mami!*"

Next I would run to find Nelson, who would invariably be lying on the bed reading a comic book while waiting for me. Nelson was a genius, and my best friend on top of being my cousin. I never got bored talking to him. He could figure out how anything worked, and together we pondered mysteries of the natural world, like gravity. He was up for any game I could devise, including jousting knights, which involved charging at each other across the living room, each carrying on his or her back a younger brother armed with a broom or a mop. Miriam tried to stop us, but it didn't prevent Eddie, her little brother, from falling off Nelson and breaking a leg. When the screams of pain brought my aunt running, the blame was assigned, as usual, before any facts were established: "Sonia! What did you do now?" Another walloping for that one.

Tío Benny, who was Nelson, Miriam, and Eddie's dad, was determined that Nelson would grow up to be a doctor. In my eyes, Tío Benny was the ideal father. He spent time with his kids and took them on outings, which occasionally included me too. He spoke English, which meant he could go to parent-teacher conferences. Best of all, he didn't drink. I would have traded fathers with Nelson in a heartbeat. But sadly, for all his brilliance, Nelson wouldn't live up to Tío Benny's dreams, and I would do well despite a less than perfect father.

Abuelita's apartment was small enough that wherever we settled down to play, the warm smells of her feast would find us, beckoning like cartoon ribbons in the air. Garlic and onions calling, still the happiest smells I know.

"Mercedes, you should open your own restaurant."

"Don't be shy, there's plenty."

The dominoes never stopped for dinner. The game was serious. Someone would have to lose the whole match and give up the seat before even thinking about food. "*¿Tu estás ciego?* It's right in front of your eyes!" They'd yell a lot and pretend to be angry.

"Benny, wake up and look at what you have!" Mami counters. She was good at this and could keep track of every bone played.

"Hey, no cheating! How many times are you going to cough? Somebody get this man a drink, he's choking!"

"Don't look at me, I'm honest. Mercedes is the one who cheats."

"I know you have that *ficha*, so play it!"

"Nice one, Celina."

Gallego's out of the game, calling foul as he goes. He picks up his *güiro* and strums a ratchety rhythm on the gourd, playing along with the record, as if he wishes someone would show up with a guitar. Instead, sooner or later someone would lift the needle off the record, cutting off Los Panchos mid-song. The voices in the living room would settle to a hush, and all eyes would turn to Abuelita, resting on the couch, having cleaned up and taken a turn at dominoes. When the music stopped, that was the cue for those in the kitchen to crowd in the doorway of the living room. Nelson and I would scramble to a spot under the table where we could see. It was time for poetry.

Abuelita stands up, closes her eyes, and takes a deep

breath. When she opens them and begins to recite, her voice is different. Deeper, and vibrant in a way that makes you hold your breath to listen.

> *Por fin, corazón, por fin,*
> *alienta con la esperanza . . .*

I couldn't understand the words exactly, but that didn't matter. The feeling of the poem came through clearly in the music of Abuelita's voice and in the look of faraway longing in the faces of her listeners.

Her long black hair is tied back simply and her dress is plain, but to my eyes she looks more glamorous than anyone trying to be fancy. Now her arms stretch wide and her skirt swirls as she turns, reaching for the whole horizon. You can almost see green mountains, the sea and the sky unfolding, the whole world being born as she lifts her hand. As it turns, her fingers spread open like a flower blooming in the sun.

> *. . . y va la tierra brotando*
> *como Venus de la espuma.*

I look around. She has the whole room mesmerized. Titi Carmen wipes a tear.

> *Para poder conocerla*
> *es preciso compararla,*
> *de lejos en sueños verla;*
> *y para saber quererla*
> *es necesario dejarla.*

¡Oh! no envidie tu belleza,
de otra inmensa población
el poder y la riqueza,
que allí vive la cabeza,
y aquí vive el corazón.

Y si vivir es sentir,
y si vivir es pensar . . .

The poems that Abuelita and her listeners loved were often in the key of nostalgia and drenched in rosy, sunset hues that obscured the poverty, disease, and natural disasters that they had left behind. Not that their yearnings were unfounded. As the poet says, "To know it, you need to see it in dreams from afar. To learn how to love it, you need to leave it." Even those of the generations following who were born here, who have settled decisively into a mainland existence and rarely have reason to visit the island—even we have corners of our hearts where such a nostalgia lingers. All it takes to spark it is a poem, or a song like "En Mi Viejo San Juan."

The parties always wound down late. The stragglers had to be fed; Charlie and Tony, Titi Gloria's sons, might stop by after their Saturday night dates. Most others would say their good-byes and go home, like Tío Vitín and Titi Judy, who typically left carrying their kids, my cousins Lillian and Elaine, fast asleep, drooped over a shoulder.

But for those who remained, what often happened next was the climax of the evening. The *velada* was something that no one ever talked about; adults would change the subject casually if a kid asked a question. The kitchen table would be cleared and moved into the living room. A couple of neighbors from downstairs would appear, joining the party quietly. My mother and Titi Gloria would retire to the kitchen. Mami thought the whole business was silly and didn't want any part of it. Titi Gloria was actually scared of the spirits.

The remaining kids—Nelson, Miriam, Eddie, Junior, and I—would be corralled in the bedroom and ordered to sleep. We knew that nothing would happen until the adults believed we were snoozing, and they were dead serious about this. Somehow they failed to reckon with the power of my curiosity, or how easily I could impose my will on the other kids. We all lay on the bed in watchful silence, perfectly still, waiting.

There was just enough light coming from the street and through the curtains on the glazed doors separating the bedroom from the living room to make the atmosphere cozy or spooky, depending on your mood. I could hear the fading rumble of the El train going by. I could hear by their breathing when Junior and Eddie both conked out.

As we lay there, my mind would rehearse what Charlie had told us: how Abuelita and Gallego call the spirits to ask them questions; how they were not evil but they were powerful, and you had to develop your own powers if you wanted their help; how Abuelita's spirit guide was called Madamita Sandorí and spoke with a Jamaican accent. His eyes got wide just talking about it. Charlie and Tony were Alfred's age, an in-between generation much older than the rest of the cousins. Charlie was adult enough that they let him sit at the table for the *velada*. Gallego, who was as skilled an *espiritista* as Abuelita, wanted to teach Charlie, but Charlie did not want that responsibility. It was one thing to have the gift, quite another to dedicate yourself and study it.

As strange as they were, Charlie's reports of the supernatural made sense. They weren't like Alfred's unbelievable stories, about the ghosts of dead *jíbaros* riding horses around San Germán, intended only to scare us. I knew that Abuelita used her magic on the side of good. She used it for healing and for protecting the people she loved. Of course I understood that a person with a talent for engaging the spirit world could equally put it to work for darker ends—*brujería*, or witchcraft. In Abuelita's own building one of the neighbors was known to put curses on people. I was forbidden to go near her door on penalty of getting smacked, which was something Abuelita had never done, so I knew she meant it.

Finally, the little bell would ring very softly. That was the cue. Nelson, Miriam, and I would climb off the bed and sneak up to the glazed doors. We'd stick our noses to the panes, peering through the tiny gaps at the edge of the curtain stretched and pinned over the glass. All I could see was the backs of chairs, the backs of heads, shoulders hunched by candlelight in a tight circle around the table. The bell would tinkle again, but except for that one clear note it was impossible to make out any sounds through the door.

I would carefully open the door a tiny crack, and we would huddle to listen. It was good to be close together, just in case. Gallego would always be the first to talk, and not in his usual voice. It didn't sound like Spanish, but it wasn't English either. It sounded like someone chewing words and swallowing them. Choking on them. Then the voice coming out of Gallego would moan louder until the table moved, seeming to rise off the floor, signaling the spirits' arrival. Miriam, trembling, would scoot back into bed fast. I wouldn't give up so easily. But no matter how hard I tried, I couldn't decipher the garbled words. After Nelson and I got tired of trying, we'd join Miriam in bed. Nelson would pull the blanket over his head and whisper in mock exasperation, "How do they expect us to sleep with a house full of spirits?" We'd all lie still for a minute. Then Nelson would pretend to snore very softly, and Miriam and I would start giggling.

EXCEPT FOR my very earliest memories, when we still lived on Kelly Street in the same tenement as Abuelita, my father hardly ever came along to the parties. It was easier that way. On the rare occasions when he did come—on Mother's Day or Thanksgiving—I was nervous, watching and waiting for the inevitable signs of trouble. Even in the midst of the wildest mayhem that Nelson and I could concoct, even sinking my teeth into Abuelita's irresistible crispy chicken, even when everyone else was lost in music and laughter, I would be watching my father from the corner of my eye. It would start almost imperceptibly. His fingers would slowly curl up into claws. Then his face gradually scrunched up, just slightly at first, until finally it was frozen into a contorted grimace.

I usually noticed the early signs before my mother did, and for an agonizing interval I watched them both, waiting for her to notice. As soon as she did, there would be sharp words. It was time to go home, while he could still walk. I didn't have a name for what was happening, didn't understand what alcoholic neuropathy was. I only knew that I saw my father receding from us, disappearing behind that twisted mask. It was like being trapped in a horror film, complete with his lumbering Frankenstein walk as he made his exit and the looming certainty that there would be screaming when we got home.

Best were the times when I didn't have to go home. Most Saturday nights I stayed over at Abuelita's. When there was a party, Mami would take Junior home; Tío Benny and Titi Carmen somehow managed to get Nelson, Miriam, and Eddie down the street and into their own beds.

When I woke up in the morning, I would have Abuelita all to myself. She would stand at the stove in the housecoat she always wore for an apron, her pockets full of cigarettes and tissues, making the thick, fluffy pancakes she knew I loved. Those mornings were heaven. When Mami came to take me home later, I would kiss Abuelita good-bye. *"Bendición, Abuelita."* She would hug me and say without fail every time we parted, *"Que Dios te bendiga, te favorezca y te libre de todo mal y peligro."* May God bless you, favor you, and deliver you from all evil and danger. Just her saying it made it so.

Three

WITH THE EXCEPTION of my cousin Nelson, who was in a category of his own, Gilmar was my best friend in elementary school. To tell the truth, he was my only real friend who wasn't a cousin. He lived in the Bronxdale projects too, in the building across from ours, and we played together outside almost every day.

We were lying down in the concrete pipes next to the far playground, our favorite hiding place, when he told me the news. His parents—Gilbert and Margaret, who'd each given him a bit of their names—had decided to move to California. They had palm trees in California, he told me, and the weather was always sunny. I had seen palm trees when I visited Puerto Rico, but beyond that I had no mental picture of California. Still, I could imagine what having to leave must have felt like to Gilmar: not seeing our corner of the world and all the people in it anymore, maybe ever.

"Gilmar, you have to say good-bye to everybody. Everybody! Come on, I'll do it with you."

The good-bye tour on which I accompanied Gilmar that day was a snapshot of our life in the projects. Pops was the first person we both thought of. We scrambled out of the pipe and ran to the gray truck he kept parked on the service road off Bruckner Boulevard. Every day when my father got home from work, he would give us each a penny, and we would run over to Pops's truck to buy candy. On Fridays we got a dime, because it was payday.

Pops was surprised to see us so early that day; Gilmar explained that he was moving to California. Pops said he was sad to see Gilmar go, and they shook hands. Then he let us each choose a candy and said we didn't have to pay.

We went to Louie's building next and knocked on his door. Louie lived with his grandmother because his parents had died in a car accident. It was a story that I'd only heard in neighbors' whispers, but it seemed to be confirmed by the fact that his grandmother always wore black. She was Jewish, but I surmised that they had the same custom we did, of wearing black for *el luto* when people die. Louie attended Hebrew school and didn't play much with the other kids in the projects, but Gilmar and I played with him because I liked his grandmother. She invited us in that day, but we only stayed for a minute, because we also had to say good-bye to another grandmother in the next building over.

Mrs. Beverly also had a grandson living with her, in this case because his mother had problems. Jimmy might have had something wrong with him too; it was hard to say. Maybe he was just different, or a little slow; anyway, it was clear to me that he was more than the typical burden an elderly woman might bear caring for a young boy, and that gave Mrs. Beverly a heroic aura in my eyes, especially since she also held down an office job. Sometimes my mother and I would run into her on the street and stop to chat. She always wore a fur coat even when the weather was mild, and I thought she was very elegant. Mami explained to me that her coat was

probably the only precious thing she owned and that's why
it was important to her. I could see that it gave her pleasure
to wear it.

Mrs. Beverly wasn't expecting Gilmar and me at the door,
of course, and when he explained about California and said
good-bye, she almost cried. I've always thought grandmoth-
ers who take care of kids are special.

In the building kitty-corner from ours was Ana, my
mother's best friend, who kept an eye on Junior and me after
school until Papi got home. Ana's husband, Moncho, and
her daughter, Chiqui, were both home. Junior was there,
too. That was no surprise. He worshipped Moncho and followed him everywhere, even to take out the garbage. Ana
called Junior Moncho's *rabo de conejo,* his rabbit tail. Ana's
next-door neighbors, Irma and Gilbert, heard the commotion, so of course they came over to see what they were missing. It became almost a party as Gilmar said good-bye to
everyone.

We decided to walk over to Blessed Sacrament next, to
say good-bye to the nuns. Junior wanted to come with us, but
Moncho asked him to stay and help him cook an octopus,
which he had in a bucket. He showed it to us, all slimy arms
and suckers. Junior's eyes widened, his mouth was hanging.
"Mami doesn't cook *that,*" he said. Moncho was a merchant
marine who brought his kids exotic souvenirs from far-off
lands. I imagined he knew all about the depths of the ocean,
as well as how to cook things we'd never even heard of. He
certainly knew how to keep Junior occupied, and we continued our good-bye tour unencumbered.

When we reached Blessed Sacrament, the school yard was
empty and silent, abandoned for summer vacation, but the

office door was open. Sister Marita Joseph and Sister Elizabeth Regina both looked up.

"Hello, Sonia. Hello, Gilmar. Is everything all right? What brings you here on a Saturday?" Sister Marita Joseph looked apprehensive. When Gilmar explained that he was moving to California and saying good-bye to everyone, she asked, "And you, Sonia? Are you accompanying Gilmar on his good-byes?" I just nodded. I might have been a compulsive talker at home, but at school I spoke when spoken to. "That's very unusual," she said, looking at me strangely. I thought she approved, but I was not 100 percent sure. Why would it be unusual to keep a friend company? It had practically been my idea, even if it was Gilmar who was leaving.

Sister Elizabeth was our teacher that year. The best I could say about third grade was that it was a more or less continuous state of dread. As hard as I tried to keep a low profile, trouble seemed to find me. At Christmas, for instance, all the students brought presents for their teachers. That year my father had chosen my present for Sister Elizabeth. He'd never once come to school, had never even met her, but he chose the present, which he proudly handed to me in a long box, already gift wrapped by him. He wouldn't even tell me what it was.

Sister Elizabeth opened her presents in front of the class; there was soap, candy, a zippered prayer book, a box of stationery, and then there was Papi's present. Inside the box was a ruler. And not an ordinary wooden or plastic ruler, but a ruler made of some indestructible metal alloy no doubt invented to build rocket ships or bank safes—the Ruler of the Future, likely fabricated at the factory where Papi worked.

The sight of it was like a punch in the stomach, and actual

ones came my way at recess, as I had predicted from the dag-
gers of hatred being shot from every pair of eyes in the class.
Pleading ignorance won me no mercy, and I cried all the way
home. Fortunately, the hatred eventually died down, because
the ruler was never to reappear, either for measurement or
for punishment. Sister Elizabeth had her merciful side, too.

Discipline was what made Catholic school a good investment in my mother's eyes, worth the heavy burden of the
tuition fees. The Bronx public schools of the 1960s were
not yet as severely troubled as they would become, though
they struggled with de facto segregation and a chronic lack
of funding and offered a rough environment compared with
the parochial alternative. Still, none of my uncles and aunts
chose the sacrifice of sending my cousins to Catholic schools.

Among the black-bonneted nuns who managed class-
rooms of forty or fifty kids in my school, discipline was virtually an eighth sacrament. It might mean my copying a prayer
in my clumsy cursive however many times it took to get
every loop perfect or submitting to slaps and blows for some
infraction. I often stewed with righteous anger over physical punishments—my own or others'—especially when they
seemed disproportionate to the crime. I accepted what the
Sisters taught in religion class: that God is loving, merciful,
charitable, forgiving. That message didn't jibe with adults
smacking kids. I remember watching as Sister continued to
slap one boy who'd disrupted class even after the braces in
his mouth drew blood that ran down his chin. Many of my
classmates have happier memories of Blessed Sacrament, and
in time I would find my own satisfaction in the classroom.
My first years there, however, I met with little warmth. In
part, it was that the nuns were critical of working mothers,
and their disapproval was felt by latchkey kids. The irony of

course was that my mother wouldn't have been working such long hours if not to pay for that education she believed was the key to any aspirations for a better life.

AFTER WE'D FINISHED saying good-bye to everyone we could think of, Gilmar and I went back to say our good-byes to the concrete pipe and to each other. Lying inside, all we could see was the circle of bright sky. Our voices bounced around in the hollow of the concrete. We shouted and stretched the words out long and loud to get a really good echo.

"Good-bye, Gilmar!"

"Good-bye, Sonia!"

"I'll miss you!"

"Write me a letter!"

"Write me a letter, too!"

"From the palm trees?"

"From the palm trees!"

I WOULDN'T GET to see California until my second summer at law school. I remember driving the freeways with palm trees in view and thinking of Gilmar, among other friends I've lost touch with who may never know what memories they've left behind in my keeping.

Four

THIS IS my mother, Sonia, your *bisabuela*," said Abuelita. "Give her a kiss." The cheek that was my target was wrinkled and translucent, so fragile that I feared my lips would bruise it. Her eyes were blank. As I leaned in to kiss her, she seemed to pull away, but it was just the rocking chair easing back from my weight. There was no spark of awareness or curiosity. I don't know if I was more disturbed by this absence that gave no hint of how I should relate to her or by the shadow of Abuelita's features that I could see arranged inanimately on her mother's face.

Bisabuela Ciriata was in her nineties, though she looked two hundred years old to me. Her rocking chair of carved wood and woven cane tilted between this world and another that was beyond imagining, wafting scents of talcum and medicinal tea, auras of lace-edged *santos* whose eyes rolled up to a heaven too close for comfort.

We were in an area of San Juan called Santurce. Abuelita visited with her sisters and brothers while I played on the balcony or in half-hidden gardens. There had been ten of them all together, she said (Diezilita, Piatrina, Angelina, Eloys . . .), but I couldn't keep track or tell sisters and brothers from cousins and uncles and aunts. We were in a city, but it seemed to teeter on the edge of dissolving into nature. Vines snaked under iron fences and up balustrades. Chickens scrabbled under hibiscus bushes and bright yellow canario flowers. I watched the afternoon rains pour down like a curtain enclosing the balcony, rutting the street below with muddy streams, pounding on the corrugated roofs and wooden walls until Abuelita called me inside to a treat for merienda—maybe a tembleque, a gelatin made of coconut milk and sweet condensed milk, or fruits that I'd never seen in New York: guavas with their sharp perfume, quenepas with pits as big as grapes and a thin layer of featherlight flesh that puckered your mouth when you sucked on it, and mangoes of a melting sweetness unlike any I had tasted back home. At night, I slept with Abuelita in a room crowded with sisters and cousins, and the mosquito nets transformed our bed into a cozy hideaway among gauzy clouds. The traffic noise gave way to the rickety rhythm of the ceiling fan and coquís—the tiny musical frogs that are a symbol of the island—chirping in the shadows as I drifted to sleep.

On my earliest trips to Puerto Rico, when I was small—including my first as a toddler—it was just Abuelita and I. My mother was determined that she would never, ever go back to the island, but then she changed her mind. Some of the best summer vacations I remember were traveling with my mother and Junior to Mayagüez to visit her family.

Traveling with Mami to Puerto Rico was a little like being around Rip van Winkle on the day he woke up. She wore an expression of constant wonderment: everything surprised her by how much it had changed, except for the things that surprised her because they were just as she remembered them.

Barely out of the airport, we would stop at the food stands

on the roadside, joining the traffic jam of people returning who couldn't wait another minute for a first taste of home. The coconuts were big and green, not like the shriveled hairy brown things in boxes on the sidewalks of the Bronx. We would shake them and listen to find one that had a lot of liquid swishing around inside. The vendor would hack a piece off the top with a single swipe of a long machete and stick a straw in the hole. We would sip the almost-sweet nectar as the cars passed by on the highway, and I would listen to my cousin Papo and Titi Aurora, my mother's elder sister, filling my mother in on the news she needed to know before we saw the rest of the family: who'd married whom, who'd had whose baby, who'd been sick . . . Though Titi Aurora lived in New York, she went often to Puerto Rico to visit friends and sort out family problems. Before she finished her briefing, I'd hand the empty coconut back to the vendor with the machete, and he would hack it in two so I could use the little top piece that he'd cut off first to scoop out the creamy flesh, which to me was the best part of all.

Another day, my mother stopped a perfect stranger with his cow in a field beside the road and asked him for a glass of milk. He looked at her as if thinking: crazy American. Even in Puerto Rico people were drinking their milk pasteurized by then, not straight from the cow. But memories of the old ways must have overwhelmed her. She pushed the tin cup at me, but I wouldn't touch it. I just watched as she drank, a look of heavenly bliss spreading over her face.

IN MAYAGÜEZ, we usually stayed at Titi Maria's house. She was the first wife of Tío Mayo, my mother's eldest brother. Titi Maria helped to look after my mother when she was small, and their family bond outlasted the marriage. My mother is close to Tío Mayo's later families too; she has a talent for not taking sides, which is handy in a complicated extended family. It is a trait I've adopted, trying never to lose contact with cousins and second cousins whose parents have separated or divorced. We visit with everybody. There were family members whom I'd never even heard of before; my mother was set on showing Junior and me off to every single one of them over a cup of coffee. At first, people would laugh because our Spanish was clumsy and limited, but within days I could hear myself improving, and people would compliment me on it. Junior would have improved too if he'd have just opened his mouth and said something once in a while. It took me years to appreciate how hard it must have been for him to be always in the company of two chatty and strong-willed women.

At Titi Maria's house, my cousin Papo always prepared a special welcome. Waiting for me under the sink would be two whole shopping bags of mangoes that he'd gathered from under the trees up the hill in anticipation of our arrival. I ate them all day long, in spite of constant warnings that I would get sick. Looking back, I suspect I was getting a higher dosage of insulin than I needed—not uncommon for juvenile diabetics in that day—making the added sugar manageable. In any case, I hated the sluggish feeling that high blood sugar brought on, and I didn't need reminding. I might have had to eat less of something else, but I could indulge my lust for mangoes.

At lunchtime, the whole family came home from work, and Titi Maria cooked a big meal for all her kids—my adult cousins—and some of their kids too. Even those who lived elsewhere would often come for that meal. After lunch we set-

tled down for a siesta. I would read a book—sleep wouldn't
come to me easily—but I loved this time when everyone was
gathered at home and quietly connected.

Papo had a job designing window displays for a number
of big stores on the island. He claimed to be the first person
doing this work as a professional designer in Puerto Rico, and
he often traveled to New York to gather ideas. Charo was a
high school teacher. Minita was the senior executive secretary
for the newspaper *El Mundo*. Evita worked in a government
office. It was clear to me even then that the people I knew on
the island had better jobs than the Puerto Ricans I knew in
New York. When we walked down the street in Mayagüez, it
gave me a proud thrill to read the little signs above the doors,
of the doctors, the lawyers, and the other professionals who
were Puerto Rican. It was not something I had often seen in
New York. At the hospital where my mother worked, there
were Puerto Rican nurses but only one Puerto Rican doctor.
At the larger shops and businesses in the Bronx, there were
Puerto Rican workers but rarely managers or owners.

Tío Mayo's *panadería* was my favorite place to visit. They
called it a *panadería,* but it was much more than a bakery.
There were loaves of bread and rolls that Tío Mayo started
making while it was still dark outside, kept warm in a special
case with a heat lamp. There were cases full of cakes and
pastries filled with cream, homemade cheese, and guava jam.
My uncle's then wife, Titi Elisa, also got up early to make
lunch and snacks to sell to the workers who sewed in the factory across the street. She fried the chicken and roasted the
pork, made stews and meat pies and pots of rice and beans.
The smells of her cooking mixed with the yeasty smell of the
bread, and the coffee, and the whole amazing cloud of flavors
spread down the street and up into the balconies.

When the noon whistle blew at the factory, the bakery would fill up in minutes. I helped with serving, and I loved the two-handed challenge of the lunch hour rush. I knew the price of every item, and I knew how to make change—I was discovering that I had a facility with numbers, which I inherited from Papi—and Titi Elisa would let me work the cash register when my uncle wasn't around. Although he had seen me in action, he couldn't quite believe it. He wasn't comfortable with the idea of girls handling money.

When I wasn't busy helping, I played with my cousin Tito in the alleyway behind the bakery, reenacting scenes from the Three Stooges. Tito was Moe and I was Curly. We could usually convince Junior or someone else to be Larry, the third *chiflado,* but only Tito and I knew all the moves and the right sound effects: a twang for a fake eye poke, a ratchety sound for an ear twist, and the all-purpose "Nyuk! Nyuk! Nyuk!"

Before she left Puerto Rico, my mother had lived in Lajas and San Germán and had seen very little of the island beyond the neighborhoods of her childhood. She was eager to show us places that she'd heard about but had never seen herself. We went to the beach at Luquillo. It was nothing like Orchard Beach in the Bronx, which was the only beach I knew. There were no traffic jams in Puerto Rico, no waiting for hours packed in a hot car to get there, no dirty sand, no standing in line for the bathroom. Progress has caught up with the island since my childhood, and it has its share of traffic jams, but the water is still warm and clear, and the sand is perfectly white. When you look down into the water, you can see the bottom, and it rolls out blue until it meets the blue of the sky.

The Parque de Bombas in Ponce fascinated me, a fantasia of red and black stripes that wouldn't go away even when you closed your eyes. The fire truck looked like a giant toy with its ding-dong bell, and I couldn't imagine it in action. How did they ever put out a real fire? "*Mi'ja*," said Mami, "all those little wooden houses burned down anyway. But they did the best they could." She would say that about a lot of things: they did the best they could.

Of all the sights, the art museum in Ponce left the deepest impression. I had never been to a museum before. The building is beautiful and seemed to me then as grand as a castle with its staircase that sweeps in a big circle on two sides. It was so magnificent that I just had to run up and down the stairs to see what it felt like. It felt horrible when the guard yelled at me. So I walked slowly and looked at the paintings one by one.

I figured out that portraits were pictures in which a person from olden times just stood there or sat, wearing fancy clothes and staring very seriously. I wondered who these people were. Why did an artist choose *them* to be in a picture? How much work was it to paint this? How long did he have to stand there like that? Other paintings were more like stories, though I didn't know what the story was. Why did she cut off his head? I could tell that dove was not just an ordinary dove that happened to be flying by. I could see that it had a meaning, even though I didn't know what the meaning was. When I got tired of not understanding the stories, I noticed other things: Sometimes you could see the brushstrokes and the thickness of the paint; other times it was smooth, without texture. Sometimes things in the distance were smaller, and it felt as if you could reach into the space; other times it was flat like a map. I wondered, were these the things I *should* be noticing? I could tell that there was more going on than I could describe or understand.

Does it seem strange that a child should be so conscious of

the workings of her own mind? I have clear memories of
many such moments, often turning on a recognition of
something I didn't know, an awareness of a gap in my
knowledge. A framed reproduction of a painting that mesmerized me hung for years on the wall in Abuelita's living
room. Who knows how it got there, but it was a scene, I'm
assuming in hindsight, from the French Revolution, a broad
staircase leading from a public square up into a stately building, with a balcony where several elegant figures formed a
cluster, including a woman—Marie Antoinette?—with a
pale blue dress and imposing hair. In the street below, many
other people approached, more poorly dressed, but my eye
was drawn to an old man on the lower steps, shabbily clad,
leaning one-legged on a cane, his back to the viewer. I knew
nothing of the history, the social and political background
that informed the painting, but I understood that a message
was somehow intended when the artist contrived to place
this man front and center. I spent a lot of time wondering
about him and trying to imagine his face. But that was as far
as I could get.

"SONIA, we're going to visit your grandfather. My father."
This got my attention. My mother had never so much as
mentioned his existence before. When I questioned her, she
answered in a voice that sounded as if she were reading aloud
from the small print on the back of a package of medicine. "I
don't know the man. He left when I was born. I haven't seen
him since then. But Tío Mayo and Titi Aurora want me to
come with them to the hospital to see him, and they say you
should come too." The unknown grandfather was not the
whole mystery. I usually knew what Mami was thinking from

the flash in her voice, the speed of her smile, as rare as it was then, the telltale arch of her brows. This woman speaking with such flat indifference was not the mother I knew.

Tío Mayo led us to the bed at the far end of the room, by the window. As we walked the length of the ward, I hardly saw the patients in the other beds, so intently was I focused on my mother and our looming destination. Nothing was going to slip by me, though I had no idea what to expect or even what I should be wondering about. Would she greet him with a kiss? How do you relate to a father you don't know?

He had Mami's light eyes. Framed by the white of his hair, the white mustache, the white of the sheets, their sea-green color seemed even lighter, bluer, more startling. He was a handsome man but gaunt. His arms were just sticks poking from the sleeves of the hospital gown. A thousand questions ran through my head, but I didn't dare speak any of them out loud: Why did you leave Mami behind? Who are you? Do you have a wife? Do you have other kids? Where have you been living?

I climbed onto the chair and watched. My mother walked up to the bed and stood looking down at the old man. In an ice-cold voice she said, "*Yo soy Celina.*" That was it. He didn't say anything to her. He didn't ask how her life had been, what it was now. There were no tears, no revelations.

Titi Aurora led me by the hand to the bedside and introduced me. I got barely a nod from him. I retreated, climbed back onto the chair, and watched as Titi Aurora chattered about nothing and fluffed his pillows. Tío Mayo was there and not there, talking to the nurses, taking care of business. But in all this nothing, I understood something: that my mother had been wounded as deeply as a human being could be.

I have carried the memory of that day as a grave caution. There was a terrible permanence to the state that my mother and her father had reached. My mother's pain would never heal, the ice between them would never thaw, because they would never find a way to acknowledge it. Without acknowledgment and communication, forgiveness was beyond reach. Eventually, I would recognize the long shadow of this abandonment in my own feelings toward my mother, and I would determine not to repeat what I had seen. The closeness that I share now with my mother is deeply felt, but we learned it slowly and with effort, and for fear of the alternative.

Five

I T WAS IN April of the year that I turned nine. I was heading straight home after school that day because Papi had stayed home sick from work. Usually, Junior and I would go to Ana's first and then play outside till Papi got home. I didn't need to check in with Ana, because she would know that Papi was home. My mother had coffee with Ana every day before she went to work; there was nothing about each other's lives that they didn't know instantly.

When we came round the corner, I could see Moncho, Ana's husband, hanging out the window on the third floor of their building, washing the windows but also looking intently at passersby. That was odd, I thought. When he saw me, he waved at me. He didn't stop. He kept on waving furiously, signaling to me, and then he yelled "Sonia! Junior! Come upstairs!" in a voice that meant business. Junior bounced ahead of me, happy to see Moncho.

But when Ana opened the door, something was terribly wrong. Her eyes were puffy from crying, and her face was pale. This wasn't some everyday fuss that just happened to reach the level of tears; something had shaken her deeply. She wouldn't explain, but she started to cry and made us wait while she phoned Mami, saying to Moncho, "Celina should tell them." Moncho was quieter than I'd ever seen him. This was all so strange that I was scared but also riveted as I watched to see what would happen next. Ana said, "Let's go," and we walked downstairs and across the way to our building. It was the shortest of walks, but it took forever. It was hard to move my legs, as if dread were weighing them down.

Alfred opened the door to our apartment. His eyes, too, were red. Tío Vitín was there, and I could hear other voices. I looked into the living room and saw many faces looking back at me with the same teary gaze. Mami was sitting in the chair by the telephone in the hallway, staring into space, her eyes wide and wet. Junior said to her, "Where's Papi?"

"Dios se lo llevó."

God took him. I could see that Junior didn't understand. I did. She meant that Papi had died. But what did *that* mean? Had he become a spirit? I didn't know what I was supposed to feel, or say, or do. As if from a far distance, I could hear my own voice joining all the other voices crying. I ran down the hall and threw myself on the bed. I was sobbing, pounding my fists, when Ana entered the room.

"Sonia, you have to be a big girl now. Your mother's very upset; you can't cry anymore. You have to be strong for your *mami.*"

So that's what I'm supposed to do? I stopped crying. "I'm okay, Ana." She left me alone. The stillness in the room was louder than the noise down the hall. I remembered that morning how Papi had called out from the bathroom, saying that since he wasn't going to work, he wanted to make us a Sunday breakfast, even though it was a weekday. Mami had yelled: "Go back to bed if you're sick, the kids don't have

time, they have to get to school, and why are you taking so
long shaving?"

WE HAD BEEN at the funeral home for hours. It felt like
forever, but my mother and Abuelita and my aunts had been
there even longer, for days. It was important not to leave the
body alone, and they all had to keep each other company.
Mami didn't want Junior and me to come, but Titi Aurora
insisted, because the nuns and Monsignor Hart were coming
from Blessed Sacrament. It wouldn't be respectful if Junior
and I weren't there when they showed up.

The room smelled of flowers, cologne, and perfume
masking a mustiness. People were speaking in whispers,
looking at the floor, shaking their heads. There was talk of
premonitions, a greeting or casual word exchanged with my
father over the last few days that now took on greater significance; the way he had shaved and dressed up that morning,
even though he was home sick. As if he had known. Everyone agreed that he was a good man, a family man, and that
forty-two was a tragically young age to go. And Celina so
young too, a widow at thirty-six with two young kids!

My aunts took turns crying. Abuelita never stopped. I sat
down next to her on the couch and held her hand. Abuelita's
crying was unbearably painful to me. I couldn't even tell if I
had any sadness of my own, because I was so full of Abuelita's sadness. I worried that her spirit had been torn apart
so painfully by Papi's death that she might never be happy
again. What would happen to me if she died too?

The nuns and Monsignor Hart came and went. Dr.
Fisher came too, and some people from the factory where

Papi worked. All the while, Mami just sat there. Her eyes were open, but she was not really present, not even answering when people talked to her. Titi Aurora had to tell her to say thank you to Monsignor Hart.

What happens next is that I'm supposed to say good-bye to Papi, Titi Aurora says. She wants me to kiss him. I want to scream "No!" but I swallow it because I don't want to upset Abuelita any more than she's upset already. "*No tengas miedo*, Sonia. Touch his hand." I'm not afraid, but I'm not okay either. This thing with a powdery white face resembles my father, but it's not him, and it's certainly not something I want to touch. But I close my eyes and get it over with.

A part of me was not surprised by what happened then. A knot that had been tied tight inside me for longer than I can remember began to come loose. Deep down, I'd known for a while that this was where Papi was heading. Looking at this thing that was not Papi, I realized that he was not coming back. From here, Mami, Junior, and I would be going along without him. Maybe it would be easier this way.

. . . Santa María, Madre de Dios, ruega por nosotros peca-dores, ahora y en la hora de nuestra muerte.

We did the *rosario* for Papi for seven straight nights at Abuelita's, and every night I thought it would never end. Abuelita cried. Mami cried. My aunts cried. The prayers went on and on, along with that horrible week. The final night should have been better because the end was in sight, and friends brought dinner instead of just pastries, but the bad news was that we had to do three . . . whole . . . rosaries . . .

Dios te salve, María, llena eres de gracia: El Señor es con-

tigo. Bendita tú eres entre todas las mujeres, y bendito es el
fruto de tu vientre: Jesús . . .

I must have fallen asleep at some point, because I woke
up with my mother standing next to me, pulling my arm out
of its socket, gripping my hand so tightly it hurt. Her whole
body was shaking with anger, and her voice trembled as she
spoke to Abuelita: "Mercedes, you can't do this! I won't let
you!" The room was silent. Everyone's eyes were on Mami,
standing there with the tears running down her face. "I swear,
I will take her away from you and you will never see us again.
Never!"

She dragged me to the bedroom and cried all night. I
had no idea what had so upset her that she would turn on
Abuelita, and she wouldn't tell me. Much later I learned the
story. As I nodded off in the midst of the prayers, I apparently spoke in a strange voice—one that sounded like Abuelita's long-dead sister to those who remembered her, a voice
my grandmother might summon during one of her séances.
The message I delivered was that my father was safely in her
company; there was no need to worry. "*Confórmate*," I said.
Accept it.

I can't explain it. Nothing like that had happened to me
before, and it hasn't happened since. Everyone there was as
exhausted as I was, and it's hard to separate what they heard
from what they wanted to hear. I know that I wanted more
than anything to make Abuelita feel better; it's very possible
I was talking in my sleep or as I drifted off. In any case, it
didn't matter. Any desire my grandmother might have had
to develop what she believed to be my "gift" was trumped by
my mother's threat to remove me from the influence of what
she saw as superstition and *brujería*.

We had been sleeping at Abuelita's every night since Papi

died, because my mother couldn't bear to go back to our apartment. That meant getting up very early in the morning so Mami could get us to school on time, after which she would go to Ana's. They would drink coffee and talk and cry together until school was out, and then she would take us back to Abuelita's. Fortunately, the building manager at Bronxdale Houses let us move into a different apartment very quickly. It was over on Watson Avenue on the second floor—much better than the seventh floor if you'd rather not see what happens in the stairwells. It was much closer to Blessed Sacrament, too. Best of all, my mother was able to change her schedule at the hospital. She didn't have to work nights anymore, so she could be at home after school.

Tío Vitín and my cousin Alfred helped us with the move. They cleaned out Papi's room and carried out a big bag of clanking empty bottles. They found those flat, half-pint bottles, drained of Seagram's Seven, under the mattress, in the closet, behind the drawers, in his coat pockets, his trousers, his shirts, in every jacket. There was even one hidden inside the lining of a coat.

It occurred to me that every day when he came home from work and sent us off with pennies for candy and fifteen minutes more to play, my father was keeping us outside just long enough to have a drink before starting dinner. Junior, who had slept in the same room with Papi, in the other twin bed, and sometimes only pretended to be asleep, now confessed that he had known all along about the bottles under the mattress. I always slept with my mother in the other room, and nothing ever woke me up once I fell asleep. I wondered what else I had missed.

I do know that my father loved us. But as much as he loved us, it wasn't enough to stop him from drinking. To the end, Abuelita and my aunts blamed my mother for Papi's drinking. It's true that Mami could say all the wrong things; neither of them knew how to stop an argument once they started. But I knew too that my mother didn't make him drink any more than she could make him stop. I knew he did this to himself; even as a child, I knew he was the only one responsible.

All those hours that he sat by the window looking out . . . I treasured those times when I stood beside him, inhaling the scent of Old Spice up close and of rice and beans bubbling in the background, and he told me what he imagined the future would be: all the different stores they would build on the empty lots around us, or how one day a rocket ship would carry a man to the full moon that was rising, low and yellow, over the South Bronx. The truth is, though, that for each of those moments, there were so many more long hours of sadness, when he stared in silence at the vacant lots, at the highway and the brick walls, at a city and a life that slowly strangled him.

On the day we moved in, it smelled of fresh paint. The view from the new apartment on Watson Avenue was different. You could see the school yard at Blessed Sacrament from our window. The kids had left for the day, but there were still two guys practicing shots on the basketball court. Farther back, one of the nuns was walking along by the buildings, but I couldn't tell who it was under the black bonnet . . . As I looked out the window, a memory came to me of something that happened the day Papi died, which I'd almost forgotten in all the commotion that followed. I was down in the school yard at recess, standing by the fence, looking this way toward the projects—and I thought about him. It wasn't a normal thought that pops into your head or one that's connected to the thought that came before it. More of a feeling than a thought, but almost not even a feeling: like the barest shadow of a mood passing over, or a breeze so perfectly soft that nothing moves. I didn't know yet what had happened, but maybe that was Papi himself, saying good-bye.

Six

I N   T H E   D A Y S and weeks following the funeral, the
release and relief I felt from the end of the fighting gave
way to anxious puzzlement. At nine, I was equipped to
understand loss, even sadness, but not grief, not someone
else's and certainly not my own. I couldn't figure out what
was wrong with Mami, and it scared me.

Every day Junior and I came home from school to find the
apartment quiet and dark, with the curtains drawn. Mami
would come out just long enough to cook dinner, leaving the
back bedroom, where she passed hour after hour with the
door closed and the lights out. (Junior and I shared the front
bedroom in the new apartment on Watson Avenue, using
the twin beds that had been in Papi's room in the old place.)
After serving dinner like a zombie, hardly saying a word, she
would go right back into her room. So even though she was
working the early shift now and getting home in the afternoon before us, we saw no more of her than when she'd been
working late. We did homework. We watched TV. We did
homework and watched TV.

On weekends, I was able to rouse Mami to go grocery

shopping, retracing my father's steps. I remembered what Papi used to buy, and that's what I put in the basket, though I wasn't sure Mami would know what to do with everything. I missed Papi's cooking. I missed Papi. Somehow, when he died, I had taken it for granted that our lives would be better. I hadn't counted on this gloom.

I wasn't the only one who was worried about my mother. I overheard some of her friends talking to Ana, and they decided one of them would pay a call at Blessed Sacrament to ask Father Dolan to come visit Celina. His refusal, as reported over coffee at Ana's, enraged me, all the more so because of the reason: my mother didn't go to church on Sunday.

It was true, but she did send her kids to church and always with money for the offering basket. And she worked long hours at the hospital so we could go to school at Blessed Sacrament. Shouldn't Father Dolan be forgiving if she needed help? Even if he thought she wasn't Christian enough, I reasoned, shouldn't he be more Christian? My reaction was of a piece with the frustration I felt when he stood there at the altar during the Mass, with his back turned to us, as priests did in those days before Vatican II. Show us what you're doing up there! I always thought. Now when he turned his back on us, it felt like just what it appeared to be: rejection. I was delighted when, a few years later under Pope Paul VI, the Church turned its priests around to face the congregants.

Another week passed in darkness and silence. Another friend of my mother's, Cristina, asked the pastor at her church to visit Mami. He'd never even met her before, and of course she'd never been to his church, which was Baptist. But that didn't stop him from coming. They talked quietly together for hours. I was impressed that he spoke Spanish; whether or not he had anything to say that could help, at least he cared enough to try. That I respected.

As spring turned to summer, Mami stayed shut in her darkened room, and I found myself on summer vacation longing for school to start. I didn't feel like playing outside. I couldn't articulate exactly what I feared, but I knew I should stay close by and keep an eye on things.

My solace and only distraction that summer was reading. I discovered the pleasure of chapter books and devoured a big stack of them. The Parkchester Library was my haven. To thumb through the card catalog was to touch an infinite bounty, more books than I could ever possibly exhaust. My choices were more or less random. There was no one in my family who could point me toward children's classics, no teacher who took an interest, and it never occurred to me to ask the librarian for guidance. My mother had subscribed to *Highlights* for Junior and me, and *Reader's Digest* for herself, but by now I was reading whole issues of the *Digest* myself, cover to cover. "Laughter, the Best Medicine," was what I sorely needed then. Sometimes when a story caught my imagination, I would search the library for the original book—I understood that these were excerpts or abridgments—but I never had any luck, and that mystified me. Now I realize that a tiny public library in a poor neighborhood would be unlikely to receive new releases.

My favorite book was one that Dr. Fisher had lent me. I had seen it, bound in burgundy red leather, on the shelf in his office and asked about it. He pulled the heavy volume down and said I could keep it as long as I liked. Those stories of Greek gods and heroes sustained me that summer and beyond. I imagined the gods of classical antiquity as versions of Abuelita's familiar spirits, who interfered in human affairs and kept open lines of communication to the Bronx. The heroes were admirable if flawed, as compelling as any comic book superhero to a kid who was hungry for escape, and there was grandeur in their struggles that the Flash could not match. Riven by conflicting impulses, these immortals seemed more realistic, more accessible, than the singular, all-forgiving, unchanging God of my Church. It was in that book of Dr. Fisher's, too, that I learned that my own name is a version of Sophia, meaning wisdom. I glowed with that discovery. And I never did return the book.

USUALLY, when I didn't understand what was going on with someone, I could listen carefully and observe until I figured things out. But with my mother, still sitting alone in darkness behind her closed door, there were no clues. As far as I knew, when Papi was alive, they did nothing but fight. If they weren't screaming, they were putting up a stone wall of bitter silence between them. I couldn't remember ever having seen them happy together. And so her sadness, if that's what it was, seemed irrational to me.

Abuelita's terrible pain seemed less mysterious, if only because I was so attuned to her feelings. The parties ended. There was no more music and dancing, no more shopping for chickens, no more calling the spirits. Abuelita didn't dream the winning numbers anymore. "My son died and my luck died too," she said. She was angry at the spirits, it seemed, for not warning her that something bad would happen to her son, for not even giving her a chance to protect him. The week after Papi died, she forgot, in her distress, to place her usual bet, only to find out later that the winning number had been the number of his gravestone. It was as if the spirits were mocking her.

And yet it had been years since I'd seen her talking to Papi as her beloved firstborn, with that glow of adoration that lit up her face. On holidays when he came with us to Abuelita's house, he would sit silently, looking out the window, the same way he did at home. He might warm up if there was a ball game on TV. Before we got our own set, he might even come just to watch the game, then one of his few real pleasures. Those baseball games, with some good shouting for a change, were such a rare semblance of normal family life that on those nights I would fall asleep with a smile that wouldn't go away.

But still, looking at it rationally—and I was a very rational child—why should the parties stop when Papi hardly ever came anyway? Why would his not being there make a difference now when it hadn't before? Why was even Titi Carmen so overcome with grief at the funeral that she tried to jump into the grave and had to be dragged out? I never once saw her eager to spend time with Papi when he was alive.

What was all this adult misery about? I had my theory. They must all feel guilty. If Papi slowly poisoned himself to death, then of course it must be Mami's fault (as had long been the theory), or maybe Abuelita now blamed herself and the failure of her spirit powers. Titi Carmen too might have faulted herself for not interceding. And how many times had I heard Titi Judy criticized for Tío Vitín's failure to visit the family more often—even though Tío Vitín was Abuelita's son and Titi Judy was just his wife? That was how their minds worked: if a man did something wrong, there was a woman to blame, whether wife, mother, sister, or sister-in-law. I recognized that it must be horribly painful to imagine you could have stopped him but didn't. But I also knew all that was nonsense. There was no saving Papi from himself.

IT IS a day like any other, and the door is still closed. My rational self hasn't yet noticed it, but I can't take another minute of this. Before I know what's happening, I'm pounding with both fists on that stupid, blank, faceless door, and when she opens it, I'm screaming in her face, "Enough! You've got to stop this! You're miserable and you're making us miserable."

Such screaming hasn't been heard in the house in months. She's just standing there, blinking at me. I can't help myself, I'm still screaming. "What's wrong with you? Papi died. Are you going to die too? Then what happens to me and Junior? Stop already, Mami, stop it!"

I turn around and march up the hall to the front bedroom, slamming the door behind me as hard as I can. I grab a book and lie down on the bed. But with my hands trembling and my eyes full of tears, there's no way I can read. I close the book and sob for a very long time. I haven't done that in ages. Crying like a stupid baby.

Seven

I T WASN'T UNTIL I began to write this book, nearly
fifty years after the events of that sad year, that I came to
a truer understanding of my mother's grief. For most of
my life, my sense of my father, and of my parents' relationship, was confined by the narrow aperture through which I
watched them as a child. That sense was frozen in time when
my father died. My theory of guilt-induced grief was hardly
more sophisticated than Lucy's psychiatric help at five cents
a pop. The vague shame overhanging my father's alcoholism
silenced any conversation among the adults that might have
caused me to question what I thought. As we grew, Junior
and I would speak more openly to each other, but he could
add nothing to my analysis. Although he was six when Papi
died, he has virtually no memories of our father or of the
time before his death. And so, with the vocabulary of hindsight, I came to assume that the intensity of my mother's
grief implied some form of clinical depression that was never
treated but that somehow resolved itself eventually.

I had never before in all these years asked that very intelligent and perceptive woman for her own version of events.
I would be startled by what I uncovered and grateful even

at this remove to meet a happier version of my father—and my mother—than I ever knew. My parents' relationship was richer and more complex than a child could imagine, and the stories that have come to light are all the more precious to me for having been captured as my mother's memory is fading fast with age.

SOMETIMES THE PEOPLE closest to us are those we know the least.

"Where should I begin, Sonia?"

"Begin at the beginning, Mami."

MY MOTHER'S BIRTH, in 1927, was bad news. It was the reason, or at least the occasion, as she understood it, for her father's abandonment of the family. Her own mother was sick, an invalid, as far back as she could remember. She believed her father was somehow to blame for that, but the story was never clear, since nobody spoke about him in their home. Toward the end, the sickness afflicted her mother's mind as well as her body, and she would wander off. Celina would wake up at night alone in the bed they shared, the door open. She would find her mother by moonlight in the sugarcane field, take her by the hand, and lead her back to bed.

Home was a little wooden shack of a house near Lajas, in the middle of the fields, with a dirt floor in the kitchen and an outhouse. There was no running water. It was the child Celina's job to draw water for cooking from the hand pump at her uncle's house by the road and carry the pail back carefully, without spilling. For washing they collected rainwater in drums.

The farm had belonged to her mother, but she had sold it to raise bail when her husband landed in some drunken trouble. A brother, he of the water pump, provided some help for the bedridden mother of six, but grudgingly. There had been a prouder time, and traces of it were still visible in the way that Celina's grandmother carried herself, in her long crinoline skirts and high lace collars in the Spanish style. "Raise your head!" she demanded if she caught Celina hunching over. "You don't have to be ashamed of anything." She was strict and insisted on manners. Even Celina's brothers, rough as they were and country people, knew how to be polite.

Celina was the youngest, and her siblings raised her, their mother helpless. Aurora found work sewing. When Celina was still a toddler, Aurora, sixteen years older, was the first to marry. That's when she left for San Germán, though she never really left behind the responsibilities that had cut short her childhood. She would come back every two weeks to collect piecework from women who sewed handkerchiefs, and to pay them; she was always in a bad mood, always a dark cloud hanging over her. She taught Celina to sew too. Celina had to make two dozen handkerchiefs a week, stitching the little hems and ironing them. She didn't get paid, of course. That work was her contribution to the household. Aurora made the clothes and paid for shoes, one pair every year.

Mario Baez, the eldest brother, who was nicknamed Mayo, fed the family. He went fishing in the mornings at La Parguera before reporting to his job loading the sugarcane wagons at the train station. When he got married, he built another little house for himself, closer to the road, and his wife, Maria, did the cooking. But Celina ate mostly fruits that fell off the trees: poking around in the grass like a little bird, looking for mangoes, *grosellas, tamarindos* . . . She didn't like fish.

In the absence of a father, discipline was in Mayo's hands, and he was rough about it. Celina got the belt for climbing a tree, for coming home late from school, having stopped to wade in the stream. For standing outside Tío Foro's store, where the men were drinking, so she could listen to the jukebox. For buying candy with the three cents they gave her to mail a letter. That was a bad one; she never did that again. Her mother would get up to put *sebo de flande* on the welts, Celina crying from the pain and her mother crying too as she rubbed the sticky salve into the child's skin. Pedro, the brother closest to her in age, never got the belt. Pedro was the dear little one, the light of Mayo's eye. Celina was only trouble.

She hated Mayo for those beatings, hated him with such a passion that she swore she would never go back to Puerto Rico after she left. But of course she did, and now my mother tempers her judgment with forgiveness: he was doing the best that he knew how; a girl gone wrong would have been a terrible load to carry. With their mother helpless and their father missing, it was kids raising kids and just her bad luck to have been the youngest. At least they sent her to school. She was grateful for that, and in her warm remembrances of school I sense the stirrings of her passion for education.

When she was very small, she went to a tiny little school nearby, and later all the way to Lajas, about an hour away if she had to walk. Walking was hard because her shoes were always too small, so she'd wind up carrying them, barefoot. But often a farmer's cart would pass and she'd thumb a ride, with the bullocks swaying ahead of her and the sugarcane behind. When she wandered home afterward, there was the temptation of streams and the house where an old woman would wave to her to come have a snack.

School was a pleasure because it got her out of the house, but it was not easy. The kids were cruel in a thousand small ways. They would attempt any kind of silly *burla*—making faces or doing a little dance behind the back of the teacher as she wrote on the board—just to make Celina laugh her nervous laugh. Then she would be the one to be punished. Whack! It was just the way she would then punish her own pupils. When she got home and there was no one to play with or talk to, she taught her lessons to the trees: "Children, repeat after me!" And when they didn't get it right, she would swat them with a stick. It helped her remember the lessons, and she liked being surrounded by the trees. Nature was a solace and a kind of freedom.

The best part of school was the library and carrying home a book. She loved to read, hoarded magazines and pamphlets, any scrap of writing she could find. When the sewing was finished, she read stories into the evening, by the light of the *quinqué* with the moths dancing around the kerosene flame.

It was an evening like that when her mother died, when she was nine, the same age I was when Papi died. People came to the house that very same night for the wake, drinking and talking until dawn, with the *quinqué* burning all night long. They brought ice to put on top of the box and under it, since there was no embalming, nothing to slow the ravages of the hot days and nights. They buried Doña Francisca Toro Torres in the morning.

After her mother died, what little remained of the household was broken up. Pedro moved in with Mayo, and Celina was sent to live with Aurora in San Germán. Her brother Abraham had already left for Mayagüez. He was young still, but old enough to run off with a woman and old enough to step into the ring. He loved boxing, but he didn't know how and he lost every bout.

The house in Barrio Bosque where Aurora lived with her husband was just one street over from the train station. From the little room by the kitchen where Celina slept, she could hear the sound of the train escaping down the tracks. It was the last link to Lajas, to so many people who vanished from her life. Pedro came to visit a couple of times but gradually lost touch. He got married, joined the army. She never saw her grandmother again. That was just the way it was. There was never any choice, so there was not much room for feelings. But it could have been worse: usually orphans got sent to work in rich people's houses. Aurora had saved her from that fate.

Aurora was busy with the handkerchiefs, working long hours and traveling to collect piecework from other women who sewed. Celina still made her two dozen handkerchiefs every week. She cleaned the house on Saturdays and did small things to make it nice, picking flowers to put beside the photographs in frames. They had electricity, though the toilet was still outside. Aurora's husband, Emmanuel, was an old man and crazy in his own way. He was a blacksmith, but he spent more time fussing over his son Alfred than he spent working. Alfred was just a baby but the center of his universe, and people talked about how Emmanuel seemed weirdly obsessed with the child.

In school Celina was lonely all the time and so quiet that practically no one knew she was there. She lived in the library and often read so long that there was no time left to study.

Her grades suffered, but she knew a wealth of words from those precious books, words that nobody would ever guess she knew.

Walking between school and home, or during the break at lunchtime, she had the freedom of the town. San Germán is like a cap on the dome of a hill, with a sky that's bigger than you'd expect in a place where the forest closes in tightly around. She would wander and look at the fine houses that seemed to be dressed in lace, with colored windows and filigreed gates and porches that wrapped around like shawls. She used to go to the post office just to watch the girls come from the college to mail their letters, with their chaperones waiting outside, lined up on the bench: nannies for young women, really. Only the rich girls or the very intelligent ones went to college. What would happen to a girl who thought herself neither?

She didn't know then how to make friends. If she had any at all, they were just the neighbors, people who recognized the same raggedy girl passing by every day. There was a lonely old lady who lived down the street in Barrio Bosque. Her granddaughter had become a prostitute and didn't visit anymore. So Celina went to sit with the grandmother in the afternoons.

Aurora was very strict, very religious, and fearful of anything fun, but she did have a few friends who came to visit. Celina would listen to the stories they told over coffee: about who was promenading in the plaza, the ladies on the left and the men on the right; about tea dances at the Hotel Parador Oasis. Walking home from school, she would peek into the entrance and catch a glimpse of shadowy pink archways, but she would never set foot inside. When she woke in the middle of the night to singing and guitars in the street, she could guess who was being serenaded: the same girl who sat there on the balcony in the afternoon, dressed like a princess with her fingernails painted.

One morning, a group of young soldiers were leaving for Fort Buchanan, and some of Celina's classmates decided to go wave good-bye to them at the train station. Ever since Pearl Harbor, Puerto Rico was in shock, and the boys were joining up as soon as they were old enough, if not sooner. She didn't even know the ones who were leaving from San Germán that day, but she liked the idea of a *despedida* to send them off. Maybe she still missed Pedro. The girls stood on the platform at the train station and waved till the caboose disappeared into the forest. When they got to school, they were all punished for being late.

Maybe a seed was planted that day. Later she saw an ad in the newspaper: Join the Women's Army Corps! She knew the instant she saw it: this was her chance. She mailed in her name and address and said she was nineteen. Celina was only seventeen. They wrote back and told her to present herself in San Juan. Celina showed the letter to Aurora.

"You're crazy," Aurora said.

"No, it's an order from the army. I have to present myself! I can't disobey. I *have* to go."

It took six or seven hours by train to get to San Juan, and that trip was the best adventure of her short life. The conductor punching the tickets looked like a general in his smart uniform. Passengers came from who knows where, all over the island, with their bags and bundles and boxes, their *fiambreras* stacked up with what they'd brought to eat. The world zipped past the windows. A car raced alongside the tracks, the driver honking and waving. The train pulled in at little flag stops, not even stations, where kids ran on the platform to sell fruits through the windows. At one crossing, a chain beside the tracks cordoned off a road leading elsewhere, a crimson tunnel carpeted with petals dropped by a *flamboyán* tree in full bloom.

Aurora's husband had a sister in San Juan, and they had called her on the telephone. She met Celina at the train station and took her to the camp the next day. High on adrenaline, Celina took a whole battery of tests and passed every one of them, mental and physical. Then they asked for her birth certificate. Panic. They said, you leave for Miami in four days. Go home and get your birth certificate. Come back in time to ship out.

She took the train back to San Germán, another whole day traveling and plenty of time to fret. At home she told Aurora what had happened: "You have to find a birth certificate, and it has to say I'm nineteen. Or else they'll put you in jail!"

"*¡Estás loca!* You're the one who's going to jail, not me." Well, *somebody* would be going to jail if the U.S. Army went to all that trouble to recruit a WAC and then found out she had lied. Aurora went to Lajas and found Mayo. Mayo found a lawyer. Somehow they did what they did, and Aurora came back with a birth certificate that said Celina Baez was born in 1925.

All of this my mother managed on impulse, without any real thought about where she was headed. She would never have much patience with the spirit world, always keeping a safe distance from such things, but in this particular turn of events, so unforeseen and ultimately so fortuitous, she still credits the guiding hand of her mother, who, she believes, continues to watch over her.

My mother boarded the flight to Miami with an incredulous excitement that would never completely fade. The stories of her army days were among the few memories of youth that she shared with friends and family when I was growing up. It was a coming of age, a sudden and sometimes comical meeting with the modern world, and, for all the military discipline, a time of unthinkable, giddy new freedom. It was also an extraordinary moment in history. My mother was recruited into one of the first Puerto Rican units of the Women's Army Corps. Over twenty thousand Puerto Rican men had already served in the U.S. armed forces before the women were included. And although the first units were kept segregated because of their limited English, it was for many of these women, as for so many of the men who served, how they came to see themselves as rightfully American.

Landing in Miami, the new recruits were transferred from the airport to the train station, where, shivering on the platform in their cotton dresses, they waited for the Pullman. It was December, but none of the girls from Puerto Rico had coats or stockings. A kindly black conductor found blankets for them to use until they got to Georgia, where they were headed for basic training.

At Fort Oglethorpe, the sergeant took the whole band to the PX and let them choose nylons and garter belts and brassieres to wear with their new uniforms. They were screaming with laughter, showing each other what to do with them. Many of that ragtag bunch had joined up wearing homemade underwear and had never touched such fancy things in their lives. And when they learned how to march, the stockings fell down, causing my mother to laugh so hard she got KP duty as a penalty.

The basic training was difficult, because there was so much to learn: not just the military life and duties, but simply functioning in a world that was new to her. Never having used a telephone on her own, she didn't know not to hang up when she went to find the officer someone was calling for. All the instructions were in English, which to her had been just another class in high school until then. Her schoolbooks had said nothing about KP duty, about how to light a chimney stove, how to peel a potato.

Though the war seemed far away, the WACs understood that every task given them would have required an able-bodied man. For every woman in the force, a man was freed to fight the war. After basic training, my mother's group was assigned to New York, and that was the real beginning of her new life. They lived in the Broadway Central Hotel and worked at the post office on Forty-second Street, sorting letters and packages for the troops in Europe. They practiced their English, learned their way around the streets and the subways, learned how to be on their own. For Celina, there was also a lesson that others already knew: learning how to have a friend.

Carmin was the first real friend Celina had, and emotionally it was like learning to walk. Together the two of them explored the mesmerizing town. In those days Forty-second Street was a beautiful place. It was classy, not yet the seedy peep-show district it would become in the 1970s or the garish tourist zone it is today. Just walking down the street you felt liberated. The restaurants and the shows—they saw Frank Sinatra and Tommy Dorsey—and so many other things were free because they were in uniform. Celina and Carmin were in a movie theater when the reel stopped and the lights came up for the announcement: the Germans had surrendered. They went out in the street, and then came the scene that my mother would describe so many times, always with the same look of wonder. "Beautiful pandemonium," she called it. Thousands of people, all the soldiers and all the girls, everybody kissing and hugging, yelling their heads off, embracing strangers, everyone so jubilant. It was magic; it was electric. Like nothing she'd ever seen.

Carmin had friends in the Bronx, and one day they braved the long subway ride to go to a party, getting up at every station so as not to miss the stop at Intervale. They had never taken the subway anywhere except back and forth between the hotel and the post office.

That was the day she met Juan Luis Sotomayor. The family called him Juli (*Juu-li*), in the typically creative Puerto Rican approach to nicknames. He saw that Celina was shy, and he was very gentle. And fine looking, *guapísimo*. She liked the way he paid attention. No one had ever paid attention to her. He talked to her about things he read in the newspaper; they both read the whole of *El Diario* every day. No one had ever talked to her about reading before either. Afterward, he would write letters, just to tell her about his day—and to ask when she was coming back. There was always a reason to come back, always another party. Even after the WACs were reassigned to Camp Shanks, somehow Celina and Carmin would find their way down to the Bronx, to 940 Kelly Street.

And at the same time as Celina fell in love with Juli, she fell in love with his mother too. "Don't call me Doña," she said, introducing herself that first day. "Call me Mercedes. Doña is for old ladies." Mercedes loved people, drew them around her, and was the life of the party. She *was* the party. She always found something to laugh at, something to argue about, news to share. Coming into that family, for Celina, was an awakening to life and energy, to the joy of being with people. She could forget about being an orphan.

Mercedes and her son were two of a kind, both of them *embusteros,* spinning tall tales that swept you along, right up to that moment when it dawned: That can't be true! And the poetry that followed after the room went quiet and each looked to the other, mother and son, to see who would begin—the pleasure of that moment of anticipation.

>*¿Qué cómo fue, señora?*
>*Como son las cosas cuando son del alma.*

As it is with matters of the heart . . . *Y entre canto y canto colgaba una lágrima . . .** Celina had always loved poems, as far back as Lajas, copying them onto little slips of paper so that she could learn them. But she had never heard anyone recite them so they came alive.

When she was coming up for discharge, she decided she didn't want to go back to Puerto Rico. Juli said: Stay in New York; we'll get married as soon as you're out of the service. They did, at city hall, with no more ceremony than a couple of signatures and a kiss. When she moved in, it was she and Juli, his brother Vitín and his sister, Carmen, all living with Mercedes and Gallego, the whole family piled into two bedrooms, girls in one, boys in the other. Until the newlyweds got their own place downstairs. The building was an old tenement, with dark and narrow rooms, but their kitchen was big and Juli made it beautiful. He put up curtains and pretty tiles. He raised a scaffold and mixed different colors and

*You ask how it was, Madam?
 As it is with matters of the heart . . .
 And between each song hung a tear . . .
 (from "*El Duelo en la Cañada,*" or "Duel in the Canefield," by Manuel Mur Oti)

painted the old plaster molding on the wall. It was glorious, bouquets of flowers on her kitchen wall. Juli had such flair.

When friends came over, he always had something to offer them, knew how to make them at home. He taught his bride to dance. Bolero. Cha-cha-cha. Merengue. She was clumsy, apologetic. "You'll do okay, Celina," he said. "You'll do okay." She was learning to be like him, and that was all she wanted.

On her birthday, she went into the bedroom, and there on the bed was a new dress, the skirt spread wide, with roses scattered around it. Juli did everything with creative exuberance; in his heart of hearts he was an artist. He'd taught himself to sculpt and made busts of Roosevelt, Truman, and MacArthur, with nothing but newspaper photographs to go by. One day he made Celina's face. It was a strange feeling to see how he saw her, with arched eyebrows, wearing a turban. That face was stunning, and yes, somehow it looked like her, even though she had never imagined herself to be beautiful. It was stranger still when she saw how they used it as a model at the mannequin factory where he worked. There they were, a whole crowd of Celinas with those eyebrows and turbans, headed for shop windows, who knew where.

My father's education was minimal, though he had demonstrated a prodigious numerical aptitude early. Sixth grade was as far as he'd got before he joined other members of the family working full-time in a button factory in Santurce. His father got sick with tuberculosis, which was endemic on the island then, with no treatment available, so Juli had to help support the family. At one point, however, something extraordinary happened. Some professors from the university in San Juan had somehow heard about his math talent and came to watch him doing calculations in his head. They wanted to give him a scholarship to go away to school, but his mother—my *abuelita*—couldn't bear to let him go. He would stay by her side until he was twenty-two, when Abuelita decided to move the entire family, which by then included Gallego, to New York in search of work. My father arrived on the U. S. Army Transport *George S. Simonds,* which then ferried workers from the Caribbean, just days before Christmas of 1944—within days of my mother's arrival.

When he worked at the mannequin factory, they recognized his talent. He loved that job, but the factory closed, and he went on to work at a radiator factory. There they realized he was good with numbers, and they took him off the shop floor to do their bookkeeping. People could see his intelligence, but with no education the opportunities were limited.

Despite having lost his own chance for an education, my father never resented my mother's ambitions. On the contrary, he encouraged her. She managed to finish high school, do a secretarial course, and study to qualify as a practical nurse in the first years of their marriage. In many ways, he defied the macho stereotype of a Latin male. It took my mother seven years to get pregnant, and though she felt the pressure of Abuelita's impatience and comparisons with others, it was never my father who gave her a hard time. When I was finally born, he was overjoyed. She was the one, not he, who doubted her ability to be a good parent.

The family has always told stories about how difficult I was as a baby, and what a terror as a toddler. They say I learned to walk at seven months and to run the very same day, ever after the hot pepper—*¡Ají!*—a menace to myself and everyone else. How many times had they rushed me to the hospital in a panic? Once a fireman neighbor had to rescue me when I got my head stuck in a bucket, trying to see what my voice sounded like in the enclosed space.

Only lately has my mother told me that my father was the one who walked me through endless colicky nights, even drove me around in the car when he found that would settle me; who was calm and patient while she felt panicked and incompetent.

So how did it all fall apart? When did the drinking become a problem? The move from the tenement on Kelly Street to the Bronxdale Houses was a turning point, and it happened around the time the mannequin factory closed, another displacement. My mother saw the new projects as a place that was cleaner and safer to raise a family. But for my father, it was exile in a wilderness of concrete and vacant lots, far from the enfolding life of family and the give-and-take of friends, far from the whole noisy, boisterous business of the streets where everyone knew everyone, watched out for everyone, and spoke Papi's own language. In the long run, the whole family would follow us, and the Bronxdale Houses would borrow a little of the old neighborhood's warmth, but when my mother insisted on making the move, we were pioneers.

He was drinking before that, she realized, but so was everyone else. In those days it was harder to tell a bit of excess from a serious problem. The beginning of the story went back much further. When his father died of tuberculosis, in the little cottage he had built to quarantine himself from the family, Juli was just thirteen. As the eldest son, and now the breadwinner too, he was the man of the house, child or no. Then, a couple of years later, Gallego came along in his *guagua* bus and swept Mercedes off her feet. Juli didn't deal with it very well. He never completely accepted Gallego, even after they all came to New York; years later you could still see the uneasiness between them in subtle ways. It was when Gallego appeared that my father first learned to drink. But it would be a long time before his drinking became the catalyst for daily fights, before my mother realized that she not only didn't know what to do but didn't know what not to do to avoid making it worse. And still she insists: whatever else her husband did, he always worked, and he always cared about Junior and me. Just not enough, because how much could you care if you're killing yourself? If you're drinking every extra penny there is?

My mother could not have even afforded to pay for Papi's burial if Dr. Fisher hadn't insisted that my father take out a life insurance policy: twenty-five hundred dollars. When my mother balked at the payments, Dr. Fisher said he would cover it himself if my parents couldn't, which was enough to shame Mami into scraping it together each month. What kind of a doctor pays for his patients' life insurance? The man was a saint. And he knew that Papi couldn't last.

A doctor could see it coming, but for everybody else it was a shock. Even as a nurse, my mother couldn't see it as it was happening right in front of her. The day they took the bus to the hospital, she was still filling out the forms as they wheeled him away. A minute later they announce a code blue over the loudspeaker. She stops and listens out of habit: someone's in trouble. But no, this is Jacobi Medical Center, not Prospect Hospital. She's not on duty, and the moment passes. It never occurred to her that they were calling the code for Juli, that he was dying then.

In the months she sat in darkness behind her closed door, it was not just the sad waste of a man with so much talent, so much charm, so much life, that she was mourning. The death of the marriage too finally had to be mourned, a recognition so long forestalled by all the tricks the mind plays in the shadows of denial and shame. And mixed in with the mourning was fear—the practical dread of raising two kids as a single mother on a tiny income, but even more the fear that echoed a much older one, of loneliness, of being cast out. A widow, an orphan—what's the difference?

No, it was not guilt that she felt at all. It was sadness and fear. "And it was no clinical depression, Sonia. I'm a nurse, I would recognize that. It was simply *el luto,* the grief that was fitting to the time."

Eight

WHEN I WOKE UP the morning after I'd screamed at my mother, she had already left for work as usual. Ana fixed breakfast for Junior and me and got us off to school as on any other day. But when we came home that afternoon, I could feel a change as soon as I opened the door. The window shades were up for the first time in many months, and Radio WADO was playing. "We're home, Mami!" Junior shouted, and then she appeared. She had on a black dress with white polka dots, and it seemed so vivacious I didn't then register that she was still technically wearing black. She also had on makeup and perfume. I felt my smile spreading, my whole body filling up with relief.

When I look back on my childhood, most of my memories are mapped on either side of certain fault lines that split my world. Opposites coexisted without ever being reconciled: the grim claustrophobia of being home with my parents versus the expansive joy at Abuelita's; a mundane New York existence and a parallel universe on a tropical island. But the starkest contrast is between the before and the after of my father's death.

The silence of mourning was over finally, but more important, the constant, bitter conflict that had filled our lives was over too. Of course Junior and I still found plenty of reasons to yell at each other, provoking my mother's familiar warning call—her *la la la la* that rose ominously in tone, step-by-step, until we got the message that we had gone too far and that justice would be swift if we didn't immediately make ourselves scarce. We were still not like a family on television, but the screaming fights that had worn me down with sadness were no more.

My mother still often worked six days a week, but she was no longer trying to escape from us. Home was now a good place to be, and so she worked the early shift at Prospect Hospital, leaving at six in the morning in order to be home by the time we finished at Blessed Sacrament. Ana came over in the mornings to fix breakfast and get us off to school. I could have managed by myself, but Junior was such a sleepyhead that we'd never have gotten to school on time without help.

The apartment was always immaculate, but it was no longer my doing. I quit my compulsive cleaning and left it to my mother, who cared about the place now. With the bit of insurance money left over after Papi's burial, she even bought a mirror that covered one wall of the living room, making it seem bright and spacious.

I didn't entirely trust this new reality, my mother's transformation included. Once in a while, not often, she would date: a friend's brother, or someone's divorced son. I wondered what would happen to Junior and me if she got married again. Would she leave us behind? Would the fighting resume with a new combatant? My anger still lingered at what I had perceived for so long as her abandonment and her coldness toward us. It would take me many years to let go of that anger completely, and just as long for her to lose the last of her chill. It just wasn't in my mother's nature at that time to show affection, give you a hug, or get down on the floor to engage with a kid. She had been deprived of the formative security that nurtures such impulses. Besides, they would have mussed up her outfit.

My mother always dressed with effortless style, which seemed almost magical given her modest means. Even now in her eighties, she still looks flawless, camera ready, perfectly put together at all times. She would never understand why I lacked this talent that came so naturally to her. There was always some fault in my appearance that was glaring to her and invisible to me, and she badgered me constantly for being sloppy. Ana's daughter, Chiqui, who was a few years older than I and idolized my mother, would say, "Celina looks like a movie star and acts like Florence Nightingale."

Chiqui cared about fashion, about looking good and dressing up; I was convinced that deep down my mother would have gladly swapped daughters with Ana. But about Florence Nightingale, too, Chiqui was right. However undemonstrative, Mami cared about people, and she served as the unofficial visiting nurse on twenty-four-hour call for family, friends, and neighbors throughout Bronxdale and beyond. She took temperatures, gave shots, changed dressings, and called the doctor with any questions she couldn't answer herself. She grumbled only when people took advantage—"Titi Celina! I need some suppositories for my hemorrhoids!" Perhaps they assumed she could pick up supplies for free at the hospital. The staff there would often help themselves, but my mother wouldn't dream of it. "Mayo beat me over a three-cent postage stamp!" she would remind us. "You think I'm going to steal a bottle of aspirin or a box of disposable needles, even for you, Sonia?" She hardly had extra money to pay for them, but it scared her to see my needles, reused to the point of bending when I tried to inject myself.

The healing wasn't limited to physical aches and pains. Some of her best medicine involved listening to people's troubles, which she could do with full attention and sympathy, while reserving judgment. I remember my mother's friend Cristina in tears over her son, who was struggling with drugs. That was a common theme, especially with the sons returning from Vietnam. Sometimes, even if there was no useful advice to give, I saw that listening still helped.

There was also John, the Korean War vet, who sat in his wheelchair in front of our building, the only spot of shade in the new projects, where the trees had barely grown. Every day, two neighbors, older men but still strong, would carry his chair down the four steps on their way to work. The kindness left him stranded until they returned, and so John spent his days watching people come and go. My mother always stopped. She'd ask him how he was, whether he'd heard from his family or needed anything. I never had the courage to stop and chat with John when I wasn't with Mami, but her compassion impressed me, and I would never neglect to smile at him or wave when I passed. The role of confidante to friends has come naturally to me, and I credit the example of my mother, who, left on a park bench, could probably get a tree to tell her its woes.

ONE MEMORY OF my mother's comforting sneaks up on me in the night sometimes. The bedroom I shared with Junior on Watson Avenue, with its one little window, was not just tiny but unbearably hot in summer. We had a little electric fan propped up on a chair, but it didn't help much. Sometimes I would wake up miserable in the middle of the night, with the pillow and sheets drenched in sweat, my hair dripping wet. Mami would come change the bed, whispering to me quietly in the dark so as not to wake Junior. Then she'd sit beside me with a pot of cold water and a washcloth and sponge me down until I fell asleep. The cool damp was so delicious, and her hands so firmly gentle—expert nurse's hands, I thought—that a part of me always tried to stay awake, to prolong this blissful taken-care-of feeling just a bit longer.

WHILE MY MOTHER seemed to find new confidence and strength after the loss of my father, Abuelita would never emerge from her *luto* at all. She had always dressed simply, but now it was simply black, as if all color had vanished from her life. The parties were over for good; the dominoes and dancing would exist only as memories. I still went to see her often, especially after she moved to the projects, just a block away from us. But her eyesight was beginning to fail, and she didn't go out unless it was absolutely necessary. Our visits became more sedate, just the two of us talking, spending time together comfortably. I would bring my homework or read a book while she cooked; it was always quieter at her house.

That year of my father's death had been incredibly hard on her. Her mother, my *bisabuela,* would die very soon after Papi. Abuelita didn't even go to Puerto Rico for the funeral, she was so overwhelmed with grief for her son. She never spoke about my father after he died, at least not in my hearing, but my aunts and uncles understood the transformation that came over her: Juli was the firstborn, the protected one. If he could be taken away from her, then nothing in the world was safe. Something in the fabric of her universe was torn beyond repair.

Her husband's Parkinson's disease had been steadily claiming more and more of him for a long time. By the time my father died, Gallego's speech was fading, and within a few months he was completely bedridden, another reason Abuelita rarely left the house. My mother went every week on her day off from the hospital to bathe him and help change the sheets. Perhaps my grandmother was mourning prospectively for her husband too, the sadness heaving back and forth between Papi and Gallego like a trapped wave. When Gallego died a few years later, she would move to the seniors' home at Castle Hill within days. In the same way that my mother refused to go back into the old apartment after my father died, Abuelita couldn't bear to be in that space where memories and emptiness collided. And so we did the *rosario* for Gallego in a brand-new, subsidized senior citizens' home.

THINGS HAD CHANGED at school, too. My fourth-grade teacher, Sister Maria Rosalie, made an effort to be kinder, and I enjoyed an unofficial respite from reprimand from April, when Papi died, until summer vacation. Not coincidentally, by the time fifth grade started, school had become for the first time something to look forward to. Until then, I had been struggling to figure out what was going on, especially since my return from being in the hospital. Now suddenly lessons seemed easier. It certainly didn't hurt that I had spent the entire summer vacation with my nose in a book, hiding from my mother's gloom, but there was another reason too. It was around that time that my mother made an effort to speak some English at home.

As early as kindergarten, Mami once told me, a teacher had sent a letter home saying that we should speak English in the house. But that was easier said than done. My mother's English was accented and sometimes faltering, though she could manage well enough at the hospital, even working an occasional weekend shift on the telephone switchboard. At home, however, she felt awkward speaking in front of Papi in a language that he didn't know well.

I don't know if my father spoke any English at all. Perhaps he was too shy to speak it badly in front of us. I'm guessing he would have picked up a few phrases to get through his days at the factory, though I never actually heard him say a word. I know that Abuelita couldn't manage in English, because my mother interpreted for her whenever she had to deal with officialdom. I doubt her daughters knew more than a few words, or else they would have been helping Abuelita themselves. I can't even begin to imagine Titi Gloria carrying on in English the way she does in Spanish. Some things just don't translate. In any case, our family life was conducted entirely in Spanish.

It sounded odd when my mother first started speaking English at home, addressing Junior and me as if she were talking to a doctor at the hospital. But as soon as she found the words to scold us, it began to seem natural enough. In time I hardly noticed which language we were speaking. Still, as easily as Junior and I shifted gears into English with the flexibility of youth, at the age of thirty-six my mother could not have steered that change without a mighty effort. Only her devotion to our education could have supplied such a force of will. "You've got to get your education! It's the only way to get ahead in the world." That was her constant refrain, and I could no more get it out of my head than a commercial I'd heard a thousand times.

One day the doorbell rang, and my mother opened the door to a man carrying two big briefcases. It wasn't the man who made the rounds of the projects selling insurance. It wasn't the old man who came to collect two dollars every Saturday for the drapes he'd sold us months before. My mother sat down with the salesman at the kitchen table, and they talked for a very long time, looking at books, adding up numbers. I was in the other room, overhearing bits and pieces: "priceless gift of knowledge . . . like a library of a thousand books . . . easy monthly payments . . ."

When the two big boxes labeled *Encyclopaedia Britannica* arrived, it was Christmas come early. Junior and I sat on the floor surrounded by piles of books like explorers at the base of Everest. Each of the twenty-four volumes was a doorstop, the kind of book you'd expect to see in a library, never in someone's home and certainly not twenty-four of them, including a whole separate book just for the index! As I turned the densely set onionskin pages at random, I found myself wandering the world's geography, pondering molecules like daisy chains, marveling at the physiology of the eye. I was introduced to flora and fauna, to the microscopic structures of cells, to mitosis, meiosis, and Mendel's garden of peas. The world branched out before me in a thousand new directions, pretty much as the salesman had promised, and when it became overwhelming, all I had to do was close the book. It would wait for me to return.

Not all of my mother's efforts to expand our horizons were as welcome as the encyclopedias. Ballet class was a brief torture that I managed to whine my way out of. I was too gangly and uncoordinated; end of story. Piano wasn't much better, and just as brief. I still can't hold a beat, even though the metronome mesmerized me. Guitar lessons, which Junior and I took together, were the worst of all. The real problem was getting there and back through a neighborhood on White Plains Road where a gang of taunting bullies made clear Puerto Rican kids were not welcome. I got smacked by one of them and tried to fight back, but eventually we just made a run for it: no way I could actually beat them.

My cousin Alfred had an answer for this menace: he would teach us self-defense, just the way he learned in the army reserves. We had to do push-ups with him shouting orders like a crazed drill sergeant. He slapped me. Again and again. He counted the slaps, fifty in all. This would build up my courage and resistance, he said. I didn't have the heart to tell him no amount of basic training was going to toughen me enough to take on a gang of much bigger kids just for the sake of playing guitar badly. Sometimes you have to cut your losses.

There was one more reason, beyond the pleasure of reading, the influence of English, and my mother's various interventions, that I finally started to thrive at school. Mrs. Reilly, our fifth-grade teacher, unleashed my competitive spirit. She would put a gold star up on the blackboard each time a student did something really well, and was I a sucker for those gold stars! I was determined to collect as many as I could. After the first As began appearing on my report card, I made a solemn vow that from then on, every report card would have at least one more A than the last one.

A vow on its own wasn't enough; I had to figure out how to make it happen. Study skills were not something that our teachers at Blessed Sacrament had ever addressed explicitly. Obviously, some kids were smarter than others; some kids worked harder than others. But as I also noticed, a hand- ful of kids, the same ones every time, routinely got the top marks. That was the camp I wanted to join. But how did they do it?

It was then, in Mrs. Reilly's class, under the allure of those gold stars, that I did something very unusual for a child, though it seemed like common sense to me at the time. I decided to approach one of the smartest girls in the class and ask her how to study. Donna Renella looked surprised, maybe even flattered. In any case, she generously divulged her technique: how, while she was reading, she underlined important facts and took notes to condense information into smaller bits that were easier to remember; how, the night before a test, she would reread the relevant chapter. Obvi- ous things once you've learned them, but at the time deriving them on my own would have been like trying to invent the wheel. I'd like to believe that even schools in poor neighbor- hoods have made some progress in teaching basic study skills since I was in the fifth grade. But the more critical lesson I learned that day is still one too many kids never figure out: don't be shy about making a teacher of any willing party who knows what he or she is doing. In retrospect, I can see how important that pattern would become for me: how read- ily I've sought out mentors, asking guidance from professors or colleagues, and in every friendship soaking up eagerly whatever that friend could teach me.

At the time, all I knew was that my strategy worked. Soon Mrs. Reilly had moved me to the row next to the window, which was reserved for the top students. My pleasure was diluted, however, when I found out that Junior's teacher had assigned him to the farthest row from the window, where the slowest kids sat. Naturally, Junior was upset, and the unfairness irked me too. It's true that I called him stupid, but that was a big sister's prerogative, and I knew that he wasn't really. He studied almost as hard as I did. He was quiet, but he listened and paid attention; nothing slipped by him.

"He's a boy," said Mami. "He'll get there when he does." The Sisters of Charity held a pessimistic view of male children: they were trouble for the most part, often in need of a good thrashing, and unlikely to amount to much. There was more wisdom in my mother's open-ended encouragement. She would never push Junior and me to get better grades, never crack the whip regarding homework or lecture us about setting our goals high, the way Tío Benny did with my cousin Nelson. When I brought my report card home for her to sign, I could tell she was delighted to see that I was getting As. That same proud smile greeted the news in later years that I'd made valedictorian or was graduating summa cum laude. It didn't matter that she didn't understand exactly what I'd accomplished to earn her pride. She trusted me, and Junior too. "Just study," she would say. "I don't care what grade you get, just study. *No me importa si trabajan lavando baños. Lo importante es hacerlo bien.*" I don't care if you clean toilets, just do it well. Achievement was all very well, but it was the process, not the goal, that was most important.

ON THAT FIRST CHRISTMAS without Papi, Alfred helped me carry the tree home. He held the base and I supported the top as we walked it all the way, retracing the expeditions my father had led in years past. People always used to stop him to ask where he found such a perfect tree. No one stopped

Alfred and me, but it wasn't until we got that sorry specimen up the elevator and into the apartment that we noticed how much it leaned to one side. It was a lesson I'd always remember, if only seasonally: make sure the trunk is straight.

I was in charge of decorating now. I did remember how Papi always said you couldn't have two lights of the same color next to each other, or two identical ornaments side by side, and you had to drape each icicle of silver tinsel separately over a branch. No tossing clumpy handfuls, which disqualified Junior from helping, since he just didn't have the patience to do it right. But what I couldn't figure out was how Papi always managed to string the lights so cunningly that the wires were invisible. I spent hours at it without success. He'd always fussed over it a long time too. So I knew it wasn't easy, but obviously it involved some particular trick that he had never let me in on. I was reminded of another Christmas when I was very young—young enough that family still came to our house for holidays, before Papi's drinking was out of control. I had gone into the kitchen, and there was a *lechón asado* occupying the entire table, with golden, crackly skin and an apple in its mouth. I was mystified: the pig was clearly too big to have fit in our oven, and I couldn't imagine how my father had cooked it. Had he carefully cut it up, roasted it in sections, and put it back together afterward? Stare as I might, I couldn't see any seams.

As the string of lights turned into a hopeless cat's cradle in my hands, Mami walked in and I gave her a desperate look of distress, but she just shook her head and said, "Juli always did the tree. I don't know how."

No good ever did come of trying to unravel Papi's sleight of hand. One year, I had been especially zealous about snooping for presents and discovered the mother lode in the back of one closet, very artfully camouflaged. A little ripping revealed an unimaginable treasure: our own TV! Before that, we used to go to Abuelita's when there was a ball game, and to watch cartoons or the Three Stooges, I went to Nelson's house. I was so excited at what I'd found I thought I would bust. I ran straight to Papi to ask if we could watch it right away. The startled look, and then the total deflation in his face—it was heartbreaking. I had ruined his surprise. That feeling of excitement crumpling into shame would ensure I was never again tempted to peek, even when, years later, my mother had me wrap gifts that I knew, from the absence of a name card, were destined for me.

I'd always taken that part of Christmas seriously. For years when I was small, I bought presents for everyone with money I saved from the penny deposits on bottles. I collected the bottles and washed them and carried them back to the store. I recruited Abuelita and my aunts to save their bottles for me too. Abuelita would even take her empties to the bodega and then just give me the money. I earned a bit more by picking up the little winged sycamore pods from Tío Tonio's backyard: five cents for each shopping bag full. Nelson labored alongside me, but everyone else thought the work was too boring. By the end of the year, I'd have a couple of dollars stashed away, and with that I went shopping at the five-and-dime: a little mirror for Abuelita, a handkerchief for Titi Gloria, some candy for Titi Aurora . . . None of my cousins did that. I was the only one desperate to do right, to be liked, to be invited over.

Finally, one way or another, the tree was finished. The cotton skirting around the base became a snowy setting for the *Nacimiento* with its tiny manger. The picture was complete, soft sparkle and twinkling color, lights peeping shyly from behind the veil of tinsel, the crowning star aglow.

A hug from Papi would have been nice just then. I couldn't deny that our life was so much better now, but I did miss him. For all the misery he caused, I knew with certainty that he loved us. Those aren't things you can measure or weigh. You can't say: This much love is worth this much misery. They're not opposites that cancel each other out; they're both true at the same time.

Nine

D R. ELSA PAULSEN intrigued me. She was tall and very polished, even regal, in her white coat. She spoke with a hint of an accent that was not from New York, but not foreign either. When she walked into the pediatric diabetes clinic at Jacobi Medical Center, everybody—interns, residents, nurses—came to attention. You could tell that they wanted to please her, that she was the boss, though she was also warm and friendly. When she checked in on me, she actually talked to me, not just to my mother.

Dr. Paulsen was the first woman in a position of real-world authority I'd encountered. At Prospect Hospital, where my mother worked, all the doctors were men. The nursing supervisors were women, but that's as far as it went. Even at Blessed Sacrament, the nuns wielded power only over kids. To Monsignor Hart and Father Dolan the Sisters deferred.

At the clinic, the nurse would weigh me and take urine samples. If I was lucky, she took my blood too. If I was unlucky, I'd have to face one of the interns doing this for the first time. Feeling now and then like a guinea pig was in retrospect a small price to pay for the benefit of the cutting-edge treatment being developed there by the Albert Einstein College of Medicine. They had a research program on juvenile diabetes, and considering how rare the disease was then, it was amazing good fortune that the clinic happened to be located in the Bronx, even though we still had to take a long subway ride and then a bus to get there.

With a strong focus on patient education, the clinic was pioneering much that is now standard practice: child-friendly lessons on how to live with diabetes, on nutrition, and on what's going on in your body. Since I'd first begun treatment, my disease had progressed to the point where my pancreas was producing no insulin at all. Without my shots, I'd have been dead within days, if not sooner. The insulin available then was long acting, a single dose given in the morning, but there were sometimes unexpected fluctuations in blood sugar throughout the day. So you had to eat on a rigid schedule and keep snacks or juice at hand in case of a sudden drop. It wasn't true that I couldn't eat sweets, or that mangoes would kill me, as my aunts warned. Fortunately, my mother had a better understanding, and we celebrated after each visit to the clinic by sharing a piece of cherry cheesecake from the hospital cafeteria. It wasn't so much a lesson in moderation; she already knew she could trust me to eat right. Nor was it really my reward: my mother was always fonder of sweets than I was, and there was maternal guilt to be fed.

For the most part, moderation with sweets came naturally to me because I so disliked the sensation caused by a spike in blood sugar. I could recognize the first hints of that slow-motion heaviness, that feeling of trying to get out of the chair with a thousand-pound barbell on my lap. Low blood sugar felt just as bad but in a different way. I would start to sweat and get dizzy; I would lose patience, and my thinking became fuzzy. Complicating matters, there was then no easy, accurate way to test your own blood sugar, no glucose meter, only urine strips that reflected what your levels had been hours earlier. So to keep track of my blood sugar, I cultivated a constant mindfulness of how my body felt. Even now, with much more precise technology at hand, I still find myself mentally checking physical sensations every minute of the day. Along with discipline, that habit of internal awareness was perhaps another accidental gift from my disease. It is linked, I believe, to the ease with which I can recall the emotions attached to memories and to a fine-tuned sensitivity to others' emotional states, which has served me well in the courtroom.

But even if I took the shots like clockwork and watched my diet carefully, there was the grim reality of the disease then: I would still probably die sooner rather than later from complications. Given the advances in treatment since I was a child, a shortened life span is no longer as likely as it was. But that was the reality at the time, and it explains why my family had received my diagnosis as a catastrophe of tragic dimensions. My mother's biggest fear was the threat of amputations, blindness, and a panoply of other complications that were then typical. As collected and professionally cool as she was in the emergency room, as confident and reassuring when helping a sick neighbor, she would fall apart when I was the patient. If I stubbed my toe, she'd be yelling about gangrene. Sometimes I would vent my annoyance through reckless antics on the playground, just to scare her. And always, since that first day, I had asserted my independence by giving myself my own shots.

It could have been worse, I realized. My cousin Elaine had one arm that was paralyzed and stunted since birth, encased in a brace. My diabetes, being invisible, seemed the lesser evil. And Elaine got even more grief from Titi Judy than I did from my mother. As soon as Elaine would muster the courage to venture the simplest move on the playground, Titi Judy would panic. Her mother's fear was contagious and I thought might be holding Elaine back from much that she was perfectly capable of doing.

My cousin Alfred was the only one who refused to believe that diabetes was a terrible disability. Perhaps that explained his drill sergeant's determination to toughen me up. It was Alfred who would get me up on a pair of skis and even put me on a horse two or three times. When he took Junior and me to the Statue of Liberty, he made us climb all the way to the crown. I was spent by the time we had scaled the pedestal, but no: "Onward and upward! All the way to the top!" The last flights were torture, my legs in such pain that I couldn't stop tears from coming. But no way was I going to let Alfred see me cry, which meant I had to stay ahead of him, and that's how I made it to the top.

Eventually, I would translate my family's fatalism into an outlook that better suited my temperament: I probably wasn't going to live as long as most people, I figured. So I couldn't afford to waste time. Once in school, I would never contemplate taking a semester or year off. Later might never come, so I'd better get to work right now. That urgency has always stayed with me, even as the threat has receded.

SITTING IN the waiting room at the clinic, I wondered, did it never occur to anyone at the Albert Einstein College of Medicine that kids who might not have long to live shouldn't have to wait endless hours with nothing to read but stacks of old *Highlights*? I should have brought my Nancy Drew book, I grumbled.

But when my turn came, they gave me something else to read—a pamphlet about choosing a profession. I am ten years old, I thought. Isn't it a little early to be worrying about this? *You can be a famous actress,* the pamphlet assured me, *like Mary Tyler Moore. You can be a professional athlete. You can be:*

> *a doctor*
> *a lawyer*
> *an architect*
> *an engineer*
> *a nurse*
> *a teacher . . .*

The list of possibilities for a diabetic didn't seem very long. And then, more darkly, there was a list of professions that were out-of-bounds. You couldn't be an airline pilot or a bus driver. Fair enough, I thought: you don't want someone flying a plane who might pass out. You couldn't serve in the military. Fine: I'd had enough of boot camp for a lifetime thanks to Alfred. And you couldn't be a police officer . . . uh-oh. That one stopped me like a slap in the face.

You couldn't be a police officer? That meant you couldn't be a detective. This was a catastrophe! It's true that Nancy Drew manages without being a police officer, but she is an exception. She was also fictional. I knew enough about the real world to know that detectives are normally cops and not eighteen-year-old girls with charmed lives. And yet Nancy Drew had a powerful hold on my imagination. Every night, when I'd finished reading and got into bed and closed my eyes, I would continue the story, with me in Nancy's shoes until I fell asleep.

The young sleuth tools around in her little blue roadster with the top down. She is an incurable optimist who cleverly turns obstacles to her own advantage. Nancy Drew's father is a lawyer. He talks to her about his cases and gives her tips that help her solve crimes. They are like partners, father and daughter.

The world they live in is a kind of fairy tale, where people own houses on winding, tree-shaded driveways; visit summer homes at the lake; and attend charity balls at the country club. Nancy travels, too. She's even been to Paris. What I wouldn't have given to see the Eiffel Tower one day! But even though Nancy Drew is rich, she isn't a snob. And even though it is fiction, I knew such a world did exist. It wasn't Cinderella and pumpkins turning into carriages. It was real, and I was hungry to learn about it.

I was convinced I would make an excellent detective. My mind worked in ways very similar to Nancy Drew's, I told myself: I was a keen observer and listener. I picked up on clues. I figured things out logically, and I enjoyed puzzles. I loved the clear, focused feeling that came when I concentrated on solving a problem and everything else faded out. And I could be brave when I needed to be.

I could be a great detective, if only I weren't diabetic.

"JUNIOR, change the channel! *Perry Mason*'s on." Okay, so I couldn't be a police officer or a detective, but it occurred to me that the solution to my quandary appeared on that small black-and-white screen every Thursday night.

Perry Mason was a lawyer, a defense attorney. He worked

alongside a detective, Paul Drake, but even so it was Perry
Mason who untangled the real story behind the crime, which
was never what it seemed. And it was once the trial started
that things got really interesting. You assume, of course, that
Perry Mason is the hero. He's the one the show is named
after, the one who gets the close-up shots, who wins the case
almost every time and gets the hugs and tears of gratitude at
the end. But my sympathies were not entirely monopolized
by Perry Mason. I was fond of Burger, the prosecutor, too. I
liked that he was a good loser, that he was more committed
to finding the truth than to winning his case. If the defendant
was truly innocent, he once explained, and the case was dismissed, then he had done his job, because justice had been
served.

Most of all it was the judge who fascinated me. A minimal but vital presence, he was more of an abstraction than a
character: a personification of justice. At the end of the hour,
when Perry Mason said, "Your Honor, I move to dismiss the
charges against my client and release him," it was the judge
who made the final decision—"case dismissed" or "motion
granted"—that wrapped up the episode. You had to watch
carefully because it was over in a flash, but I knew that was
the most important moment in the show. And even before
that final decision, it was the judge who called the shots, who
decided whether it was "overruled" or "sustained" when a
lawyer said, "Objection!"

There was a whole new vocabulary here. And though I
wasn't sure what every detail meant, I followed the gist of
it. It was like the puzzles I enjoyed, a complex game with its
own rules, and one that intersected with grand themes of
right and wrong. I was intrigued and determined to figure
it out.

I could be a great lawyer, I decided. But a part of me, I knew, would have preferred to be the judge rather than Perry Mason. At the time, with no knowledge of what either aspiration might entail, the one didn't seem any more outlandish than the other.

Ten

I WAS DOING my homework in front of the TV one night when my mother and her friends piled in to watch *The Ed Sullivan Show*. Ana, Cristina, and Irma were all there, chattering away. They used to give my mother a hard time for letting Junior and me do homework with the TV on, but she always answered them: "Those kids are a lot more intelligent than I am. They study four, five hours every night, and they bring home good grades. Who am I to tell them how to study?" They couldn't argue with that logic. Still, they were not alone in their anxieties. The nuns at Blessed Sacrament had their own theories about the dangers television posed to impressionable minds. They could tolerate Ed Sullivan but not *The Man from U.N.C.L.E.*, a godless Russian spy in the role of a good guy being too great a threat to the received cold-war narrative. It seemed lost on everyone that television helped broaden our horizons beyond the Bronx, where I was unlikely to have encountered a lawyer in action, or much else I could aspire to.

In any case, it wasn't as if I was actually watching the TV most of the time. It had now become just background noise, where once it had been a talisman to ward off the suffocation of an engulfing silence in the house. I'd long since learned how to concentrate with other things going on around me. Sometimes a bomb could have dropped on Bruckner Boulevard, and it wouldn't have distracted me. So Mami and her friends probably thought I had totally tuned them out that night in 1965 when Tom Jones was grinding his hips and growling, "It's not unusual . . ."

"*¡Qué guapo!*" Ana said, whistling under her breath.

"If he asked me for a date, I wouldn't say no." My ears perked up. Did my mother just say that? Okay, maybe it's not true that nothing could distract me.

Cristina topped them both: "I wouldn't mind finding his slippers under my bed." I must have turned beet red.

Not that I was innocent. I knew that my new friend Carmelo and his girlfriend did more than kiss in our bedroom when they came over; it was one of the reasons they liked visiting our house. Kids gossiped. Donna showed off her hickeys. Stuff happened. Stuff happened all the time, whether you wanted it to or not. But I, for one, wasn't there yet.

I was beginning to find my own role in the social scene of middle school, and Carmelo had a lot to do with it, especially his nickname for me: Computer-Head, or Compy for short. He meant it as a compliment: I was rational and methodical. When my mind went to work, he imagined, lights blinked and tapes whirred, men in white coats with clipboards feeding me punch cards for breakfast. Carmelo saw the benefit of being friends with a nerd and would always sit beside me for every quiz and test, even though I didn't make it easy for him. He must have pulled his share of neck muscles trying to get decent grades. But he was still grateful: in turn, he looked out for me and wouldn't let me be bullied by anyone.

Carmelo was one of the most popular kids at school. He

had the special ease of a cute boy: tall, with close-cropped curly hair and a dimple on one side when he smiled. He and Eileen, another one of the cool kids, were both good friends of mine, which did wonders for my social standing. Both lived in the Rosedale Mitchell-Lama co-op on the other side of the highway, a notch up from the Bronxdale Houses. (Or several notches, if you listened to Titi Judy and Tío Vitín, who lived there too.)

The gang liked to hang out at my place because my mother, happy to have her kids nearby and under her surveillance, made everyone feel at home. There was never a hint of disapproval about anyone I might choose to invite: all were welcome, with plenty of rice and beans to go around. Often, Eileen's stepsisters, Solangela and Myra, came too, even though they were older, in high school. They were Mami's friends as much as mine, endlessly discussing their love lives with her.

"Mami, if I invite some kids over tomorrow, can you make your *chuletas*?" I stuck my nose in the refrigerator, taking stock of what we had, what we needed to buy. My mother gave me a look as if I'd just asked her to address the United Nations General Assembly in five minutes. For all her willingness to welcome my friends, she remained convinced that she was a lousy cook, ever since the Thanksgiving after Papi died, when she roasted her first turkey with the paper packet of giblets left inside. It was a mystery how someone who never enjoyed cooking made such heavenly pork chops.

I was more than happy to handle the shopping and the rest of the preparations. Hosting a party came naturally to me. I loved it when the apartment was full of talk and laughter, music and cooking smells. It reminded me of Abuelita's parties, even if it was just a bunch of middle school kids. I tried to remember how Abuelita had made it happen and translate that for seventh graders. No rum but plenty of Coke and heaps of rice and beans and Mami's pork chops.

Junior stuck his head in the kitchen door and chanted a whiny taunt, "Sonia's in love with Ringo, nyeah, nyeah, nyeah . . ."

Junior was still my cross to bear, perpetual pest of an unshakable little sibling. When my friends came over, he listened to every word we said, pretending to be doing homework or watching TV. Sooner or later anything I said, even a confession of my favorite Beatle, would be used against me.

At that age, we fought routinely, and our fights were physical. At least that's how it worked at home. Outside, at school or on the street, I was still Junior's protector, and I took it as a grave responsibility, suffering lots of bumps and bruises on his behalf. For these I would settle with him later, privately. We continued in that manner until the day I recognized the beginning of a growth spurt I knew I could never match. He would always be three years younger, but he was a boy, with all that entailed hormonally, and a boy who spent hours every day on the basketball court. The time had come for war by other means: "Junior, we're too old for this. Let's be civilized, we can talk things out and"—though I don't remember saying this last bit in so many words—"we can always blackmail each other." Henceforth that was the form our hostilities took. We tracked each other's trespasses, we snitched to Mami, or threatened to, whichever availed the greater advantage. Our snitching often entailed phone calls to the hospital that must have driven my mother nuts, not to mention her supervisors, bless their forbearance. I've always believed phone calls from kids must be allowed if mothers are to feel welcome in the workplace, as anyone who has worked in my chambers can attest. Eventually, in high school, Junior and I outgrew our warring ways, and over time we've become very close. We don't talk all that often, but when something really matters, each of us naturally reaches out to the other before anyone else. Still, to this day my brother claims a deep resentment that he spent his childhood waiting to get big enough to beat me up and on the threshold of his triumph I changed the rules.

WHEN POPE PAUL VI CAME TO New York in the fall of 1965, Monsignor Hart arranged for a group of students from Blessed Sacrament to go see him. I wanted more than anything to be included. This wasn't just a field trip—not that we ever went on field trips at Blessed Sacrament. It was history in the making, the first time a pope had visited the United States. And Paul VI wasn't just any pope. He was elected the summer after my father died, when I had spent so much time reading. Everything I'd read about him inspired me, and now once again there were magazine and newspaper articles appearing almost daily, describing the plans for his visit and the ideas he had—about ending the war in Vietnam and using the money from disarmament to help poor countries, about dialogue between religions, and about continuing the work of Vatican II to make the Church more responsive and open to ordinary people.

I was often moved and excited by books, but how often does a newspaper article give you chills? I had to look up unfamiliar words—"ecumenism," "vernacular"—but all his impulses resonated deeply with me. I loved this pope!

So I was especially upset and disappointed at not being allowed to see him—though not surprised: only kids who had attended church regularly were included. Ever since

Father Dolan had refused to pay a call on my mother in her misery, my Sunday attendance at Blessed Sacrament Church had faltered. I often went to St. Athanasius with Titi Aurora instead. That didn't count at Blessed Sacrament, though. And so I would conclude that I had to figure out for myself what really counted.

"So what was it like? Did you shake hands? Did he talk to you?" I interrogated my classmates. Despite the bitterness of exclusion, I was hungry for details. It was a relief to learn that I hadn't missed much. The kids from Blessed Sacrament were among a crowd of thousands, and they saw less than I did on television. The cameras had followed the pope through the thronged streets of Manhattan, into St. Patrick's, to a meeting with President Johnson, and to a Mass at Yankee Stadium. Best of all, they had captured his address to the UN General Assembly: "No more war, never again war. Peace, it is peace that must guide the destinies of people and of all mankind." All in one amazing day.

IT OCCURRED TO ME that if I was going to be a lawyer—or, who knows, a judge—I had to learn to speak persuasively and confidently in front of an audience. I couldn't be a quivering mess of nerves. So when they asked for volunteers to do the Bible reading in church on Sunday, I spied an opportunity to test myself. Girls reading was a new thing, a small ripple from Vatican II along with the tidal wave that had changed the Mass from Latin to English. We couldn't be altar servers, though; that was still for boys only.

Doing the Bible reading was not the same as giving a speech, of course, because you didn't need to worry about what you would say or even memorize it. It was a long way from arguing a case in a trial, but a small step in the right direction. And I had to start somewhere.

As I walked up the few stone stairs to the pulpit, my knees were buckling. I watched my hand tremble as it came to rest on the banister, as if it belonged to someone else. If I couldn't even keep my hands still, what would happen when I opened my mouth to speak? Every pew was packed, rows and rows of faces looking at me, waiting, it now seemed, for me to make a fool of myself. I could feel a faint gagging reflex. Suppose I threw up right there, all over the Bible? I had practiced the night before, read the passage aloud so many times—would it all be for nothing?

Wobbly at first, my voice soon steadied, and so did my knees. The words started to flow. I knew it was important to look up at the end of each sentence, but I didn't dare. The faces terrified me. If I looked in their eyes, I'd be lost, maybe even turn into a pillar of salt. So at the end of each sentence I looked at the ceiling instead: the wooden beams marking off rectangular coffers, gold spiral edges, lamps hanging from black metal rings. But soon the weirdness of looking up made me even more self-conscious, and I began to worry how this was coming across: "Does this kid think she's read-ing to God?" Fortunately, after the next verse or two came inspiration: to avoid the trap of their eyes, I would focus on their foreheads . . .

Before I knew it, I made it down the stairs and back to my seat. I had done it, and I knew I could do it again.

I SPENT EIGHT YEARS at Blessed Sacrament School, far more than half my life by the time the last bell of eighth grade rang. Ted Shaw, a high school friend who later became the legal director of the NAACP Legal Defense and Educational Fund, describes Catholic school as his salvation and damnation: it shaped his future and terrified his heart. I identify with this depiction. The Sisters of Charity helped to shape who I am, but there was much that I wouldn't be sad to leave behind.

IN THE MIMEOGRAPHED PAMPHLET that was our eighth-grade yearbook, each child wrote a "last will and testament" to the life being left behind at Blessed Sacrament; the Sisters responded in turn with a few words of "prophecy" about each child. Looking over those pages, I am struck by how low were their expectations for their young charges. Of one girl, for instance, it is written that she had "hopes of becoming a fashion designer but we think she'd make a better mother with six children." Sadly, such discouragement, directed even at the many girls who aspired to more traditional occupations like secretaries, was not unusual. And yet for a tiny school with very limited resources, in a poor neighborhood where many young lives were fatally seduced by drugs and alcohol or cut short by violence, Blessed Sacrament launched so many of my classmates toward a productive and meaningful existence, success often well beyond those mimeographed prophecies. There is no denying that credit is due to the Sisters of Charity and the discipline they instilled, however roughly.

My own yearbook entry surprises me with its self-assurance. I was confident by then of my own intellect:

I, Sonia Sotomayor, being of sound mind and body, do hereby leave my brains, to be divided evenly, to the incom-

ing class of 8-1, so they will never have to know the wrath
of Sister Mary Regina because of lack of knowledge.

And here, less confident but still hopeful, is what Sister
Mary Regina wrote:

> This girl's ambitions, odd as they may seem, are to become
> an attorney and someday marry. Hopefully, she wishes to
> be successful in both fields. We predict a new life of chal-
> lenges in Cardinal Spellman, where she will be attending
> High School, we hope she will be able to meet these new
> challenges.

I RECENTLY RETURNED to Blessed Sacrament for a visit.
It has many fewer students and much smaller classes than
when I attended. It is also clear that the teachers, now more
laypeople as well as nuns, subscribe to a more nurturing
approach since abandonment of the rod. Every generation
has its own way of showing it cares.

Eleven

CARDINAL SPELLMAN HIGH SCHOOL WAS a good hour's ride from the Bronxdale Houses, assuming the trains and buses were running on time. The school building was divided right down the middle by a crack in the wall, girls on one side and boys on the other. On each floor, a nun stood guard at the crack to make sure that neither sex crossed over into the other's side without a teacher's permission slip. The nuns were Sisters of Charity, the same as at Blessed Sacrament, but by the time I entered high school in 1968, many had shed the black bonnets and long black habits, looking a lot less menacing than they used to.

Girls and boys were allowed to mix in the lunchroom, but we had separate classes, except for religion and a very few upper-level courses, mostly Advanced Placement. Another exception was freshman Spanish. All the kids who spoke Spanish at home were in one accelerated class, taught by a nun recently arrived from Spain. It was her plan, she told us, to condense three years of high school Spanish into one month of "review" and then start teaching us literature.

We were only a week into the semester when the class was on the verge of mutiny. A desperate mob surrounded Eddie

Irizarry and me—the two biggest mouths—asking us to plead the class's case.

"Tell her we aren't Spanish, we're American."

"Forty-five minutes and nobody understood a word that she said!"

Our teacher was totally unaware that Puerto Rican kids raised in the Bronx would have had no formal instruction in their native language. As for the acquired tongue, many of us had struggled in earlier years through a sink-or-swim transition in schools that had provided no support for kids who'd first enrolled speaking little or no English. And so I started high school having never studied Spanish grammar, conjugated a verb, or read more than a few sentences at a time: an advertisement, or a newspaper headline, maybe a very short article. I had certainly never read a book in Spanish. None of us could understand the teacher's proper Castilian accent or her elegant diction. We looked on blankly, unable even to follow her instructions, let alone do the assignments.

My Spanish was so deficient that I wasn't even pronouncing my own name properly. She called me on it. "You have the most regal of Spanish names," she said. "Don't you ever let anybody mispronounce it. You are *Sonia Sotomayor—Soh-toh-mah-yor*—and anything less is disgraceful. Say it correctly, and wear it with pride."

I could tell that her heart was in the right place. And sure enough, when Eddie and I explained the situation, she was very understanding and accommodating. The very next day she came back with a gentle apology and a new plan that was much more realistic: we would still go twice as fast as the regular Spanish class, but we'd cover the basics and learn grammar first, then start Spanish literature the second year. It was a good lesson in the value of learning to express your basic needs and trusting you will be heard. Teachers, I was finally realizing, were not the enemy.

Not most of them, anyway. There was the geometry teacher nicknamed Rigor Mortis. Word had it she'd been at Cardinal Spellman since before the invention of the triangle, standing before eons of freshman classes, like a prehistoric scarecrow, skinny and wrinkled with a bright thatch of red hair.

I was shocked when she called me into her office and accused me of cheating. The basis for her accusation was my perfect score on the Regents geometry exam. No one in all her centuries of experience had ever scored a hundred on the Regents.

"So who did I cheat from?" I asked indignantly. "Who else got a hundred that I could have copied from?"

She looked flummoxed for a moment. "But you've never scored higher than eighties or low nineties on the practice tests. How could you get a hundred?"

The truth, as I explained, was that I'd never once got an answer wrong on the practice tests; points had been deducted only because I hadn't followed the steps she had prescribed. I had reasoned out my own steps, which made sense to me, and she had never explained what was wrong with them. On the Regents exam we only had to give the answer; no one was checking the steps.

What happened next truly amazed me. She dug out my old tests and reviewed them. Acknowledging the validity of my proofs, she changed my grades. Even Rigor Mortis, it turned out, wasn't quite as rigid as all that.

PERHAPS THE MOST IMPROBABLE turn of events in those first months: my cousin Miriam and I signed up to be mari-

time cadets. On Friday nights, we went to P.S. 75 at Hunts
Point and marched around the gym. We wore uniforms. We
memorized nautical terms and learned how to tie knots. We
would never actually set foot on a boat, but we did march in
the Puerto Rican Day Parade.

Our ulterior motive for joining the cadets was to chaper-
one her brother Nelson, who played trumpet in their marching band. Nelson, my childhood accomplice, my genius
sidekick, had grown into a girl magnet. He was incredibly
handsome, as smart as ever, with a wicked sense of humor.
He'd also become an impressively talented musician. In fact,
he was desperate to pursue this love, even though Tío Benny
had always wanted him to be a doctor. He'd only agreed to
let Nelson join the marching band because he thought the
discipline was good for him and it would keep him off the
street.

The seductions of girls and music weren't the only reasons Tío Benny felt someone had to keep an eye on Nelson.
Nelson had started at Bronx Science the same year I entered
Cardinal Spellman, and already he was struggling. There was
no question of his scientific aptitude. By the time he got to
high school, he'd won several prestigious awards for his science fair projects, and his teachers had recognized him as
a prodigy, equally talented at science and music. No, Nelson's real difficulties were not intellectual but emotional: Tío
Benny and Titi Carmen were breaking up.

I myself couldn't bear to hear people gossiping about
it. I'd cover my ears against any talk of who had wronged
whom. And I certainly didn't subscribe to the theory of
Abuelita and my other aunts, who were convinced that a
hex put on the couple by means of some chicken guts left on
their doorstep had caused the breakup. It was heartbreaking

enough whatever the reason, and I couldn't imagine what it was doing to Nelson, Miriam, and little Eddie, too.

Especially Nelson.

When we were little, Miriam always found a thousand reasons to say no to any new game or plan that I suggested. Eventually, she would agree, but it was such an effort cajoling her. We would have a lot of fun together in high school, but she'd been one prissy little kid growing up. Nelson, on the other hand, never said no to me. He was game for anything, sticking his neck out for a friend without thinking twice. Those were qualities that I loved in him when we were little, but those same qualities would leave him vulnerable to the worst temptations, especially in a neighborhood that was drowning in drugs.

Sometimes when I watched Nelson practice for the band, I'd imagine him standing on the bow of a boat, blowing his trumpet with all his heart, only for that boat to drift slowly out to sea and leave me standing on the dock.

THE SUMMER VACATION between freshman and sophomore years, I was working my way through the summer reading list when *Lord of the Flies* brought me to a halt. I wasn't ready to start another book when I finished that one. I'd never read anything so layered with meaning: it haunted me, and I needed to think about it some more. But I didn't want to spend the whole break doing nothing but reading and watching TV. Junior was happy shooting baskets all the daylight hours, but there wasn't much else going on around the projects if you were too old for the playground and not into drugs. Orchard Beach still beckoned, roasting traffic and all, but getting there was a trek you couldn't make every day.

Besides, without Abuelita's laugh and the anticipation of her overgenerous picnic in the trunk, without Gallego gunning the engine of a car packed with squirming kids, somehow it just wasn't the same.

So I decided to get a job. Mami and Titi Carmen were sitting in Abuelita's kitchen over coffee when I announced my plan. There were no shops or businesses in the projects, but maybe I could find someone to hire me in Abuelita's old neighborhood. Titi Carmen still lived on Southern Boulevard and worked nearby at United Bargains. The mom-and-pop stores under the El wouldn't hire kids—leaning on family labor rather than paying a stranger—but the bigger retailers along Southern Boulevard might. I proposed to walk down the street and inquire in each one. "Don't do that," said Titi Carmen. "Let me ask Angie." Angie was Titi Carmen's boss.

My mother meanwhile looked stricken and bit her lip. She didn't say anything until Titi had gone home. Then, for the first time, she told me a little bit about her own childhood: about sewing and ironing handkerchiefs for Titi Aurora since before she could remember, for hours every day. "I resented it, Sonia. I don't want you to grow up feeling like I did." She went on to apologize for being unable to buy us more things but still insisted it would be even worse if I blamed her one day for depriving me of a childhood.

I didn't see that coming. Nobody was forcing me to work. Sure, a little pocket money would be nice, but that wasn't the main motivation. "Mami, I *want* to work," I told her. She'd worked too hard all her life to appreciate that leisure could mean boredom, but that's what I knew I'd be facing if I sat home all summer. I promised never to blame her. In that moment, I began to understand how hard my mother's life had been.

Titi Carmen reported back that Angie was willing to hire me for a dollar an hour. That was less than minimum wage, but since I wasn't old enough to work legally anyway, they would just pay me off the books. I would take the bus, meet Titi Carmen at her place, and then we'd walk over to United Bargains together. That became our routine. It wasn't a neighborhood where you walked alone.

United Bargains sold women's clothing. I pitched in wherever needed: restocking, tidying up, monitoring the dressing rooms. I was supposed to watch for the telltale signs of a shoplifter trying to disappear behind the racks, rolling up merchandise to stuff in a purse.

Junkies were especially suspect. They were easy to spot by the shadow in their eyes, though the tracks on their arms were hidden under long sleeves even in summer. There was never an argument, never a scene. Once in a while I had to say, "Take it out." Most of the time I didn't need to utter a word. She would pull the garment out of her bag, put it back on the hanger, or maybe hand it to me, our eyes never meeting as she slinked out. We always let them go. There wasn't much choice: in a precinct that had come to be known as Fort Apache, the Wild West, the cops had their hands full dealing with the gangs. Besides, the management understood that the shame and pity were punishment enough, and I naturally agreed. I abhorred feeling pitied, that degrading secondhand sadness I would always associate with my family's reaction to the news I had diabetes. To pity someone else feels no better. When someone's dignity shatters in front of you, it leaves a hole that any feeling heart naturally wants to fill, if only with its own sadness.

On Saturday nights the store was open late, and it was dark by the time we rolled down the gates. Two patrol officers would meet us at the door and escort us home. I don't know how this was arranged, whether it was true that one of the saleswomen was sleeping with one of these cops, but I was glad of it anyway. As we walked, we could see the SWAT team on the roofs all along Southern Boulevard, their silhouettes bulging with body armor, assault rifles bristling. One by one the shops would darken, and we could hear the clatter of the graffiti-covered gates being rolled down, trucks driving off, until we were the only ones walking. Even the prostitutes had vanished. You might trip on tourniquets and empty glassine packets when you got into the courtyard area at Titi Carmen's, but you wouldn't run into any neighbors. I would spend the night there, talking the night away with Miriam. I wished Nelson were there too, but he was never home anymore.

I remember falling asleep thinking again about *Lord of the Flies*. It was as if the fly-crusted sow's head on a stick were planted in a crack of the sidewalk on Southern Boulevard. The junkies haunting the alley were little boys smeared with war paint, abandoned on a hostile island, and the eyes of the hunters cruising slowly down the street glowed with primitive appetites. The cops in their armor were only a fiercer tribe. Where was the conch?

The next morning, in daylight, Southern Boulevard was less threatening. The street vendors were out, shop fronts were open, people were coming and going. On the way home I stopped at a makeshift fruit cart to buy a banana for a snack. I was standing there peeling my purchase when a police car rolled up to the curb. The cop got out and pointed here and there to what he wanted—there was a language barrier—and the vendor loaded two large shopping bags with fruit. The cop made as if to reach for his wallet, but it was only a gesture, and the vendor waved it off. When the cop drove away, I asked the man why he didn't take the money.

"*Es el precio de hacer negocios.* If I don't give the fruit, I can't sell the fruit."

My heart sank. I told him I was sorry it was like that.

"We all have to make a living," he said with a shrug. He looked more ashamed than aggrieved.

Why was I so upset? Without cops our neighborhood would be even more of a war zone than it was. They worked hard at a dangerous job with little thanks from the people they protected. We needed them. Was I angry because I held the police to a higher standard, the same way I did Father Dolan and the nuns? There was something more to it, beyond the betrayal of trust, beyond the corruption of someone whose uniform is a symbol of the civic order.

How do things break down? In *Lord of the Flies,* the more mature of those lost boys start off with every intention of building a moral, functional society on their island, drawing on what they remember—looking after the "littluns," building the shelters, keeping the signal fire burning. Their little community gradually breaks down all the same, battered by those who are more self-indulgent, those who are driven by ego and fear.

Which side was the cop on?

The boys need rules, law, order, to keep their worst instincts in check. The conch they blow to call a meeting or hold for the right to speak stands for order, but it holds no power in itself. Its only power is what they agree to honor. It is a beautiful thing, but fragile.

When I was much younger, on summer days I would sometimes go along with Titi Aurora to the place where she worked as a seamstress. Those must have been days

when Mami was working the day shift and, for some reason, I couldn't go to Abuelita's. That room with the sewing machines whirring was a vision of hell to me: steaming
hot, dark, and airless, with the windows painted black and
the door shut tight. I was too young to be useful, but I tried
to help anyway, to pass the time. Titi Aurora would give me
a box of zippers to untangle, or I'd stack up hangers, sort
scraps by color, or fetch things for the women sewing. All day
long I'd keep an eye out for anyone heading toward the door.
As soon as it opened, I'd race over and stick my head out for
a breath of air, until Titi saw me and shooed me back in. I
asked her why they didn't just keep the door open. "They just
can't," she would say.

Behind the closed door and the blackened windows, all
those women were breaking the law. But they weren't crimi-
nals. They were just women toiling long hours under miserable conditions to support their families. They were doing
what they had to do to survive. It was my first inkling of
what a tough life Titi Aurora had had. Titi never got the
schooling that Mami got, and she'd borne the brunt of the
father Mami was spared from knowing. Her married life
would have many challenges and few rewards. Work was the
only way she knew to keep going, and she never missed a day.
And though Titi was also the most honest person I knew—if
she found a dime in a pay phone, she'd dial the operator to
ask where she should mail it—she broke the law every day
she went to work.

One evening at United Bargains, the women were making
crank calls, dialing random numbers out of the phone book.
If a woman's voice answered, they acted as if they were having an affair with her husband, then howled with laughter at
their poor gull's response. Titi Carmen would join in, tak-

ing her turn on the phone and laughing as long and hard as any of them. I couldn't understand how anyone could be so cruel—so arbitrarily, pointlessly cruel. What was the pleasure in it? Walking home, I asked her, "Titi, can't you imagine the pain you're causing in that house?"

"It was just a joke, Sonia. Nobody meant any harm."

How could she not imagine? How could the cop not imagine what two large shopping bags full of fruit might measure in a poor vendor's life, maybe a whole day's earnings? Was it so hard to see himself in the other man's shoes?

I was fifteen years old when I understood how it is that things break down: people can't imagine someone else's point of view.

Twelve

THREE DAYS BEFORE Christmas and midway through my freshman year at Cardinal Spellman High School, we moved to a new apartment in Co-op City. Once again, my mother had led us to what seemed like the edge of nowhere. Co-op City was swampland, home to nothing but a desolate amusement park called Freedomland, until the cement mixers and dump trucks arrived barely a year before we did. We moved into one of the first of thirty buildings planned for a development designed to house fifty-five thousand. To get home from school, I had to hike a mile—down Baychester Avenue, across the freeway overpass, and through the vast construction site of half-built towers and bare, bulldozed mud—before reaching human habitation. An icy wind that could lift you off your feet blew from the Hutchinson River. Flurries of snow blurred the construction cranes against an opaque sky of what seemed like Siberia in the Bronx.

At least now we lived close enough for me to walk to school, and I was glad of that. The hour-long trek by bus and train from Watson Avenue had been tedious. Poor Junior, who was only in sixth grade when we moved, would make

the commute in reverse from Co-op City to Blessed Sacrament for another two and a half years. No one we knew
had ever heard of Co-op City. My mother learned about it
from some newspaper article on the city's plans for building
affordable housing. The cost of living there was pegged to
income, and at the same time you were buying inexpensive
shares in a cooperative, so in theory there was a tax break.

My mother was eager to get us into a safer place because
the Bronxdale projects were headed downhill fast. Gangs
were carving up the territory and each other, adding the
threat of gratuitous violence to the scourges of drugs and
poverty. A plague of arson was spreading through the surrounding neighborhoods as landlords of crumbling buildings chased insurance. Home was starting to look like a war
zone.

It was Dr. Fisher who made the move possible. When he
died, he left my mother five thousand dollars in his will, the
final and least expected of the countless kindnesses that we
could never repay, although we tried. When Dr. Fisher was
hospitalized after his wife died, Abuelita made Gallego stop
on the way to work every morning to pick up Dr. Fisher's
laundry and deliver clean pajamas to him.

Yes, Co-op City was the end of the earth, but once I saw
the apartment, it made sense. It had parquet floors and a big
window in the living room with a long view. All the rooms
were twice the size of those cubbyholes in the projects, and
the kitchen was big enough to sit and eat in. Best of all, my
mother's friend Willy, a musician who did handiwork too,
was able to partition the master bedroom into two little
chambers, each big enough for a twin bed and a tiny bureau,
so Junior and I could finally have separate rooms. Each had
its own door, and Willy even let us each choose our own wall-

paper. Junior chose something neutral, in a restrained shade of beige. Mine had constellations, planets, and signs of the zodiac in an antique style, as if a Renaissance cartographer had drawn a map for space travel.

I was reading a lot of science fiction and fantasizing about travel to other worlds or slipping through a time warp. It had been only the summer before, in July 1969, that two astronauts had walked on the moon, and I was awestruck that it had happened in my own lifetime, especially when I remembered how Papi had predicted this. From the earth's leaders, Neil Armstrong and Buzz Aldrin carried messages etched in microscopically tiny print on a silicon disk, messages that could fit on the head of a pin, to be deposited on the surface of the moon. Pope Paul's was from Psalm 8: "I look up at your heavens, made by your fingers, at the moon and stars you set in place. Ah, what is man that you should spare a thought for him? Or the son of man that you should care for him? You have made him a little less than an angel, you have crowned him with glory and splendor, and you have made him lord over the work of your hand."

I STARTED a new job at Zaro's Bakery, in the small shopping center right across the street from our building in Co-op City. On the days that I worked the morning shift, I would open the shop along with the manager and her assistant. I'd fire up the machine that boiled the bagels and fill the display cases with the pastries and breads. Then, while waiting to open, we all settled down together for coffee and a snack, always a chocolate-covered French cruller for me, offset by a low-starch lunch, of course. I loved those few minutes every day, laughing over the stories amid the smells of fresh bread and coffee. It carried me back to Tío Mayo's bakery in Mayagüez.

Soon the customers would be lining up for the familiar ritual of making change and small talk. I would shake my head when they tried to engage me in Yiddish. "What, no Yiddish? A nice Jewish girl like you?" I heard that so often that I knew the routine: my boss would explain with a bit of Yiddish I did recognize. "Shiksa" was technically derogative, but she said it so affectionately that I couldn't fault it. At least it wasn't "spic"—elsewhere I'd get that often enough too.

Co-op City gradually transformed from a construction site to a community. When the harshest days of winter had passed, you could see young couples strolling, little kids playing, senior citizens watching from the benches. A fair portion of the residents were Jewish, as the bakery's clientele indicated, but you saw people of every imaginable background, drawn from across the five boroughs, a slightly more prosperous population than we were used to in the projects: teachers, police officers, firefighters, and nurses like my mother. The buildings were pristine and flawless then, the shoddiness of their construction not yet apparent. The grounds were landscaped with trees and flowers, and the whole place was lit up at night.

Once Mami planted the flag in Co-op City, it started to look like a good idea to everyone else. Alfred, married and with kids by then, ended up in a building not far from us. Eventually, Titi Carmen arrived with Miriam and Eddie; Charlie with his new wife, Ruth; and finally Titi Gloria and Tío Tonio came too. Titi Aurora had beaten them all to the punch: as soon as we were settled, my mother's sister moved in with us.

As fond as I'd always been of Titi Aurora, this was not

good news. No sooner had we finally acquired enough space to breathe than we were overcrowded once again. Titi slept on a daybed in the foyer. She was an early riser and grumbled if Junior and I stayed out past ten. If we had friends over, she would retire to my mother's bedroom. Titi was also a bit of a pack rat. I couldn't open a closet to grab a towel without triggering an avalanche on my head. And to say Titi Aurora was frugal would be an understatement. I don't think she ever spent a penny on her own pleasure or bought anything that wasn't strictly necessary. She wore the same clothes year after year and mended them expertly until mending was a lost cause. The very idea of eating out in a restaurant, of spending a dollar for eggs and toast, was deeply upsetting to her. Titi's frugality, in turn, was deeply upsetting to my mother, who took pride in dressing well and delighted in splurging on small pleasures. Mami never saved, never put money away, and she would overextend herself for something that really mattered—like the encyclopedias or keeping us in Catholic school. She often had to go into debt, but she worked long and hard to pay off those commitments.

They were an odd couple, those two sisters. Neither of them showed affection, and Titi especially could be austere and forbidding, but it was also clear that they were bound to each other in a way that I didn't entirely understand. They were like two trees with buried roots so tangled that they inevitably leaned on each other, and also strangled each other a bit. The sixteen-year difference between them made them more like mother and daughter, which was how they'd begun and how they would remain. Junior and I both suspected that one of Mami's motivations for inviting Titi Aurora to move in was to enlist her as a spy or at least as a deterrent.

Surveillance was maintained, and Mami ducked the blame. They did have an understanding, however, that Titi was not permitted to discipline us directly. She had to report to Mami whatever terrible thing we had done—or rather, Mami, who wasn't eager to hear bad news, would reluctantly extract a report from Titi's pointedly sullen mumbling—and then it was up to our mother to decide what punishment was warranted. This often worked in our favor. When Titi phoned the hospital in a panic to report that Junior had committed an unspeakable offense, how could Mami be anything but relieved to learn that no, he hadn't committed a crime, or turned to drugs, or landed in jail? Catching him with a girlfriend in the bedroom was almost good news if you framed it like that.

JUST AS in the projects, our home was still my friends' favorite hangout. And even with Titi grumbling, the party continued, my mother coming in for a cup of coffee at regular intervals, just to remind us of her presence. If we got too noisy, though, one of the neighbors was bound to call Co-op City security. The first time that happened and a uniformed guard was banging at the door, we scrambled, looking for somewhere to hide two whole six-packs of beer. But the next thing I knew, Mami came bounding out of her bedroom like a tigress, fire in her eyes. She threw open the door and yelled into the hallway, "You tell those neighbors that these are young kids having fun in my house! That's why kids get into trouble, because people don't let them have fun at home!" Then louder still, "If anyone has a problem with that, they can come talk to me! Not call security!" When she was done shouting, she invited the guard in for coffee and told the kids already gathering their stuff that they could stay, but just keep the volume down, please.

And so, thanks to Mami, our home became party central as well as campaign headquarters for student council elections. We threw poster-making parties, painting slogans on banners stretched all the way down the halls. We threw victory parties when we won and consolation parties when we lost. Throughout my high school years, apartment 5G, 100 Dreiser Loop, was the place to be.

MARGUERITE GUDEWICZ AND I both had a crush on Joe. He was messing around with both of us, being straight with neither. What did he think, that girls don't talk? When he dumped us both for someone else, Marguerite and I became best friends.

There was something about going to Marguerite's house that stirred memories of Abuelita's when I was small. The place was like a village, with grandparents living downstairs, Marguerite and her brother and parents upstairs, and Uncle Walter in the basement apartment. I felt right at home.

Marguerite's father, John Gudewicz, was not one to censor himself, but at least he made an effort to tone down his remarks when I was in earshot. He still had his views on "those Puerto Ricans," but his kindly laugh made it impossible to take offense. In 1971, when Archie Bunker first appeared on *All in the Family,* we all joked that Mr. Gudewicz could sue CBS for copyright infringement. Still, when push came to shove, he stood up for me. One night at a party, his brother asked pointedly, "Who's the spic?"

"She's a guest of ours, and if you don't like it, you can

get the hell out," he said. And he wasn't just being a good host. I learned that when Marguerite's parents married, in their communities a match between a German and a Pole was virtually miscegenation. What's more, Marguerite's mother, Margaret, a modest woman who never talked about herself, had hidden Jews in wartime Germany. The Gudewiczes were not people who needed any lessons on the evils of prejudice.

Beyond the very circumscribed world of my family and our few blocks of the South Bronx, a much wider world was opening up to me, if only in a New York sort of way. If you grow up on salsa and merengue, then polkas and jitterbugs look as if they jumped off the pages of *National Geographic*. To Puerto Rican taste buds, the blandness of German, Polish, and Irish food left something to be desired, but it did seem we had a lot to learn about preparing vegetables. I noticed too that the *mishigas* on display in the hallways of Co-op City or at Zaro's more than matched the volubility of Puerto Rican family life, but if we'd slung the kinds of insults that our Jewish neighbors regularly did, the dishonor and acrimony would have stuck for generations. I was always amazed to hear them laughing together again within minutes of a flare-up.

The differences were plain enough, and yet I saw that they were as nothing compared with what we had in common. As I lay in bed at night, the sky outside my window reflecting the city's dim glow, I thought about Abuelita's fierce loyalty to blood. But what really binds people as family? The way they shore themselves up with stories; the way siblings can feud bitterly but still come through for each other; how an untimely death, a child gone before a parent, shakes the very foundations; how the weaker ones, the ones with invisible wounds, are sheltered; how a constant din is medicine against loneliness; and how celebrating the same occasions year after year steels us to the changes they herald. And always food at the center of it all.

JUST AS my emotional world was growing in Co-op City, my intellectual horizons were beginning to expand at school. Miss Katz, who taught us history my junior year, was different from any teacher I'd had before, different, in fact, from anyone I had ever known. Compared with the nuns, she seemed young and vibrant. She warned us against getting stuck in rote learning, about how we needed to master abstract, conceptual thinking. The meaning of all this would be revealed once we'd written our first essays. Our first what? There we sat, rows of blank faces in our regulation navy skirts, white blouses, and sweater vests. Eleven years of memorization had molded our minds to be no less uniform. Essay? Somehow we had reached junior year in high school without having written anything beyond book reports. The nuns had always fed us facts, and we had always parroted them back. I was very good at it. I prided myself on being able to soak up vast oceans of facts. No teacher had ever asked anything more in exchange for an A.

Miss Katz asked something more. Her pronouncements and challenges intrigued me. What would it mean to think critically about history? How do you analyze facts? At least I'd learned by then the value of asking for help. If I went to talk to her after class, she wouldn't slam the door on me.

In fact, the door was wide open, and we had several long and fascinating conversations. She told me about her boyfriend, a Brazilian she described as a freedom fighter working on behalf of the poor and oppressed under the military dictatorship. I asked how, being Jewish, she'd come to work at a Catholic school, and she told me she was inspired by the nuns and priests she'd encountered in Latin America. They put their lives at risk for the sake of helping the poor. She talked in a similar way about Father Gigante, too, which took me by surprise, but it made sense.

Father Gigante was our priest at St. Athanasius, where I'd attended Mass with Titi Aurora before the move to Co-op City. I would only gradually become aware that the familiar figure at the altar was a larger-than-life presence beyond the sanctuary, an activist for tenants' rights who famously walked the mean streets with a baseball bat as he negotiated with gangs and landlords. In the same parish where Abuelita and all my family had lived until my mother led the exodus, Father Gigante was working to reclaim buildings that were abandoned or gutted by arson and renovate them as low-cost housing. It wouldn't have occurred to me to call him a freedom fighter, but why not?

Miss Katz was the first progressive I'd ever encountered up close. There certainly weren't many others at Cardinal Spellman High School in those days, and she would last there only one year. I remember wondering what made her so intriguing. How could one become an interesting person? It wasn't just having a boyfriend you could describe as a hero, though that certainly got my attention. It had more to do with her questioning the meaning of her existence, thinking in terms of a purpose in life. She was a teacher but still educating herself, learning about the world and actively engaged in it. I began to have an intimation that education could be for something other than opening the doors of job opportunity, in the sense of my mother's constant refrain.

I wish I could say that the same kind of reflection that lit up my conversations with Miss Katz had thrown some light on the problem of writing a history essay. Somehow her prescription for critical thinking and analysis remained abstract, if tantalizing. Though I did well enough in her class, I would have to wait till college before I could really understand what she meant.

IT HAD BEEN established that Sonia Sotomayor was not much to look at. I had a pudgy nose. I was gawky and ungraceful. I barreled down the halls of Cardinal Spellman, headfirst, unlike those who knew how to amble with a sexy sashay. My own mother told me that I had terrible taste in clothes.

I did get asked out occasionally. Usually, a friend's boyfriend had a friend, and they were looking for a fourth to double-date. Sometimes he would ask me again, and sometimes it would last for a while but never as long as going steady. Once I was the one to put an end to it: as his contribution to a meal that some friends were making at my house, my date decided to shoplift the bacon for the BLTs. Making matters worse, it wouldn't have happened except that Mami didn't have enough money to put together a meal for us that day. She was terribly ashamed, but she would have been horrified to learn about the shoplifting. I wanted nothing more to do with that guy.

Mostly, I felt like everybody's second choice, which is why a compliment could catch me off guard, especially an unconventional one. For instance, according to Chiqui, I had "baseball bat legs." Thanks a lot, Chiqui.

"No, that's good! You see how your ankles are small and the calves curve? You've got good legs."

I would hear worse: Kevin told me that Scully's dad said I was "built like a brick shit-house."

"It's a compliment, Sonia."

"What kind of compliment is that?"

"It's just an expression," Kevin insisted. "It means you're well built. Not like some flimsy wooden job." I couldn't believe my ears. Was that what they meant by Irish wit?

Apart from dubious flattery, the truth was that Kevin Noonan made me feel attractive in a way that was new to me and not unwelcome. I, in turn, was entranced by his blue-gray eyes. I found myself scanning the hallway on the far side of Cardinal Spellman's divisive crack to catch a glimpse of that frizzy halo of sandy curls that made his slight figure stand out in the uniformed crowd.

On our first date, we took the train down to Manhattan. We walked the entire city, walked for hours, talking as he showed me his favorite spots. The first place he took me was a tiny park on East Fifty-third Street where a curtain of water still runs down a stone wall. The sound of the fountain makes the city seem far away and turns the vest-pocket park into a private cove.

From that first date, we were inseparable. For the first month that I knew Kevin, he brought me a rose every single day. One time after school I was walking with him to the stop where he caught the bus home to Yonkers. We passed by Titi Gloria's house, and I dragged Kevin in to meet her and Tío Tonio. Really, I just wanted to postpone our parting, but as soon as we got there, Kevin turned pale and clammed up. I thought maybe he was put off because Titi Gloria and Tío Tonio kept switching to Spanish, even though they were making quite an effort, welcoming us with cake and cookies and sodas. But Kevin remained stony, and I was more than a little upset by this.

The next day when I got to school, there was no rose. I was getting seriously worried that things were over between us. But finally Kevin confessed: he had been stealing my daily roses from Tío Tonio's garden! He looked at me with a hangdog expression that didn't go with his sparkling eyes and said, "There's a lot of them, Sonia." It was true: Tío Tonio's rosebushes were magnificent. I laughed so hard I almost choked. I was happy to accept that the rose-colored phase of our romance was over. Now we were just a couple.

Kevin practically moved in with us except, of course, that my mother made him go home at night. We couldn't afford much dating beyond the local pizzeria. Instead, we hung out at home, studying together or watching TV. He loved reading as much as I did, and we might silently turn the pages side by side for hours at a time. We went for walks, or visited my family, or worked on Kevin's car. And we talked constantly about everything imaginable.

We didn't go over to his house much, because his mother had a hard time accepting me. She wouldn't say it to my face, but the message came through with a tightening of the lips, a slant of the eyebrow, a slam of the door. She would have been happier if I were Irish, or at least not Puerto Rican. I'd seen this before. One guy I'd dated before Kevin had ducked a teacup thrown at his head when his mother found out I was Puerto Rican. Kevin's mom was not so kinetic about her distress, seeking the counsel of her priest. He either shared her opinion of my people or else lacked the backbone to tell her that it was not a very Christian view. Kevin defended him. The parish in Yonkers was 100 percent Irish, he rationalized, and the priest had no choice but to affirm his community's values. I disagreed. Bigotry is not a value.

At some point I introduced Kevin to Abuelita, which made the relationship official. From then on it was taken for granted that we would get married. Whatever the differences between Puerto Ricans and Irish, among our friends and families a common expectation prevailed: you married your first sweetheart. The only question was whether we would do it right after high school or wait till we finished college.

I REMEMBER STANDING at the bedroom window. Beyond the parking structure, at the corner of the empty lot where junk was strewn among the weeds, I could see Kevin's Dodge, his skinny legs stretching from under the chassis. An assortment of parts and tools were laid out carefully on the sidewalk beside him. The engine had recently taken its last gasp, and he was swapping it out for one that he'd bought at a salvage shop. Much closer, on the basketball court below, there was Junior alone with the ball, doing his endless private dance.

Mami came into the room and stood beside me. She saw what I saw and laid a hand gently on my shoulder. "My two sons," she said.

Thirteen

Cerveza Schaefer es la mejor cuando se toma más de una . . .[*]

Kenny Moy was sitting next to Titi Aurora in front of the TV, belting out the beer jingle. That was pretty much the extent of his Spanish, but it didn't prevent him from bonding with Titi Aurora. They conducted bizarrely bilingual conversations while watching pro wrestling together. Titi would be bobbing up and down, screaming at the referee, cheering on her favorite of the day. I loved to watch her: wrestling was the only thing that made her loosen up and enjoy herself. It reminded me of Papi's periodic emergence from his mournful silence to root for the Yankees on Abuelita's little black-and-white TV. But the Sheik? The Crusher? Killer Kowalski? Gorilla Monsoon? How could Titi believe this was for real?

Ken Moy was the student coach of the girls' team of the Forensics Club at Cardinal Spellman. I signed up as part of my self-imposed preprofessional program in public speaking, which advanced whenever an opportunity presented itself.

***

[*] "Schaefer is the one beer to have when you're having more than one"

The dozen or so girls on the team were an especially interesting bunch of self-selected high-functioning nerds, and Kenny coached us in debate and extemporaneous speech. He was brilliant at debate. His mind was an analytic machine that could dismantle an opponent's position, step by inexorable step. His affirmative arguments would make a concrete bunker look like a house of cards. And he was utterly untainted by emotion. I aspired to Ken's unflappable, rational cool, though I feared that I came across more like Titi Gloria in the usual nervous tizzy that accompanied her every mundane decision—red dress or blue?

"Sonia, I don't care if you have to cut off your hands, get that gesture out of your goddamn repertoire!" That was Kenny ringside. Tell a Puerto Rican not to talk with her hands? Ask a bird not to fly.

Ken should have gone to Bronx Science, but his mother made him come to Cardinal Spellman to keep an eye on his sister. Janet was a radical individualist with a completely uncensored approach to the world, a ticking time bomb in a Catholic school. She even cursed the principal to his face in the cafeteria when he caught her holding hands with her boyfriend. Ken had to tax his mighty rhetorical powers to win her a reprieve. But the truth was that if Janet had been expelled, Ken would have left too, and the school would have lost a star pupil.

They lived in East Harlem, where their parents ran a Chinese hand laundry. I never visited Ken's home or met his parents. His dad was trouble three ways, he said—heroin, gambling, and a violent temper—and since they lived almost an hour away by subway, we hung out at my place. Ken claimed they were the only Chinese family in the barrio, and he was a barrio kid through and through, slamming down dominoes with the best of them. He was skinny as a knife blade, but he could eat more of Mami's rice and beans and *chuletas* in one sitting than the rest of us together.

In philosophy class, we were studying logic. I'm not sure what I expected of philosophy, but formal logic took me by surprise. I loved it. I perceived beauty in it, the idea of an order that held under any circumstances. What excited me most was how I could immediately apply it down the hall in debate practice. I was amazed that something so mathematically pure and abstract could transform into human persuasion, into words with the power to change people's minds.

Forensics Club was good training for a lawyer in ways that I barely understood at the time. You got handed a topic, as well as the side you had to argue, pro or con. It didn't matter what you believed about the issue; what mattered was how well you argued. You not only had to see both sides; you had to prepare as if you were arguing both in order to anticipate your opponent's moves. In your allotted five minutes, you had to use language carefully to paint a picture for those who would decide the match. Then you had to listen. "Half a debate is listening to what the other person says," Ken advised. It was easy to present your own points, much harder to listen well enough to respond effectively to your opponent.

Listening was second nature to me. My friends confided in me, unloaded their problems, and leaned on me for advice, the same way my mother's friends leaned on her. When I was little, listening and watching for cues had seemed like the key to survival in a precarious world. I notice when people hesitate or get defensive, when they care more about what they're saying than they'll admit, or when they're too quick about brushing something off. So much is communicated in tone of voice, in subtleties of expression, and in body language.

What Ken taught us was a different way of listening, more formal than my own intuitive skill. He taught us to pay attention for the vulnerable links in a chain of logic, the faulty assumptions and the supposed facts that you know you can challenge when your turn comes. But even as I absorbed Ken's logical strategies, I knew instinctively that emotion doesn't disappear. Much as you had to keep your own in check, there was still that of your listeners to consider. A line of reasoning could persuade, but so could a sequence of feelings. Constructing a chain of logic was one thing; building a chain of emotions required a different understanding.

I'VE MADE IT to the finals of the extemporaneous speech competition. The timer starts, and I pick a slip of paper blindly. Three topics based on current events: choose one. I have fifteen minutes to brainstorm and organize a five- to seven-minute speech. Two of the three are so loud with the din of the nightly news—outrage at My Lai, the killings at Kent State, the war spreading across borders, the protests spreading across campuses—that it's hard to hear myself think. The third topic catches my eye: the cold-blooded murder of Kitty Genovese and the neighbors who witnessed it but did nothing. Closer to home—Queens instead of Cambodia—and it touches a nerve.

The clock is running. What can I recall of the news reports? Where do I want to take this? What's my purpose? What's the best point of entry? I'll start by painting a picture . . . and remember to keep my hands still.

"On a cold night in early spring, six years ago, a young woman drove home from the bar where she was working to her apartment in Queens. It was around 3:00 a.m. She parked her car in a nearby parking lot and was walking up the alley toward her building when a stranger appeared out of the shadows and approached her. Frightened, she ran, but he caught up with her. He stabbed her in the back. She screamed and cried for help. Several neighbors heard her cries and the struggle that ensued as Winston Moseley assaulted Kitty Genovese."

I look out and observe a rapt stillness in the room. I've got them.

"But the night was cold, and windows were closed. Those who heard thought it was probably just a lovers' quarrel or a couple of drunks getting rowdy. Kitty Genovese screamed and screamed for help as her assailant punched her and beat her over the head, stabbed her repeatedly, and bruised her all over her body. Finally, he raped her as she lay dying. When it was all over, one of the neighbors called the police. They arrived within minutes, but Kitty Genovese died in the ambulance on the way to the hospital.

"Winston Moseley got away that night. He was apprehended later on a burglary charge and confessed to the murder. He's locked up for life. That's not what I'm concerned with today. No, what concerns me is this: Thirty-eight neighbors also confessed. Each one of them heard or witnessed some part of the attack, which lasted over half an hour. Thirty-eight neighbors did nothing to intervene. They looked on and let this young woman die a horrible death."

When I pause to look at the faces before me, I see an

opening: These are the bystanders, I imagine, sitting right here in the auditorium. How do I get past whatever it is that paralyzes them? How do I get them to step up and take responsibility?

"Thirty-eight neighbors did nothing. How does this happen? It happens when we become apathetic about our roles in society. It happens when we forget that we are a community, that we are connected to one another and have an obligation to engage with other human beings." Okay, I have to unpack this a bit, cover the bases, then circle back. "A crime like what happened to Kitty Genovese may be the act of a deranged individual. Other crimes may be different in their causes, pointing to broader failures of society. But in the moment of opportunity, when a criminal grabs his chance and a victim is suffering, our own responsibility is the same. When the criminal finds his victim in a dark alley, an observer too has a moment of opportunity. Will you see the victim not as a stranger or a statistic but as another human being like yourself? Will you be fully human in that moment and feel the obligation to care, to act, to get involved? Will you be fully a citizen and rise to the responsibility?"

They're still with me, every one of them. So I start to sum up and come in for a landing . . . "There was a young woman at the threshold of her life, a budding flower ready to open." And there's my hand, almost as if it doesn't belong to me, the fingers cupped and opening in bloom, then closing to a hard fist: "We destroyed that flower."

The applause carries me down the steps. Ken is grinning broadly, proudly. They announce that I've won first prize! A little cocky, I tell Ken that sometimes talking with your hands is fine. It's who I am, where I come from.

I WAS DOING my homework at the kitchen table and Junior was doing his, as usual, in front of the TV, when the door opened. Mami made a dramatic entrance, slamming the stack of books in her arms straight down on the floor.

"I'm not going back!" she announced, her voice trembling. "It's too much for me. I'm sorry, I can't do it."

"Junior, get in here!" I yelled. He appeared in the doorway instantly. "If you can't do it, Mami, then we can't either. Take a break, Junior, no more school for us." With both hands I snapped shut the textbook I was reading—a very satisfying sound. I did glance at the page number first, though.

This mutiny was incited only a few months after my mother had sat Junior and me down at that same kitchen table and asked whether we would be willing to make some sacrifices so that she could study to qualify as a registered nurse. She had wanted years before to continue her schooling, but that hope was dashed when Papi died. Over time, the salary she earned as a practical nurse lagged further and further behind what registered nurses were earning. She was worried that with her Social Security survivors' benefits ending when Junior and I finished school, she wouldn't be able to manage on her own. She certainly didn't want to lean on us to support her. We would have to tighten our belts for a while, while she took leave from the hospital to attend school.

The money was not an insurmountable problem. My mother took a Saturday shift at a methadone clinic to make up a bit of lost income. I had worked the previous summer in the business office at Prospect Hospital, and they let me continue on weekends during the school year. Junior was working at Prospect too, in reception, and he had a second job as a sacristan at St. Patrick's Cathedral. All the little pieces added up.

No, the problem was not money. The problem was that my mother was scared out of her wits. Never mind that she was one very intelligent and ambitious woman. Never mind that Hostos Community College, where she enrolled, was specially created to serve the South Bronx Latino community with a bilingual program for students like my mother. Never mind that she had done the work of a registered nurse unofficially for years, if only because Prospect Hospital was so tiny, and she was so well trusted there. Never mind even that she had nursed half the residents of Hunts Point, Bronxdale, and Co-op City at one point or another. Do I exaggerate? Not much.

My mother was tortured by lack of confidence in her own mental ability. She was especially terrified as soon as anything could be labeled a math problem, instead of just a matter of calculating a dosage. The word "quiz" was to her a stun gun. Most of the time, she beat back her fear with furious effort. She would crack the books as soon as she walked in the door, and midnight would find her still studying. Occasionally, though, anxiety got the better of her, and it was then that a bit of reverse psychology—some might say emotional blackmail—was in order. The idea that Junior and I might quit too, however improbable, was far more terrifying than any quiz.

Seeing my mother get back to her studies was all the proof I needed that a chain of emotion can persuade when one forged of logic won't hold. But more important was her example that a surplus of effort could overcome a deficit of confidence. It was something I would remember often in years ahead, whenever faced with fears that I wasn't smart enough to succeed.

Fourteen

As much as I aspired to Kenny's cool, dispassionate rationality, *Love Story* succeeded in sucking me in, along with every other high school girl in America. But there was something on the screen that mesmerized me even more than the heart-tugging story of Ali MacGraw's sickness or Ryan O'Neal's blue eyes. The college campus where the movie was set, supposedly Harvard, seemed a wonderland. Set among pristine snowy fields, here was a cathedral of learning whose denizens lived out what seemed like an antiquarian fantasy, debating under pointy arches, scaling book-lined walls, and lounging on leather couches. Apart from Camden, New Jersey, and the alternate reality of Puerto Rico, I had never traveled far from the Bronx, and I had certainly never seen anything like this. If I had known then that many scenes of *Love Story* were actually filmed at Fordham University in the borough where we lived, my future might have turned out very differently.

Until those darkened hours in a movie theater, I hadn't given much thought to what life at college might be like or how it might be different from high school. Then, in the fall of my senior year, the phone rang. It was Kenny, the familiar deep, steady voice calling long-distance from Princeton, where he was a freshman. As he fed coins into the box every few minutes, he described the strange new world he was navigating. He advised me that it was time for me too to be thinking about applying to college, and one thing he said sticks clearly in my memory, because I had no idea what he meant: "Try for the Ivy League." Ken was the first student we knew from Spellman ever to have crossed into that world, and it wasn't a term that had ever come up in conversation. He explained that this was the finest college education available and that it would open every door, which sounded oddly like a more knowing version of Mami's claim for higher education generally. I jotted down the names of the colleges as he rattled them off, tossing in Stanford for good measure.

The next day the guidance counselor had only one question as she was thumbing through the thick catalog she'd taken down from the shelf: "Have you thought about Fordham?" A couple of pages of the book were devoted to each college: a mission statement in blandly aspirational code, a few statistics, generic black-and-white photographs of students looking earnestly engaged. When I said no to Fordham, she offered the names of several more Catholic colleges.

I told her that I wasn't really interested in parochial colleges; I wanted to apply to Harvard, Yale, Princeton, Columbia, Stanford . . .

She looked at me. "Okay." And that was the extent of her guidance. This was an occasion when it would never have occurred to me to ask for advice. At a Catholic high school that served the kids of Irish and Italian immigrants, a focus on parochial colleges made perfect sense: just getting into college was already more than most students' parents had accomplished. I happened to be graduating on the cusp of a change that would soon see many of Spellman's students going on to the most highly competitive schools. But that fall, Kenny Moy at Princeton was pretty much the first Spellman student to walk on the moon.

I got the application forms and wrote my essays, scribbling in the dark with not a clue as to what might be a worthy subject or how to shape such a thing. I tackled the SAT in much the same way. The brochure that came with the registration form was the only hint I had of what to expect on the test. Anyway, I could not have afforded a prep course, even if I'd known there was such a thing.

It is hard for students today to imagine the void before the Internet and how common my naïveté was at the time. If you attended an elite prep school, no doubt there was valuable information swirling in the air, impossible not to inhale. And obviously, those applicants whose parents had attended the same college had access to insider knowledge, to say nothing of eligibility for legacy admissions. If your own parents had gone to college at all, they still had some firsthand experience to draw on. The rest of us, for the most part, just blundered into it.

Qualifying for financial aid was the easiest part. With my mother enrolled at Hostos Community College at the time, we were living mainly on the Social Security survivors' benefits, supplemented slightly by Mami's part-time work at the methadone clinic, her summer pay at Prospect Hospital, and the little that Junior and I contributed from our part-time and summer jobs. There were no assets to report. None of us even had a bank account. On paydays I would walk five blocks from Prospect Hospital to the check-cashing place near the train station to cash my paycheck, just as my mother had always done, just as the rest of the staff at the hospital did. To pay the phone bill, you could get a money order there too. Cash was good enough for everything else.

It's just as well I had no idea how selective the colleges I was applying to were. If I had known, I might have hesitated. I did understand enough to hedge my bets, though: CUNY could serve as my safety school, since it was public admission. Among the alternatives, I figured it likeliest I would end up at the state university at Stony Brook, at which Kevin was aiming. I had quickly given up on Stanford as being too far away. Flying cross-country to have a look would have already cost more than I could afford, never mind coming home for Christmas.

Come November, a postcard arrived from Princeton with three boxes, a cryptic message beside each—"likely," "possible," and "unlikely." On my card, the first was marked with an X. This seemed more like communication from a Magic 8 Ball than from a university. I wasn't sure what I was expected to do with this occult clue, so I trooped off once again to the guidance counselor's office.

Behind the look of utter surprise that completely rearranged her features, the oracle pronounced: " 'Likely' means just what it says. There's a very good chance you'll get in." I thought to myself, really?

I was still getting my head around this when a couple of days later I happened to walk by the school nurse's office. "I heard you got a 'likely' from Princeton," she called out to me as I passed.

I stopped in my tracks. "Yes, I did."

"Well, can you explain to me how you got a 'likely' and the two top-ranking girls in the school only got a 'possible'?"

I just looked at her. What did she mean by that? Not to mention that accusatory tone. My perplexed discomfort under her baleful gaze was clearly not enough; shame was the response she seemed to want from me.

Sometimes in such situations, an apt answer only occurs to you hours later: "Because of what I've accomplished on the forensics team and in student government. Because I work part-time during the school year and full-time during the summers. I may be ranked below them, but I'm still in the top ten, and I *do* much more than the others do." But even that undelivered comeback was far from complete. Her question would hang over me not just that day but for the next several years, while I lived the day-to-day reality of affirmative action. At the time I was applying to college, I had little understanding of how the admissions process functioned generally, let alone how affirmative action might affect it in particular. Barely a decade had passed since affirmative action had been implemented in government contracting. It was still experimental in Ivy League college admissions, and few of the first minority students to benefit from it had even managed to graduate yet.

Soon, those fat envelopes I came to recognize as acceptance packages stuffed the mailbox almost daily. Now that the choice was real and imminent, I sat down to more serious deliberation. Columbia, I realized, a mere subway ride away, was too close for comfort: I'd have no choice but to live at home, unable to justify the extra expense of a dorm room. That left Radcliffe (Harvard's sister school), Yale, and Princeton, each worth a visit.

With *Love Story* still lodged in my mind, I scheduled Radcliffe first. I was told that after an interview at the admissions office, a student group would show me around. But first I had to find my way to Massachusetts. As close as we had lived to Manhattan my whole life, I had only been there on special occasions—that first date with Kevin; the Christmas and Easter shows at Radio City Music Hall; Alfred's death march to the summit of Lady Liberty. On the miserable rainy day that my visit was scheduled, the cavernous hall of Grand Central seemed cold shelter, its vault dark with decades of grime. The railways then were staggering back following a long decline, only recently rescued by the establishment of Amtrak and, in New York, the long reconstruction of Penn Station as Madison Square Garden. My nine dollars and ninety cents bought me a seat in a tattered car carpeted in cigarette butts.

A sooty rain fell uninterrupted from New York to Boston, and by the time I had navigated the Boston subway and walked the last few blocks to the admissions office, I was dripping like a sewer rat. I was also feeling a shade of disappointment. There was neo-Gothic architecture aplenty, but the campus was no idyllic haven set apart from the world. Harvard and Radcliffe were fused with Cambridge, densely urban, tangled with honking traffic.

Inside the waiting room, when the inner door finally opened, I found myself face-to-face with a creature such as I had never encountered: a woman with a hairdo—no, "coiffure" would be the word—of sculpted silver, in a perfectly tailored black dress, a pearl necklace and earrings, beautiful little pumps. This is different! I thought.

I followed this apparition into her office and was stunned again by what met my eyes. I had never before seen an Oriental rug, its intricate pattern the most gorgeous of puzzles meandering across the floor. And I had never before seen a white couch. To be honest, I had probably never seen a couch that wasn't covered in plastic. I was ushered into an elegant, high-backed, winged throne of a chair, in which I felt as small as Lily Tomlin's Edith Ann, surprised to feel my feet touch the floor. I had never seen such a room with my own eyes, but I knew: This was good taste. And this was money.

That's when the yapping dogs shattered my trance. They must have been barking since I'd walked in, but now they were jumping up at me, all bare teeth and bony claws. They were just lapdogs, really, one black and one white, but they scared me. She called to them, and they scrambled onto the white couch and sat beside her, and there the three of them completed a surreal tableau, three pairs of eyes gazing at me, a vision in black and white.

That may have been the shortest interview of my life, perhaps all of fifteen minutes. The flow of words that always came to me naturally, and still does whenever I meet a stranger, mostly dried up. When I found myself back in the waiting room, too early for the students who were to meet me, the numbness dissolved into a suffocating panic: I don't belong here! For the first and, so far, the last time in my life, I did the unthinkable: I fled. Asking the receptionist to leave word for the students who were coming to get me, I said, "I'm sorry, but I have to leave."

It was early evening by the time I retraced my journey in reverse. My mother looked up from her homework at the kitchen table. "What's wrong? You were supposed to be away for a couple of days."

"Mami, I don't belong there."

Her gaze seemed inclined to question this conclusion, but after a moment's thought she said, "You know best, Sonia." She would say it often hereafter, to confess the limits of her judgment in the world I was entering and acknowledge my having reached the stage of adult self-determination. And that was the last we would speak of Radcliffe. I was convinced they would retract their offer. They didn't, but my list was now shorter by one.

My visit to Yale was a very different story. When I arrived at the station in New Haven, an old hand at Amtrak by now, the two Latino students sent to pick me up said they were coming from a campus protest. Eager to jump back into the fray, they apologized, saying that they would just be dropping me off for now. They would give me the tour later . . . unless, perhaps, I'd like to come along to the protest?

My experience of the antiwar protests was limited to the television screen. Though friends worried plenty about their luck in the draft lottery and Vietnam would come up as a topic in Forensics Club, debates weren't boiling up spontaneously in the lunchroom. Cardinal Spellman, the archbishop of New York for whom my school was named, was also vicar to the armed forces and a fervent supporter of the war, spending Christmases in Vietnam with the troops. As the bombings escalated and spilled over into Cambodia and Laos, the protesters on the steps of St. Patrick's Cathedral called it Spelly's war. But the closest we had ever come to protesting at Cardinal Spellman High School was to lobby for a smoking room and the occasional no-uniform Friday.

That's not to say I didn't understand the reasons underlying the cause, but raising voice and fist against Yale's involvement in the war effort didn't seem a smart way to prepare for an interview there. Instead, I went for a walk. The inner city of New Haven was impoverished then, depressed and threatening, no better than the South Bronx and a lot less lively. Actually, it made Co-op City seem idyllic.

When my guides found me again, they were buzzing from the protest and eager for a rap session. We joined up with a larger group of Hispanic kids, some from New York, others from the Southwest, all of them more radical than anyone I had ever known before. For two days I camped in the dorm and scouted the campus in their company, listening to talk of revolution, Cuba, and Che Guevara and feeling generally uninformed. At least Fidel Castro was a familiar name, and news of the Cuban missile crisis had penetrated even the cocoon of my Catholic school childhood, where communism was deemed a godless threat, more cosmic than political. I could tell purgatory from limbo better than I could recognize the distinctions between socialism and communism that spurred the arguments during those two days at Yale. So embarrassed was I by my innocence that I would go to the library and read up on Che Guevara after I got home.

I was embarrassed, too, by all the "down with whitey" talk. It wasn't an attitude I shared, nor one I was eager to adopt. Many of my friends, most of my classmates, and virtually all of my teachers were white. Whether it was due to the indeterminate color of my skin or my very determined personality, I moved easily between different worlds without assuming disguises. Yes, I'd experienced prejudice aimed straight at me, from the blatant taunts of my street-fighting days to the cold shoulder of Kevin's mom, to the subtler barb from the school nurse more recently. Of course I knew that the painful consequences of bigotry—then so common, even endemic—went far beyond the sting of being called a spic, as I had often been. But I couldn't see such narrow-mindedness as the workings of systemic forces of history and certainly not as fitting neatly into a master narrative of perpetual class struggle, the way these Yale kids did. This stuff simply didn't define me in any meaningful way: if somebody called me a spic, it told me a lot about them, but nothing about myself. And how could it help the situation to hurl a slur in reply?

It was difficult to picture myself spending four years in this environment, especially with Kevin coming to visit on weekends. I left Yale thinking: not here—though I didn't feel the same panicked urge to flee that I had felt at Radcliffe. Even if I didn't share their attitudes, I knew where these kids were coming from, and when they talked of family and home, I recognized how much we did share.

BY THE TIME I went to see Princeton, I was down to gathering loose change for bus fare, Amtrak now beyond my budget. When Kenny met me at the bus station, I was surprised to see his hair grown very long, an expression of his new freedom. We dropped my bag at his dorm before heading out to tour the campus.

As we entered the main gates from Nassau Street, the sunlight on that balmy spring day danced magically on the sandy Collegiate Gothic architecture and the emerald lawns and the surrounding woodlands, a prospect that has enchanted generations of Princeton students but that took me completely unprepared. Even the bronze tigers flanking the entrance to ivy-covered Nassau Hall, while reminding me of the stone lions that guard the New York Public Library, seemed more pensive and more elegant.

Kenny had gathered a very small group of friends. Like him, they were exceptionally bright but slightly offbeat inner-city kids, radical in their politics, though quietly so, who conducted their lives at arm's length from Princeton's preppy mainstream. We sat up late together in a dorm room that night, talking easily. "Socially, it's a wasteland here," Kenny said, his judgment affirmed by solemn nods from the other freshmen. "It's a bunch of very strange, privileged human beings, and you're not going to understand any of them. But intellectually, you can deal with these people. They're not *that* smart." Nobody seemed to mind, or even notice, that I didn't join in when the pipe was passed. I didn't feel a need to make excuses or explain about being diabetic. This group was mellow through and through.

At my interview the next morning I felt just as comfortable chatting with the admissions officer in his tiny corner office. He was professorially tweedy, down to his leather elbow patches and little horn-rimmed glasses, but he was open and easy to talk to.

Before the weekend was over, my decision was firm. A full scholarship capped it.

I didn't begin to understand the power of those Ivy names Kenny had first disclosed to me until I saw the reactions of people when they learned that I was headed to Princeton. Prospect Hospital was abuzz with the news, and all day long the staff—not just the nurses and orderlies, but the doctors too—were popping into the business office: "Congratulations! Sonia, how wonderful! We're so proud of you!" All those women I had spent long summer lunch hours with in the cafeteria over card games and surprisingly good roast chicken as soap operas droned in the background and the women shared their own incrementally unfolding family dramas—they all came to give me a hug. Mr. Reuben, the comptroller, who had never been thrilled to have a kid working in the office, softened his habitual scowl. Even Dr. Freedman, who owned the hospital and who had overridden Mr. Reuben's objections when I asked for a job more challenging than candy striper, stopped by just to join the well-wishers. All this left me a little shaken. Other kids had gotten into

college too. I had certainly expected to. Was Princeton really
so special?

WHEN, at the end of summer, it finally came time to say
good-bye, the women at the hospital had taken up a collec-
tion. "Sonia, go buy yourself some new shoes for college.
Please!"

"But these shoes are comfortable," I said, my usual line.
It wasn't the first time they had begged me to upgrade my
footwear. My feet blistered easily in new shoes, so once I had
broken in a pair, I would never give them up. Everyone in
the office had heard me on the phone defending my raggedy
shoes to my grandmother. "Buy some new shoes already!
Make your grandmother happy" was an old story. New shoes
for college was just the latest twist.

On Kenny's advice, I planned to get a bicycle once I got
to Princeton. The only other purchase he advised was a raincoat. Mami offered to buy it and came shopping with me. We
searched up and down Fordham Road without finding anything I liked. We even stepped into Loehmann's, my first time
there. Though it was a discount house, and popular in Co-op
City, the prices, to us, were a shock. So we went—where
else?—to La Tercera, the Latino shopping heart of the South
Bronx on Third Avenue.

No luck at Alexander's. I wasn't being fussy; I was just
having a hard time picturing myself in that magical land
of archways and manicured lawns wearing anything I saw
on these racks. On the other side of the street, which was
divided by the elevated train line rumbling overhead, were
the slightly more upscale dress shops, places where you might

shop for a wedding or some other very special occasion. In this case, a last resort.

There it was: glowing white with toggle buttons and a subtle flair of fake fur trim up the front and around the hood. As improbably white as a white couch, white as a blanket of snow on a college lawn.

"You like it, Sonia?"

"I love it, Mami." This was another first. Unlike my mother, or Chiqui, or my cousin Miriam, or many of my friends, I'd never cared enough to fall in love with a garment. But wrapped in this, I knew I wouldn't feel so odd. Unfortunately, it was a size too small. I tried on a couple of other coats, but my heart had been claimed, and Mami knew it.

I was ready to leave and try elsewhere, but she said, "*Espera* . . . Sonia, wait, maybe they can order it." She went to the counter and waited in silence as the saleswoman helped another customer. And then another and another. My mother is a very patient woman, so I knew what it took for her to finally say, "Miss, I need help."

"What do you want?" she snapped without turning.

"Do you have this in a twelve?"

"If it's not on the rack, we don't have it."

"Do you have another store? Can you order it?"

The woman finally turned and looked at her. "Well, that would be a lot of trouble, wouldn't it?"

I was halfway to the door, fully expecting my mother to give up, but she stood her ground. "I know it's a lot of trouble, but my daughter's going away to college and she likes this coat. I want to give it to her as a gift. So would you please look to see if you can find this coat for my daughter."

Her silent shrug spoke loudly enough: You're a pain in

the ass. But as she turned away, she asked indifferently, "So where's she going to college?"

"To Princeton."

I saw the saleswoman's head swing round as in a cartoon double take. The transformation was remarkable. She was suddenly all courtesy and respect, full of praise for Princeton, and more than happy to make a phone call in search of my coat, which, as it turned out, would arrive in a week. Mami thanked her profusely and left a deposit. It was a lot of money, but that coat would last me all four years of college. It had to.

As we were walking back to the station, I commented on the saleswoman's change of attitude. My mother stopped in the shadow of the elevated track and said to me, "I have to tell you, Sonia, at the hospital I'm being treated like a queen right now. Doctors who have never once had a nice word for me, who have never spoken to me at all, have come up to congratulate me."

Overhead, the train rumbled loudly, and I had to pause for a long moment before I admitted that I had never dreamed what a difference Princeton would make to people.

She looked at me steadily. "What you got yourself into, daughter, I don't know. But we're going to find out."

Fifteen

I N THE WEEK since Alfred drove off with Mami waving good-bye out the window, a look of doom overcoming her firm-set jaw, the collegiate fairy tale in my mind was becoming something more akin to science fiction. In part it was the record-breaking heat that summer of 1972, which silvered Princeton's leafy vistas, endowing everything with a more unearthly aura than I had remembered. But I was also finding that many of my classmates seemed to come from another planet and that that impression was reciprocated.

Waiting outside Dillon Gym, where we were to meet our advisers, I struck up a conversation with another freshman sitting beside me. She was from Alabama, she said. I had never before heard an accent like that in real life. I listened spellbound as she explained how her father, her grandfather, and her elder brother were all Princeton alums. She couldn't have been more delighted to be there representing her generation. "And it really is just the friendliest, most welcoming place you'll find," she gushed. "I mean, look at all the unusual people that come here!" She was indicating an approaching pair, their heads together, laughing loudly.

I recognized my roommate, Dolores, and our friend

Teresa. Dolores was vaguely Mexican looking, with light brown skin and Indian-black hair. Teresa was barely a shade darker than I am, hardly dark at all, but her features were distinctively Latina. They both looked pretty normal to me. Without premeditation, I greeted them exuberantly in rapid-fire Spanish, though we usually spoke English together. I meant no malice toward the girl from Alabama, but my pulse was speeding with a sense of purpose. Nothing more needed to be said.

Dolores Chavez was from New Mexico. We must have been assigned to room together because someone had assumed two Hispanics would have a lot in common. But all Dolores knew of Puerto Ricans came from *West Side Story*, and I suspect that initially she was half afraid I'd knife her in her sleep. I knew even less of New Mexico than she knew of New York. Dolores seemed to me a country girl, sweet-tempered, shy, and very far from home. One night soon after we'd arrived, she got her guitar out and sang softly for a while before we went to sleep, such deep longing in her voice.

As social as I am, I was quiet in those early days, trying to make sense of the conversations flowing around me. One evening, I found myself with a group of girls sitting in our resident adviser's dorm room. One of them mentioned being invited to a wedding and that she'd decided just to choose a gift from the bridal registry. What the hell is a bridal registry? I wondered. Our adviser, a senior, allowed that her father sometimes received wedding invitations from people whose names he didn't even recognize, probably strangers hoping he would blame his memory and send a gift anyway, she figured. Who invites strangers to their wedding? For that matter, who sends them gifts? Where I came from, you handed the couple an envelope with money at the reception. Were people here so rich they could afford a wedding without gifts of cash?

Whenever I felt out of place or homesick, I took refuge at Firestone Library. Books had seen me through an earlier time of trouble, and their presence all around me was both a comfort and an answer to the question of why I had come here. From my first day on campus, I'd enviously eyed the carrels in Firestone, which were reserved for upperclassmen. One day, one of those would be mine! Meanwhile, I reveled in the vastness of the main catalog room, riffling through the drawers full of cards, rows and rows of cabinets running almost the full length of the ground floor. And above them, like cathedral spires, rose the stacks, shelf after shelf, carrying a book for every card below, books ranging in subject from the majestic to the comically arcane. Here, in one of the world's great libraries, was my first exposure to the true breadth of human knowledge, the humbling immensity of what was known and thought, of which my days spent pawing the *Encyclopaedia Britannica* had offered only a foretaste.

My grazing in Firestone that first week was not at random, however. The course offerings at Princeton seemed a bewildering buffet: so many unfamiliar subjects that whetted my appetite. I dug into the library catalog to get a taste of each subject that tempted me before committing to a whole meal. At the same time, I was already well aware that in our freshman class, some, like me, were far fresher than others. Many from across the United States and abroad had gone to high schools that sounded more like mini-colleges, with library buildings of their own and sophisticated electives. I had made it into Princeton but, in this way too, with far more meager resources than most. I was under no illusions about how much remedial education could be accomplished skimming a few books in the stacks.

That there was no official pre-law curriculum turned out to be a blessing of sorts. I had to decide for myself what would be the most useful way to fill in the wide blank areas in my understanding. Having negligible prior knowledge of practically everything, I planned with each course to gulp down as much as I could. And so introductory surveys seemed ideal. I was drawn to psychology and sociology, having always been interested in the patterns of individual behavior, as well as the structure of communities; history, especially American, seemed essential and promised to reveal how a larger scheme of things had developed over time. Moral philosophy sounded a lot like what I imagined legal reasoning to involve. And just from reading the newspaper since entering Spellman, I knew that one day I would need to grapple with economics. An art history survey seemed like just the way to answer the many questions that had lapped at my mind since my childhood visit to the Ponce museum. But I would err on the side of practicality for now, saving that one for a sophomore treat.

My adviser approved my course load without question, and I felt I was on my way. But back at the dorm, deflation awaited. Everyone had returned from taking care of the same business, and the freshman floor was abuzz with talk of exotic upper-level courses my classmates were taking thanks to their Advanced Placement work in high school, which had allowed them to leapfrog ahead. By comparison, my course selections sounded boring, even lazy. Was I squandering an opportunity to really challenge myself? Maybe I just wasn't as smart as they were?

That tide of insecurity would come in and out over the years, sometimes stranding me for a while but occasionally lifting me just beyond what I thought I could accomplish. Either way, it would wash over the same bedrock certainty: ultimately, I know myself. At each stage of my life, I've had a pretty clear notion of my needs and of what I was ready for. There would be time enough in those four years at Princeton to sample Chinese Politics and Roman Law, to delve into Social Disorganization, Crime, and Deviant Behavior. Meanwhile, the introductory surveys would involve just as much work, given their broad scope, as more specialized advanced courses and would allow me for the first time to cultivate the critical faculties that Miss Katz had tried to instill: understanding the world by engaging with its big questions rather than just absorbing the factual particulars. This was the way to be a student of anything, and learning it has served me ever since. As a lawyer and even more as a judge, I would often be called upon to make myself a temporary expert in some field for the duration of a case. From the sciences to technology to the arts, the variety of industries and other endeavors that come before the courts is vast, and often there is no determining how the law applies without a working knowledge of the field in question.

I still had to choose a science lab course to meet a core requirement. Those in the natural sciences were known to be backbreakers, requiring a share of one's waking hours more appropriate for a pre-med or a budding scientist than an aspiring lawyer. I did notice, however, that Introductory Psychology included a lab that met the need. An introduction to Freud and other schools of thought, as well as an overview of brain function, seemed as if it might prove very handy over time. There was only one challenge to overcome, but one far more daunting than any rigors of organic chemistry or molecular biology labs: rats.

I have always had a deathly fear of anything that scurries or crawls: bugs, rodents, what have you. It isn't just the stereotypical fear of a lady standing on a chair, though I've done that. The special revulsion I feel goes back to childhood. The giant cockroaches that infested the projects one year—we called them water bugs—brought me to hysteria. How many times had I seen my mother take the whole place apart trying to locate the nest? The very thought of their proximity would keep me awake all night. And so when I realized that the psych lab would oblige me to handle rodents while I studied their reactions, I decided, a little perversely, to make the most of it. Undertaking a course of what psychologists call exposure therapy, I devised an experiment that required me not only to hold the rats but to implant electrodes in their brains.

It was going surprisingly well at first. I had steeled myself to picking the rats up by the tail and holding their furry bodies as I gave them a sedative injection. Once they were drugged, implanting the electrodes wasn't so bad. Tracking their behavior was no fun: it meant watching them continuously, without turning away in disgust. But I was doing it. It wasn't until the final weeks of the semester that everything went awry. I came into the lab one day to find all my rats milling around the same spot in the cage in an oddly intent way. I couldn't see what the attraction was, but the sight of their frenzied huddle was enough to stir the old revulsion: I certainly wasn't going to stick a hand in that cage. I found a stick and poked one of them off the pile. He turned to look at me, and in the gap that opened up, I saw the rat they were gnawing at, its abdomen already half devoured.

The grad student overseeing my efforts intercepted me as I ran out of the room screaming. Trying to contain my hysterics, he explained that cannibalism is normal rat behavior, that it had evolved as a way to control disease in the population and, as such, was a widely recognized sign of plague. Somehow that didn't help. He suggested I calm down and come back tomorrow.

The next day my state of mind was no better: the trauma had done its damage. It was horrifying even to imagine handling a rat as I had been doing for months, and no less so to think I had botched a whole semester's work. Fortunately, my professor took a philosophical view when I explained why I was utterly incapable of seeing my project through. As a psychologist he credited the motive of trying to cure my phobia by means of this experiment, and as a teacher he could see I had been at it diligently from the start. My grade wouldn't suffer much because of this fiasco. "Your plan was perfectly suited to what the course was intended to teach," he allowed. "Not every experiment is a success. That's the nature of doing science." The nature of doing many things, I might add: success is its own reward, but failure is a great teacher too, and not to be feared.

PART OF my financial-aid package committed me to weekly hours in the work-study program. At the start of freshman year, I was assigned to food service at the commons, but a lingering case of mononucleosis took me off the cafeteria line. I needed a desk job where I couldn't cause an epidemic. I was eager, too, to explore something new. The food service job was standard student fare in a predictable environment. But when I saw a posting for a keypunch operator at the Computer Center, I was intrigued.

Computers were a brave new world when I started work there in 1972, and access to their powers was confined to cavernous campus centers. Judith Rowe, head of the center's social sciences division, was a pioneer; among the first to envision the potential of quantitative analysis in the social sciences, she saw that computers would be the key to realizing it. To advance that vision, she encouraged graduate students to use the computer in analyzing their research data, an effort she facilitated by hiring work-study students like me to do the data entry. One project I worked on was with the historian Vernon Burton, who had discovered a treasure trove of old census records near his hometown in South Carolina. (There is such serendipity in historical research: Vernon had stopped on a back road to buy a soda when he spotted the stacks of ledgers holding up a shelf; he offered to build the shopkeeper some proper shelves in exchange for the ledgers.) My job was to key all the census data onto punch cards and help Vernon run the analysis.

I'd taken a typing class in high school, figuring that I could always get a job that way if necessary. That was qualification enough to start, as no one beyond the programmers themselves had any computer skills. Under Judith's guidance I learned a bit about programming and became skilled at keypunching. Because the work was specialized, I earned double what I had been making in the cafeteria. There were other perks too: we could set our own hours and come as we were, in jeans and T-shirts. It was a student's dream job, and I kept it all four years at Princeton, working there ten or fifteen hours a week on top of other jobs that came and went.

The mainframe computer housed in the center gave off so much heat that its room was cooled to frigid temperatures, and I wore a jacket and gloves whenever I went down into the basement to feed my stacks of punch cards into the machine. If the program crashed, I had to inspect each card individually to find the error. Often that meant perusing hundreds or even thousands of punch cards for a single mistaken keystroke, a maddening effort. Next to the monitor that showed the jobs queuing to run on the computer was a metal post that seemed to serve no purpose. It was a while before someone explained it to me: after repeatedly replastering the wall, the administration had decided to install the post for the convenience of frustrated students, who invariably needed something to kick when their code crashed.

Later, in my senior year, I was taking a break from writing my thesis to catch up on a couple of hours of keypunch work when an idea occurred to me: Why not enter the text of my thesis on the same types of punch cards that we were using for data analysis? That way, I could make changes as needed to individual cards without having to retype all the subsequent pages. Judith was intrigued. She thought it was a worthwhile experiment, and she assigned another operator to do the data entry for me. It's hard to be certain, but I might have submitted the very first word-processed senior thesis in Princeton's history, and I didn't even have to type it myself.

In my freshman year, however, I had cause to doubt that I would be able to write a senior thesis eventually. My very first midterm paper, for American history class, came back with a C, a grade I couldn't remember getting since the fourth grade. I was flattened, but even worse I had no idea where I had gone wrong. I'd fallen in love with the subject—the

Great Depression and Roosevelt's New Deal—pursuing it with everything I had. And the professor had been so inspiring that I wanted to impress her. Nancy Weiss was chair of the department, one of the first women in the whole country to hold such a post; later, as Nancy Malkiel, she would become the longest-serving dean of the college.

Professor Weiss told a familiar tale: although my paper was chock-full of information and even interesting ideas, there was no argumentative structure, no thesis that my litany of facts had been marshaled to support. "That's what analysis is—the framework of cause and effect," she said. Her point was a variation of what Miss Katz had been getting at, though now it was coming across more clearly and consequentially. Obviously, I was still regurgitating information. It was dawning on me that in all my classes I was so concerned with absorbing the facts in the reading that I wasn't marshaling them into a larger argument. By now, several people had pointed out where I needed to go, but none could show me the way. I began to despair of ever learning how to succeed at my assignments when quite unexpectedly it occurred to me: I already knew how.

Running into Kenny Moy outside Firestone one day got me thinking about my days in Forensics Club. Suddenly I realized that what had made me a winner on his team was precisely what I needed to do in my papers. I would not have dreamed of opening my mouth in a debate without first mapping out a position, anticipating and addressing objections, considering how best to persuade my listeners. Seeing the task in the context of another I already performed well largely demystified the problem. In my next few papers I would start doing in prose what I learned how to do in spoken words. But before I could do that really well, I'd have to face up to another obstacle: the general deficiency of my written English.

Whether it is a pregnant pause or even talking with her hands, a debater has many expressive tricks in her repertoire, some of which may cover a multitude of sins against the language. In writing, however, one's words stand naked on the page. Professor Weiss had minced none of her own informing me that my English was weak: my sentences were often fragments; my tenses erratic; and my grammar often just not grammatical. If I could have seen it myself, I would have fixed it, but what was wrong sounded right to me. It wasn't until the following year, when I took Peter Winn's course in contemporary Latin American history, that the roots of my problem were uncovered: my English was riddled with Spanish constructions and usage. I'd say "authority of dictatorship" instead of "dictatorial authority," or "tell it to him" instead of "tell him." Peter's corrections in red ink were an epiphany: I had no idea that I sounded so much like my mother! But my English wouldn't be as easy to fix as the lack of an argument in my essays. I bought some grammar handbooks and, as part of the same effort, a stack of vocabulary booklets. Over summer vacations spent working at Prospect Hospital, or later at the Department of Consumer Affairs in Spanish Harlem, I'd devote each day's lunch hour to grammar exercises and to learning ten new words, which I would later test out on Junior, trying to make them my own. Junior was unfazed by my semantic challenges. He was just happy to be out of my shadow in his final years at Cardinal Spellman.

I CAME TO ACCEPT during my freshman year that many of the gaps in my knowledge and understanding were sim-

ply limits of class and cultural background, not lack of aptitude or application as I'd feared. That acceptance, though,
didn't make me feel less self-conscious and unschooled in
the company of classmates who'd had the benefit of much
more worldly experience. Until I arrived at Princeton, I had
no idea how circumscribed my life had been, confined to a
community that was essentially a village in the shadow of a
great metropolis with so much to offer, of which I'd tasted
almost nothing. I was enough of a realist not to fret about
having missed summer camp, or travel abroad, or a casual
familiarity with the language of wealth. I honestly felt no
envy or resentment, only astonishment at how much of a
world there was out there and how much of it others already
knew. The agenda for self-cultivation that had been set for
my classmates by their teachers and parents was something
I'd have to develop for myself. And meanwhile, there could
come at any moment the chagrin of discovering something
else I was supposed to know. Once, I was trying to explain
to my friend and later roommate Mary Cadette how out of
place I sometimes felt at Princeton.

"It must be like Alice in Wonderland," she said sympa-
thetically.

"Alice who?"

She was kind enough to salvage the moment with a quick
grace: "It's a wonderful book, Sonia, you must read it!" In
fact, she would guide me thoughtfully toward a long list of
classics she had read while I'd been perusing *Reader's Digest*.
What did my mother know of *Huckleberry Finn* or *Pride and
Prejudice*?

Later, at the Computer Center, I would enter data for a
project that Judith Rowe described as a study of how people
paid for college. My fingers froze on the keys as I read what

I was typing: financial figures of the most well-off at Princeton. This was my first glimpse of trust funds; tax write-offs and loopholes; summer jobs at Daddy's firm that paid the equivalent of a year's tuition; incomes in the millions, disbursed a half million here, a few hundred thousand for that poor guy there. Between her own salary from Prospect Hospital and her survivors' benefits, which would end very soon, my mother's income was never more than five thousand dollars a year. Nothing could have clarified as starkly where I stood in relation to some of the people among whom I was now living and learning.

I never deluded myself that I could fill in everything I had missed growing up. Nor did I fail to appreciate that I'd had experiences of my own to prize or that I'd seen some aspects of life of which my classmates were sometimes naively unaware. Suffice it to say that Princeton made me feel that long after those summers spent first discovering the world's great books, I'd have to remain a student for life. It has been my pleasure to be one, actually, long after the virtue has ceased to be such a necessity.

Sixteen

EVERY WEEK, like clockwork, a small, square envelope arrived in the mail, addressed in a familiar, scratchy hand. Inside the envelope was a paper napkin and inside that a dollar bill. Abuelita wasn't much of a correspondent. She might sign the napkin, or not, but the loving gesture was reliable and steadfast. It meant a lot to know she was thinking of me, and a dollar was no small thing, for her or for me. Once in a rare while she would send a five-dollar bill, and I could see her smiling from seventy miles away.

Kevin came to visit with an equally reliable regularity. Driving down to Princeton from SUNY at Stony Brook every single weekend, he would make a detour through Co-op City to pick up a care package of fruits and juice from my mother. He would arrive around midnight frazzled and exhausted, still not accustomed to freeway driving, but as the weeks passed, he became more confident at the wheel.

When I asked my roommate, Dolores, if she would mind Kevin sleeping on our floor, she offered to spend weekends in a friend's room. I thought that was so generous of her, so graciously thoughtful. She meanwhile was thinking I was incorrigibly wild. She never let on, but later, after we'd gradually warmed to each other and become good friends, we'd have occasion to laugh about our first impressions of each other.

Actually, I wasn't wild at all: Kevin and I spent our wild weekends studying side by side. Stony Brook was a party scene, and he was glad of the chance to catch up on work. I offered many a time to come visit him there and save him the drive, but I don't think he wanted me to see just what a party scene it was. Only once did he accept, and that was on a holiday weekend when the campus was deserted. I could see why he preferred Princeton to the institutional, nondescript concrete of Stony Brook. He fell in love with the environment the same way that I had; later he would find his way back there for graduate school.

My mother came to visit me on campus once or twice each year. The first time, my cousin Charlie drove her and Junior down, along with Charlie's girlfriend. Kevin came too, of course. Nassau Inn, where many of my classmates' families would stay, was unimaginably expensive, so we had a slumber party. I gave Mami my bed and borrowed sleeping bags, mattresses, blankets, and pillows to make the rest of us comfortable on the floor. Charlie had a moment of profound shock in the bathroom, having forgotten that this was a girls' dorm. I sent him over to the male dorm next door, but their informal policy of sharing the showers with girlfriends was even more shocking to him. He's talked about it ever since.

If you happened to visit Princeton on a weekend, the cafeteria food in the commons was a crapshoot. Most of the regular staff was off duty, and students cooked. They laid on steak when there was a football game, but there was no game when my family first came to visit. My mother was aghast at what was on her plate, afraid that I might starve to death, a very bland death, before I could graduate. "I have to take you out tonight, Sonia," she said grimly after her first bite. I didn't know what to suggest. The hoagie shop on Nassau Street was the only place in town I could routinely afford. Advice from friends sent us ten miles out on Route 27, to the A-Kitchen and the beginning of a tradition. Just reading the menu downwind from the kitchen, I was jumping out of my skin with excitement, my mouth watering at descriptions of ginger, garlic, and chilies. The prices were right, and judging by the crowd, the fare was authentic. Chinese food of that quality and spiciness was new to me, a far cry from the spareribs and egg foo yong of the Bronx.

WHEN I CAME HOME from Princeton for a midterm break in my first year, Mami was panicking. She was in the final stretch of getting her nursing degree. The bilingual program at Hostos Community College included an English writing requirement. It wasn't as terrifying to her as the math, but it was onerous and she was struggling with it. She conceived the insane plan that I should write her paper for her.

"No way! That's cheating!" Facing dire threats that she would quit, I compromised. I agreed to look at what she had written and give her advice. We spent untold hours of my brief vacation at the kitchen table poring over her sentences. "There's no structure here, Mami. It wanders."

"I don't know, Sonia, I'm not good at embellishing."

"Forget about embellishing. What's the story you're trying to tell? What's your theme?"

"Ay, Sonia, please just write it for me!"

I didn't say it out loud, but I thought: Please, Mami, I don't have time for your insecurities. I have my own to deal with.

Her final exams were a torture worse than the English papers. Studying was not the problem. She had been doing that relentlessly for two years; she was used to it. But when exams loomed, the tension rose to a pitch higher than human ears could bear, the whips and chains came out, and the self-flagellation began in earnest. "I'm never going to pass," she moaned. I reassured her. She knew the material inside out. She had been doing these same procedures at Prospect Hospital for years.

"No, Sonia. I must have had some brain damage when I was small. Nothing stays in my memory."

"Don't be ridiculous! You're going to pass. Do you want to bet on it?"

"Yeah, I bet I'll fail."

We wagered a trip to Puerto Rico and shook hands on the stupidest wager I'd ever heard of: The winner would be the bigger loser. If she passed the exams, she would buy me a plane ticket. If she failed, I would pay for her trip.

I don't know if the bet was reverse psychology or a perverse good luck charm, but it seemed to steady her resolve. In the end, of course, I won: my mother passed all five of her qualifying exams on the first try, which doesn't happen very often.

LATE IN THE FALL SEMESTER of my sophomore year, I sensed that something wasn't right. For two weeks in a row, no envelope had arrived in the mail. I was worried and phoned my mother: "Where's Abuelita? Why haven't I heard from her?"

There was a long silence before Mami finally spoke. A tone of blustering hesitation in her voice told me that I was the last to hear the news. No one had the courage to tell me. Abuelita was in the hospital, at Flower–Fifth Avenue. She had ovarian cancer. Like so many older women, she had stopped seeing a gynecologist long before. She thought—and she was sadly wrong, I want to stress—that routine checkups were pointless since she was past having children. And so the cancer was far advanced when they found it. I was ready to get on the next bus, but Mami said, "No, wait till you come for Christmas. Hopefully, she'll be home by then."

That was a few weeks away. I had no experience with cancer of any kind then, no point of reference, no way to guess at how serious it might be. All I knew was that winter had set in and the sky hung lower with each passing day.

By the time I got there, Abuelita was delirious and hallucinating. I spent the days at her side, just being there, studying while she slept. Aunts and uncles and cousins squeezed into her hospital room, and then at some point on Christmas Eve the crowd vanished. People were anxious because the oil embargo meant hour-long lines at every gas station and they needed to fill up before the pumps closed for the holiday. Titi Gloria said, "Come, you'll get stuck here." My cousin Charlie and I looked at each other: no way were we leaving.

We decided to go get a Christmas tree for Abuelita; Charlie was the one who always decorated her apartment for the holidays, just as I had done our tree ever since Papi died. It started to snow as we walked down Lexington Avenue in the fading light. We'd gone all the way to Ninety-sixth Street before finding a florist that was open. We picked out a small tabletop tree that was beautifully decorated and took turns carrying it back, our hands freezing. The snow was already sticking; it was that cold.

"Do you remember . . . ?" The whole way there and back,

Charlie talked. His voice is gentle, musical; just the sound of it was a comfort. He had so many memories of Abuelita, many from before I was even born. He was very close to Gallego too and had stories to tell from when they all lived in Puerto Rico, some he'd heard others tell. When Abuelita was just twelve years old, the parish priest in Manatí recognized that she could heal people who were suffering mentally. He used to bring her to the asylum to exorcise their demons. She couldn't help with physical ailments, but if an unclean spirit possessed someone's mind, she could order it to leave. Even the patients she couldn't cure found a sense of peace in her presence.

Charlie has always had complete faith in Abuelita's spiritual powers. I'm too rational for that. You don't need to credit any superstition to feel how Abuelita protected the people she loved. Charlie confided in me a particular experience, his eyes getting bigger and bigger as he told the tale: One time, he had walked his girlfriend home to her place in Brooklyn, only to fall asleep on the train back up to the Bronx. Suddenly he woke, the sound of Abuelita's voice calling to him urgently, and he jumped off at the next station, just in time for the doors to close on three men who were about to mug him. The next day he saw Abuelita in person, and without any prompt the first thing she said was that he'd better give up that girl in Brooklyn!

Her fierce protectiveness also showed itself in ways that had nothing to do with spirits. She was wildly jealous of Gallego. Once at a party, he was dancing a slow merengue with the wrong woman. Abuelita grabbed the record from the Victrola and smashed it on the floor; then she kicked off her shoes and chased the woman down the stairs screaming. That was before my time, but I can imagine it easily. Mercedes was famously impulsive: joyrides at midnight, picnics on the highway median . . .

At her bedside, Charlie was trying to feed Abuelita a few spoonfuls of Jell-O, but she wouldn't take any. She kept asking for her clothes, as if she were going home. I was sitting in the chair by the door, and she looked right through me, talking to someone who wasn't there. "Angelina," she said. A chill went down my spine. I recognized the name: her sister, who'd passed away years ago. Charlie left the room for some reason, and then Abuelita said to me, "*Sonia, dame un cigarrillo.*"

It was the first time she'd said my name since I'd arrived from Princeton. "Abuelita, this is a hospital," I said gently, hating to deny her. "You can't smoke in here."

She said it again, imperiously: "Sonia, give me a cigarette!" The voice of the matriarch. I found my purse, pulled out a cigarette, lit it. I held it to her lips. She took a puff and gave a little cough. Then, as I watched, the life left her face.

I gave her a hug. "*Bendición, Abuelita.*" And then I yelled for the nurse. People came running, shooed me out of the room. It was just as well. I didn't go back in. I needed to be alone.

At the funeral, Charlie in his grief assumed an irrational added burden of guilt. He remembered Abuelita's having told him the year before that she wouldn't live to see another Christmas. "We should never have bought that tree, Sonia," he said, shaking his head. "We should have kept Christmas out of that room." My own sorrow flared into rage when I saw Nelson appear briefly, a spectral presence on the fringe of the mourners. I hadn't set eyes on him for three years, and now here he was, nodding in a doped-up daze. It was disrespectful of him to show up in that state, I fumed in silence. And it was desperately sad, sadder than I could bear just then. Nelson had got himself addicted to heroin while he was still in high school and then flunked out of half a dozen colleges while his father refused to accept the reality right before his eyes. His test scores were stellar, off the charts, so he'd get in the door easily enough, but he couldn't bring himself to show up for class or do the work. He slipped away from the funeral before we could say anything to each other, and I wouldn't see him again for several more years.

In the weeks that followed, I understood for the first time Abuelita's devastation when Papi died, how it had cut into her spirit. Her death did the same to me. A piece of me perilously close to my heart had been amputated. The sense of loss was startling, physically disorienting. It occurs to me that Flower–Fifth Avenue is the same hospital where I was born. "Full circle" is the phrase that pops into my mind, as if we were one person. *"Mercedes chiquita."* I can still hear her voice sometimes, all these years later. "Don't worry, *mi'jita*," she says, and I feel her protection.

Seventeen

I MET MARGARITA ROSA a few weeks after arriving at Princeton, and we soon became fast friends. Coming from a poor neighborhood of Brooklyn and a traditionally conservative Puerto Rican family herself, Margarita understood instinctively the path I had traveled to Princeton. We rarely needed to talk about the incongruities of our being there, and so our rapport progressed quickly to more urgent matters.

"Three guys for every girl, and I can't get a date! What's wrong with this picture?"

"Don't take it personally," I'd say. "They didn't want to let women in the door, and now that we're here, they don't know what to do with us." Princeton had turned coed just three years before, and the presence of women on campus was still a thorn in the side of many old-school diehards.

"Not true, Sonia. If you're a blue-eyed blonde, they know what to do with you. If you're black, there's at least a handful of brothers ready to stand up and say you're as beautiful as they are. But a *café-con-leche* Latina with a 'fro? That they don't know what to do with."

Margarita's tough luck with men mystified me. To my

eyes, she was indeed attractive, petite, and lively, as well as being eloquent and passionate about making the world a better place. She was a junior when I was a freshman, and I could only hope to become like her.

"At least you don't have a pudgy nose," I offered.

"At least you've got Kevin," she returned.

We often studied at Firestone Library until closing time, when we would walk back to the dorms together. About once a week, before going home, we would stop off at the pub to continue the conversation over a glass of sangria and a slice of pizza. Margarita was pushing me to join Acción Puertorriqueña, the Latino student group that she was involved in, and I was pushing back. It was no reflection on the group; nor was I being standoffish. I just wasn't inclined to join anything until I'd gathered my bearings and felt more comfortable with my course load.

I've since come to recognize a personal tendency. In high school, I hadn't tried anything like student government or the Forensics Club until my second year, and it would be the same at Princeton and again at law school. The first year that I face the challenges of any new environment has always been a time of fevered insecurity, a reflexive terror that I'll fall flat on my face. In this self-imposed probationary period, I work with compulsive intensity and single-mindedness until I gradually feel more confident. Some of the looming panic is no doubt congenital; I often see in my reactions something of my mother's irrational fear of being unequipped for nursing school. I have gone through this same kind of transition since becoming a judge, first on the federal district court, then on the appeals court, and finally on the Supreme Court.

Sure enough, I would join Acción Puertorriqueña during my sophomore year. I would bicycle out to the far edge of campus, where the architecture descended from Gothic Revival heights to the more human scale of colonial, and then on to the less-than-human industrial modern of graduate student housing. Just before the campus dissolved into suburban New Jersey, you reached the modest redbrick building of the Third World Center: headquarters and party central not just for Acción Puertorriqueña but for all the minority student groups on campus. I knew the area well: across the avenue were the Computer Center and Stevenson Hall, a relatively new dining facility that offered alternatives to the exclusive Princeton eating clubs. I'd embarrassed myself once in Stevenson asking for a glass of milk with my meal in the kosher canteen there, but after that I felt right at home. In fact, that part of campus became my neighborhood.

A space where one had a natural sense of belonging, a circle of friends who shared the same feeling of being a stranger in a strange land, who understood without need for explanation: it amounted to a subtle but necessary psychic refuge in an environment where an undercurrent of hostility often belied the idyllic surface. *The Daily Princetonian* routinely published letters to the editor lamenting the presence on campus of "affirmative action students," each one of whom had presumably displaced a far more deserving affluent white male and could rightly be expected to crash into the gutter built of her own unrealistic aspirations. There were vultures circling, ready to dive when we stumbled. The pressure to succeed was relentless, even if self-imposed out of fear and insecurity. For we all felt that if we did fail, we would be proving the critics right, and the doors that had opened just a crack to let us in would be slammed shut again.

We were different: not only from the generations of Princetonians who had walked through Nassau Gate before us, but, increasingly, from the friends and classmates we had left behind. I couldn't shake the feeling of having been admitted because of some clerical oversight. Margarita felt it too, Ken said the same thing, and the sentiment has been expressed countless times by minority students everywhere: by some accident of fate, we few among the great many had won the lottery. As the winners we stood in for all those not so lucky—some truly brilliant kids like Nelson, who slipped up, or others who'd never crossed paths with someone who could point the way, or who'd never even heard there was a way. Many of us experienced our election as survivor's guilt. I tried to frame it more optimistically: when she'd won a big pot, Abuelita used to say it was important to share the luck with others. Still, the sense of arbitrariness—unfathomable and irreducibly unsettling—would linger so that even in the best of times you could never be entirely sure that you were home safe.

It was because of this uneasy climate that so much of the work of Acción Puertorriqueña and other such groups focused on freshman admissions. In those early days of affirmative action—again, the practice was so new to Ivy League admissions that the first Latino students had yet to graduate when I arrived—many factors that complicate the cost-benefit analysis a generation later were at the time non-existent.

Until we would raise kids of our own, no minority students had alumni for parents, and rare indeed were those who had not come from poor communities. The typical undergraduate had been guided to Princeton by relatives, by prep school guidance counselors, or else by teachers savvy about the system. Minority kids, however, had no one but their few immediate predecessors: the first to scale the ivy-covered wall against the odds, just one step ahead ourselves, we would hold the ladder steady for the next kid with more talent than opportunity. The blacks, Latinos, and Asians at Princeton went back to their respective high schools, met with guidance counselors, and recruited promising students they knew personally. Then, every time a minority application landed in the pile of potential admissions, they'd reach out to make the applicant feel welcome or at least a little less intimidated.

This outreach was vital because disadvantaged students often had no idea that they stood a chance at a place like Princeton, assuming they'd even heard the name. In high school, I was vaguely aware that affirmative action existed, but I had no idea how or to what extent it worked in practical terms. When the two Hispanic students met me at the station in New Haven to show me around Yale, I was inclined to see their ethnicity as more a matter of pleasant coincidence than a programmatic effort. At most, I figured, they were being nice to one of their own kind, rather in the way Ken had encouraged me to consider Princeton and the other Ivy League colleges, not out of any political agenda. My innocence was the result of being unaware of just how few Latinas there would be in a place like Princeton, or for that matter that my being one could have figured so much in my admission.

Beyond freshman recruiting, Acción Puertorriqueña and similar groups were vocal in campus protests relating to national issues. It was an honorable tradition, most recently involving resistance to the Vietnam War and Princeton's entanglement with the military, but the war was over, and being a rabble-rouser did not appeal to me. Not that I didn't care passionately about the group's causes; rather, I had my doubts that linking arms, chanting slogans, hanging effigies, and shouting at passersby were always the most effective tactics. I could see that troubling the waters was occasionally necessary to bring attention to the urgency of some problem. But this style of political expression sometimes becomes an end in itself and can lose potency if used routinely. If you shout too loudly and too often, people tend to cover their ears. Take it too far and you risk that nothing will be heard over the report of rifles and hoofbeats.

Quiet pragmatism, of course, lacks the romance of vocal militancy. But I felt myself more a mediator than a crusader. My strengths were reasoning, crafting compromises, finding the good and the good faith on both sides of an argument, and using that to build a bridge. Always, my first question was, what's the goal? And then, who must be persuaded if it is to be accomplished? A respectful dialogue with one's opponent almost invariably goes further than a harangue outside his or her window. If you want to change someone's mind, you must understand what need shapes his or her opinion. To prevail, you must first listen—that eternal lesson of Forensics Club!

One of our most pressing objectives was to convince the administration to honor its commitment to increase the hiring of qualified Hispanics. There were almost sixty of us enrolled as students, a huge increase over just a few years ago, thanks mostly to the efforts of groups like ours. But there was not one Hispanic on the faculty or the administrative staff. It was hard, they said, to find qualified scholars, but could they not locate even one Latino janitor? You would never have known that Puerto Ricans made up 12 percent of the population of New Jersey. Quotas had not been declared illegal by the Supreme Court then, but we were not arguing in their favor. We were arguing only for some good faith effort to correct historical imbalances.

There were no actual villains, just inertia. The administration genuinely wanted more diversity for reasons of its image as well as fairness, notwithstanding the cranky alumni letters in *The Daily Princetonian*. The university's long-standing reputation as the northernmost school for southern gentlemen, which had bred resistance to desegregation, eventually gave way to some healthy soul-searching. Consequently, efforts to recruit black students were earnest and energetic. Faculty and administrative hiring of blacks still lagged, but it was going well compared with efforts among Puerto Ricans and Chicanos. Hiring committees had not a clue where to look for or how to attract suitable candidates. And so, though a high-level recruitment plan existed on paper, there was only foot-dragging and defensive excuse making. The administration wouldn't even respond to our letters.

It was not until we filed a formal complaint with the Department of Health, Education, and Welfare that we got President William Bowen's attention and a dialogue opened. Within a month, the Office of Civil Rights at the Department of Education had sent someone to meet with us in the provost's office. Before you knew it, Princeton had hired its very first Hispanic administrator—and not just any administrator: the assistant dean of student affairs, whose role was to advocate for students like us.

When I first joined Acción Puertorriqueña, the Mexican-Americans had their own separate group, the Chicano Organization of Princeton. Clearly, numbers as small as ours were better not divided, so we often joined forces on issues of mutual concern, and the two groups almost always partied together. (They outnumbered us, so tortillas and *refritos* were more typically the fare than *arroz con gandules,* but our salsa dancing was more than a match for their *rancheras.*) There were a handful of nonaligned minority students—Filipinos, Native Americans, and other Latinos—so we at Acción Puertorriqueña invited them in, tacking "y Amigos" onto the end of our name. I liked the indiscriminate amiability of how that sounded, but even more the inclusiveness in practice. As much solace and strength as we gathered from group identity, it mattered greatly to have an open door. After all, the failure to include was our raison d'être.

All of the different minority student groups at Princeton shared the Third World Center, and together they elected a governance board to run the facility. To assure balance, equal numbers of seats were allotted to African-American, Hispanic, and Asian students. In addition, there was an "open" section usually filled by African-Americans, by far the largest minority on campus. I took the risk of running outside the Hispanic category, becoming the first nonblack to win one of the open seats. I was proud of that victory, seeing it as a tribute to how well I listened and brokered compromises between factions.

For all the sense of accomplishment and the embrace I felt at the Third World Center, I had no wish to confine myself to a minority subculture and its concerns. The Latino community anchored me, but I didn't want it to isolate me from the full extent of what Princeton had to offer, including engagement with the larger community. I would warn any minority student today against the temptations of self-segregation: take support and comfort from your own group as you can, but don't hide within it.

My opportunity to venture out came with the chance to

serve on the student-faculty Discipline Committee. The body typically dealt with the predictable lows of student behavior: stolen library books, dorm rule infractions, intoxicated rowdiness. Sometimes I wanted to cringe, as when a pair of our "amigos," Native Americans, had had a few too many and started tossing furniture out the window at the Third World Center. I shook my head in despair: drunken Indians? Talk about making it easy for the cranky old letter writers! A more serious incident involved a brilliant student wrongly accused of hacking into the university's computer system. Getting to the bottom of that one proved a challenge more technical than any other we would face, but I was able to draw on my experience at the Computer Center for clarity, in what was arguably my first judicial role.

THERE ARE FEW PLACES in this country where institutional history overlaps the national narrative as self-consciously as it does at Princeton. The cannon in the center of the green saw action in the Revolutionary War. Among the über-alumni: James Madison, class of 1771, author of the Constitution. The Continental Congress of 1783 sat in Nassau Hall to receive news of the Treaty of Paris. Those self-assured people surrounding me, who had traveled the world confident of having an influential role in it one day, were no less certain of themselves as the rightful inheritors of this history. It was not something on which I could ever hope to have the same purchase. I needed a history in which I could anchor my own sense of self. I found it when I began to explore the history of Puerto Rico.

I had studied American, European, Soviet, and Chinese history and politics, but I knew next to nothing about the

history of my own people. Every people has a past, but the
dignity of a history comes when a community of scholars
devotes itself to chronicling and studying that past. In the
course offerings in Latin American history and politics, however, Puerto Rico was barely mentioned. Fortunately, it was
possible for students to initiate courses. Years before, I discovered, a Princeton student had put together a course on
Puerto Rican history, and now, under the guidance of Professor Winn, I set out to revive it, bringing the syllabus up-
to-date and recruiting the necessary quorum of students. I
didn't make it easy on those who might be interested: my
reading list was ambitious, to say the least.

The history that emerged from our reading was not
a happy one. Under Spain, Puerto Rico suffered colonial
neglect and the burden of policies designed to enrich distant
parties at heavy cost to the island. Little effort was made to
develop the natural resources or agriculture beyond what was
needed to provision and mount the conquistadores on their
way to Mexico and South America. Poor governance was
compounded by bad luck—hurricanes and epidemics—as
well as state-sponsored piracy by the British, French, and
Dutch. For the Spanish settlers, as for the enslaved indigenous
tribes and those from elsewhere in the Caribbean who took
refuge on the island, it was a precarious existence that would
not begin to improve until well into the nineteenth century.
There was negligible civic life and minimal economic activity
beyond smuggling. Any liberties the Spanish crown granted
were often quickly revoked.

When Spain ceded Puerto Rico to the United States in
1898, along with Cuba and the Philippines as the spoils of
the Spanish-American War, Puerto Ricans held an optimistic faith in American ideals of liberty, democracy, and jus-

tice. But that optimism would yield to a sense of betrayal for many. Governed without representation, exploited economically, some islanders came to feel they had merely exchanged one colonial master for another.

It was clear that the idea of Puerto Rico as the "rich port" was never anything but a fantasy. The island had always been poor. At the same time, it was tied to an old culture and several continents. One didn't have to romanticize the past or succumb to mythology to appreciate its thread in the fabric of history.

One of the books on our reading list to make a profound impression on me was Oscar Lewis's *La Vida*. It was a contentious inclusion, an anthropological study of one family that stretched from the slums of San Juan to those of New York. Many Puerto Ricans have been offended by its airing of dirty laundry: the granular view of prostitution and a culture that seems preoccupied with sex. But there was much else going on in the lives Lewis described and in his argument about how the culture of poverty persists by virtue of being adaptive, a set of strategies to cope with difficult circumstances. I couldn't deny that the book triggered powerful moments of recognition, often painful but nonetheless fascinating, as I saw my own family reflected in its pages. I was beginning to understand my family lore in a cultural framework, to spot sociological patterns in what had seemed mere idiosyncrasies, and dark ones at that.

What *La Vida* was lacking, I realized, was an appreciation of the good, the richness of our culture, however long overshadowed by poverty. There are strengths in our collective psyche that account for our resilience and that equally hold the potential for our renewal, if properly nourished and cultivated. I could see it in my own mother's reverence for education, her faith in community, her infinite capacity for hard work and perseverance; in Abuelita's joyful generosity, her passion for life and poetry, her power to heal. Such strong women are no rarity in our culture. I could see resilient strength, too, in the way that Spiritism and the Catholic faith have accommodated each other rather than clashing.

THE CLASSROOM DISCUSSIONS were heated and often loud. We hadn't resisted our colonial masters in any meaningful way, some would claim. Others responded: El Grito de Lares had rallied rebels against Spain. And in the 1950s members of the militant Puerto Rico Nationalist movement, who pursued armed revolution against the United States, went as far as an attempt on the life of President Truman and a deadly shoot-out in the U.S. Congress. And yet others retorted: These moments of resistance were fleeting and never led to the kind of sustained struggle that had won independence for Cuba or the Philippines. If identity arises from struggle, and trauma spurs growth and change, did not the frailty of our opposition threaten to define us historically? Cuba's revolution, like the wars of independence fought in the Philippines, had forged those national identities in a crucible of violence. Many in the class would ask what it was in our character that had led us to a more peaceable accommodation with colonial power.

Again and again, the conversation returned to the island's political status. Did we want to remain a commonwealth, with some self-rule and a preferential trade relationship with the mainland? Half the class believed that was no better than being a colony of the United States, living as second-class citizens. But if we should aspire to statehood, the full rights of citizenship would come at the price of the full obligations, including a tax burden that, arguably, might have crippled our economy at the time. Some proposed, with passionate conviction, that full independence was the only way to preserve our culture and the proper dignity of self-determination. The economic repercussions of each position were as inscrutably complex as they were critical to the arguments. And for those who are eager to discern my own present views on the status question, I can only advise not to give too much weight to whatever ideas vied for prominence in a young student's mind.

WHEN MY MOTHER made good on our wager of a plane ticket and I found myself in Puerto Rico for two weeks, I had my first chance to view the island through adult eyes and with an evolving new consciousness of my identity. Some things hadn't changed since childhood visits. We still made the ritual stop for a coconut on the road from the airport, but now the vendor would add a bit of rum to my libation from a bottle he kept out of sight. I still began the trip with a round of visits to every family member in order of seniority, still feasted on mangoes fresh off the tree. But instead of playing the Three Stooges, my cousins and I enjoyed dominoes, dancing, and the ubiquitous bottle of rum. The kindness of strangers was still striking: a flat tire fixed, cups of coffee offered while we waited.

Much of what I saw was familiar but now made more sense. The poverty documented in *La Vida* was visible to me now in the slums of San Juan. Compared with my family in New York, my family in Puerto Rico was modestly prosperous; they had shielded me as a child from realities that I could now reckon with, though certain aspects of the island's social stratification would remain hidden from me until very recently. San Juan also has its gracious homes, its old money, and its high culture.

The stunning natural beauty of the island, which I had barely registered as a child, also made a deep impression on that trip as I played tourist. In the rain forest at El Yunque, waterfalls trick the eye, holding movement suspended in lacy veils. Wet stone gleams, fog tumbles from peaks to valleys, mists filter the forest in pale layers receding into mystery. On the beach at Luquillo, when the sun appears under clouds massed offshore and catches the coconut palms at a low angle, the leafy crowns explode like fireworks of silver light. At night there is liquid stardust swirling in the dark waters of the phosphorescent bay. Almost every evening there are sunsets of white gold where the sky meets the sea.

At Cabo Rojo, a little motorboat came puttering to shore after a long wait and ferried a handful of people across the lagoon to La Isla de los Ratones. There was nothing there—no food stalls, no vendors, no "amenities"—nothing but the skirt of pure white sand and a coral shelf that let you walk chest-deep in crystal translucence for what seemed like miles before the floor dropped into the ocean. I looked down into water so clear that it was invisible, except for the rocks and sand and sea fronds rippling on the floor as at the beginning of a dream sequence in a movie.

As a New Yorker of profoundly urban sensibilities, I was never very attuned to nature. During my first week on campus, a cricket had me tearing the dorm room apart, searching for the source of the chirp until Kevin explained that it lived in the tree outside my window. I've been known to confuse cows for horses. The ocean was always the one grand exception. Even in the chaos of Orchard Beach, the circus of family picnics, crowded surf, and traffic jams, I could find in the rhythm of the waves a transcendent serenity. And anyone who could find peace in the beaches of the Bronx would find heaven in Puerto Rico.

Another revelation of my adult trips to the island was how much the political questions broached in my course, especially about the island's status, infused everyday life. You'd see party symbols everywhere, the straw hat for the faction supporting commonwealth, the palm tree for those supporting statehood, the green flag with the white cross for those who favored independence. Everyone pored over the newspapers, dissected the candidates' positions on economic development, education, health care, corruption . . . During one election season, in the plaza of Mayagüez—and in many other towns too, I'm sure—traffic jams proliferated as cars honking horns and flying one party's flags refused to give way to other cars honking horns and flying the other party's flags. It was chaos, but at least people cared. I learned that 85 percent of the island's population had gone to the polls in recent elections.

This manic enthusiasm that gripped the island in election years, and still does, was a marked contrast to the political despondency felt by Puerto Ricans on the mainland in those years. The summer that I won the bet with my mother, I worked as usual in the business office at Prospect Hospital before going to Puerto Rico. For a couple of weeks, however, Dr. Freedman, as part of his community outreach efforts, lent me out as an intern to Herman Badillo's ultimately unsuccessful campaign for mayor of New York City. Badillo was our congressman, the first Puerto Rican ever elected to the House of Representatives. It was then I first saw how difficult it was to energize a community that felt marginal and voiceless in the larger discourse of a democracy.

Puerto Ricans in New York then felt their votes didn't count. And so why should they take the trouble even to register? Having experienced discrimination intimately, they knew they were seen as second-class citizens, as people who didn't belong, with no path to success in mainland society. Their chances of escaping from the underclass, from the vicious cycle of poverty, were no better than those of their similarly alienated black neighbors and probably worse for those who didn't speak English.

Puerto Ricans on the island, by contrast, didn't have full consciousness of being a minority because they'd never had to live as one. There were inequalities in their world, but no one's dignity suffered merely on account of his being Puerto Rican. Whether content with commonwealth status or aspiring to statehood, or even independence, they took it for granted that they were fully American: American citizens born to American parents on American territory. To be mistaken for foreigners—aliens, legal or otherwise—would have been a shock.

It was dawning on me that if the Puerto Rican community in New York ever hoped to escape poverty and recover its self-respect, there were lessons to be learned from the island. The two communities—islanders and those on the mainland—needed to work together for their mutual benefit.

FOR THE FINAL PAPER in the Puerto Rican history course, Peter Winn suggested a marvelous project, a family oral history. It was a challenge befitting any serious student of history: going mano a mano with primary sources, my cassette recorder planted on the kitchen table. Not everyone warmed to it: "You're wasting your time! Nothing interesting ever happened to me." For some, it was a grudging surrender to interrogation, slow and halting; others, the natural storytellers, proved surprisingly eager and voluble.

I was amazed by how many of these stories I'd never heard before. People had left their past behind when they came to New York. Memories of hardship and extreme poverty were of no use starting a new life on the mainland. With so much to deal with in the present, who had the luxury of dwelling on the past? My mother had told me very little about her childhood. Now it unfolded, hesitantly at first—her mother's death, her orphan loneliness—and then, with more confidence, she recounted joining the army, coming to New York, falling into a new family at Abuelita's. She said very little about my father. Those stories, as I've said, came out only recently.

The experience of hearing my Princeton reading echoed in family recollections had the effect of both making the history more vivid and endowing life as lived with the dignity of something worth studying. When, for instance, I had read that "a woman who takes ten hours to finish two dozen handkerchiefs earns 24 cents for them," I could picture Titi Aurora holding the needle, my mother leaning over the iron. Nor were these lives lived beyond a broader scheme of historical cause and effect. It was America's wars that would transform us into real Americans, not only by reason of my mother's decision to enlist, but even earlier, with the granting of American citizenship to Puerto Ricans in 1917—after two decades of limbo—just in time for Abuelita's first husband, my grandfather, to be drafted into World War I with a wave of young Puerto Rican men. After the war, that same grandfather rolled tobacco in a factory in Manatí, listening all day as a reader read from novels and newspaper stories to keep the rollers entertained. From my reading I knew that a tobacco factory worker made between forty cents and a dollar a day and that tuberculosis, from which my grandfather died, was the most common cause of death on the island, and particularly lethal to those who worked long hours in air heavy with tobacco dust.

Everyone agrees what a shame it is to have lost the chance to gather the stories of Abuelita's mother. Bisabuela's memories of Manatí, the town where Abuelita grew up, vividly recalled Puerto Rico when the island still belonged to Spain. Still older stories survive in hand-me-down recollection beyond any living soul's direct experience: The Sotomayors, I heard, might be descendants of Puerto Rican pioneers. On my mother's side, once upon a time, there had been property too. I heard rumors of family ties to the Spanish nobility. Somehow there was a reversal of fortune. Was it a gambling debt that had cost them the farm? Disinheritance? The tatters of old stories are tangled, weathered, muted by long-held silences that succeeded loud feuds, and sometimes no doubt re-dyed a more flattering color.

My family's shifting fortunes followed the island's economic currents: coffee plantations sold off piecemeal until yesterday's landowners took to laboring in cane fields that belonged to someone else. Child labor and illiteracy were normal; girls were married at thirteen or fourteen. We moved from mountainside farms to small towns like San Germán, Lajas, Manatí, Arecibo, Barceloneta; and after a time, on to what were then the slums of Santurce in San Juan; from there the mainland beckoned, and we answered, boarding the venerable USAT *George S. Simonds,* the army transport that carried so many Puerto Ricans to New York, until Pan Am offered the first cheap airfares and we rode *la guagua aérea*, the aerial bus, between mainland and island. We were not immigrants. We went freely back and forth. We became New Yorkers, but we did not lose our links to the island.

Of all the links, language remains strong, a code of the soul that unlocks for us the music and poetry, the history and literature of Spain and all of Latin America. But it is also a prison. Alfred talked about moving from Puerto Rico to the South Bronx in third grade. His experience was common: no help in the transition, no remedy for his deficiency but to be held back. After that, teachers just shrugged and passed him from one grade to the next, indifferent to whether he'd understood a word all year. The sharpest kids would eventually pick up the language on their own and come out only a few years behind. Still, Alfred said, "the white kids were always the most advanced. The black kids were behind them, and the Puerto Ricans were last."

My cousin Miriam was listening in on our recording session, nodding in recognition. At the time, she was studying for a degree in bilingual education at Hunter College, and today she is no less passionate about that calling with decades of teaching experience behind her. "I want to become the kind of teacher that I wish I'd had," she told me. She'd had it rough in the public schools, where the teachers knew so little of Latino culture they didn't realize that kids who looked down when scolded were doing so out of respect, as they'd been taught. Their gesture only invited a further scolding: "Look at me when I speak to you!"

I felt my own shiver of recognition too, remembering my early misery as a C student at Blessed Sacrament, in terror of the black-bonneted nuns wielding rulers, a misery that didn't abate until after Papi died and Mami made an effort to speak English at home. It seems obvious now: the child who spends school days in a fog of semi-comprehension has no way to know her problem is not that she is slow-witted. What if my father hadn't died, if I hadn't spent that sad summer reading, if my mother's English had been no better than my aunts'? Would I have made it to Princeton?

Recently, those recordings I made have resurfaced. As I listen to them now, too often I hear my own voice. There I go again, inserting opinions and jumping on the faintest hint of racism in their comments. It was my campus conditioning: I found it unfathomable that people who'd themselves been subject to so much prejudice on the mainland still clung to ideas about color as a gauge of status, as the way to keep score of how many of your ancestors had come from Spain, how many from Africa. I also cringe to hear myself lecturing Ana and Chiqui about how women's roles are culturally constructed and therefore changeable. "Read Margaret Mead!" I yell at them. "In certain tribes in Papua New Guinea, it's completely reversed. What you consider male, the women do. And what women do here, the men do over there."

"That's over there. It's different over here," Chiqui says with finality. She wasn't taking guff from a college know-it-all. It's embarrassing, sad, and amusing, all at the same time. My own biases were exposed every bit as much as those of my informants. In those moments when arguments flared on the tape, the distance I'd traveled at Princeton was revealed, but it could also be erased in a moment when someone pushed my buttons. I could be yanked for a time into one world or the other, but mostly now I would be living suspended between the two.

FOR THE TOPIC of my senior thesis I chose Luis Muñoz Marín—the island's first governor to be elected rather than appointed by a U.S. president—whose efforts at industrialization brought Puerto Rico into the modern world. I was inspired by his work in marshaling the *jíbaros,* politically marginalized peasants, into a force that could win elections. Some part of me needed to believe that our community could give birth to leaders. I needed a beacon. Of course I knew better than to let such emotion surface in the language and logic of my thesis; that's not what historians do. But it kept me going through the long hours of work, and it counterbalanced the fact that Muñoz Marín's story had no happy ending, as initial success generated other economic challenges. How could this have happened? It was hard to imagine a more fruitful area for study.

ONE MORNING, a small headline in the local paper caught my eye. A Hispanic man who spoke no English had been on a flight that was diverted to Newark airport. No one there knew enough Spanish to explain to him where he was or what had happened, and in his frustration and confusion he made a scene. He was taken to Trenton Psychiatric Hospital and held there for days before a Spanish-speaking staff member showed up and helped him reach his family. This, I fumed, is not acceptable.

When I called the hospital and asked some questions, I found that there were a number of long-term patients who spoke no English and had only intermittent access to

Spanish-speaking staff. I could imagine nothing crueler than the anguish of mental illness compounded by mundane confusion and being unable to communicate with one's keepers.

The Trenton Psychiatric Hospital was beyond any influence of Acción Puertorriqueña. There was no way we could pressure the administrators to hire more Hispanics as we had the university. So I resolved to take a different approach, organizing a volunteer program under which our members spent time at the hospital on a continuous rotation so that there was always someone who could interpret for the patients and intercede with the staff if necessary. We also ran bingo nights and sing-alongs, finding that some very uneasy minds were nonetheless able to dredge their memories for the comfort of old songs their parents had sung. And before heading home for Thanksgiving and Christmas, we threw holiday parties for the patients, recruiting our mothers and aunts to prepare the traditional foods that were too complicated to attempt in dorm kitchens.

The program in Trenton was my first real experience of direct community service, and I was surprised by how satisfying I found the work. Modest as the effort was, I could envision it working on a grand scale—service to millions. But the operations of major philanthropy being then beyond my imagination, government seemed the likely provider. And so it was I began to think that public service was where I was likely to find the greatest professional satisfaction.

UNDER A BANNER reading "*Feliz Navidad*," we had set out the stacking chairs for the patients, and on the folding tables we'd arranged a bounty of *pasteles* and *arroz con gandules*. This was not an audience you could expect to settle down and listen attentively, but when Dolores strummed the strings of her guitar, the harsh fluorescent light seemed somehow to soften. We mustered some Spanish carols, Nuyorican *agui-naldos*. But it was when she turned to old Mexican favorites that Dolores's voice truly shone as she serenaded those broken souls on a silent winter night in New Jersey:

> *Dicen que por las noches*
> *no más se le iba en puro llorar . . .**

They say he survived the nights on tears alone, unable to eat . . . Dolores sings the Mexican ballad of a lover so bereft that after he dies, his soul, in the form of a dove, continues to visit the cottage of his beloved. Even my heart, as yet untouched by such passion, is captured, and I am transfixed as Dolores coos the song of the lonesome dove: *cucurru-cucú . . .*

In the audience, an elderly woman is staring into space, her face as devoid of expression as ever. She is always the unresponsive one, who has not spoken a single word since we've been coming to Trenton. Tonight, even she is tapping her foot gently as Dolores sings.

---

*They say that all those nights
All he could do was cry . . .
(from "Cucurrucucú Paloma," a popular Mexican song)

Eighteen

FELICE SHEA WAS SITTING at my desk, waiting for me to walk over to the commons with her for dinner. She was that very fair-skinned Irish type, blushing at the slightest discomfort, and I had gotten pretty good at reading her reactions. Seeing at this moment a virtual red tide, I asked her what was up.

"I really hope you don't think I was snooping, Sonia, but I couldn't help noticing that letter in your wastebasket . . ."

"It's just junk mail from some club. They want you to pay for membership, and then they want more money for some trinket engraved with your name. What a scam!"

Felice now looked more embarrassed than ever as she tried to explain that Phi Beta Kappa was totally legitimate. More than legitimate, in fact: an honor of such prestige that she insisted I had to accept the membership even if she had to pay for it. Felice was not only exceptionally kind and generous; as the daughter of two college professors, she knew all the ins and outs of academia and had guided me through many such blind spots. After four years at Princeton, I thought I knew the terrain pretty well, but every once in a while, even as a senior, I'd hear about something that made me feel like a freshman. I wasn't going to take Felice's money, but I did take her advice.

Something similar had happened not long before. I was asleep when the phone rang; the voice on the other end said it was Adele Simmons, dean of student affairs, calling to congratulate me on having won the Pyne Prize. You'd have thought it was Publishers Clearing House from the excitement in her voice describing this honor I'd never heard of, obviously not paying attention to it in *The Daily Princetonian,* but inferring it was important from her tone, I found the presence of mind to express how astonished and grateful I was. It wasn't until after I hung up and dialed Felice's number that I got a full briefing on the Moses Taylor Pyne Honor Prize. It seemed I would have to give a speech at an alumni luncheon where the award was presented. Felice and I were already into a discussion of appropriate attire, and planning a shopping trip, when she let drop the most important detail: "It's the highest award that a graduating senior can receive."

I had not shopped for clothes seriously since the day I acquired my going-to-Princeton raincoat, which was now eligible for retirement. My complete wardrobe fit in one laundry bag, easy to carry home on the bus. It consisted of three pairs of dungarees, one pair of period plaid pants, and an assortment of interchangeable tops. When my summer job demanded a more professional look, I managed to avoid the problem by wearing a hospital uniform. Felice and her mother took me to Macy's and helped me pick out a gorgeous suit for fifty dollars. It was the most expensive outfit I'd ever worn, but to judge by how I felt wearing it, it was a good investment.

The gymnasium was transformed by tables dressed in white linen, flatware, and flowers. The crowd was vast—

alumni, professors, and deans, all abuzz with greetings and congratulations, their hands extended, smiling broadly, glasses raised. A part of me still felt uncertainty—or was it disbelief?—about all this fanfare and how to take it, but there was no denying that whatever it meant, it felt great. I had worked hard, and the work paid off. I had not disappointed.

Among the recent graduates were those who, as women or as other minorities, had already altered that old image of a Princeton alumnus long cherished by some. There were friends who had graduated a year or two ahead of me, like Margarita Rosa, who came down from Harvard Law School for the occasion. Others were only names to me until that day. Nearly every living Hispanic who had ever graduated from Princeton showed up, overflowing with pride and camaraderie, for what amounted to a triumphant reunion. My family, of course, was there en masse, Mami sitting there with a dazed smile that burst into beams of happy recognition with each friend or acquaintance who came over to congratulate her. My own face was sore from all the grinning.

The vault of the gymnasium and the blank scoreboard were a distant frame, filled with the upturned faces of many hundreds of strangers. This was the view as I took to the podium to give my speech, stricken with the usual bout of nerves. With the exception of our small cluster of "Third World" friends and family, the faces were uniformly white. It was a fitting reminder of what I was doing up there. The Pyne Prize, often shared by two students, recognizes excellent scholarship but also leadership that provides "effective support of the best interests of Princeton University." My efforts on the Discipline Committee had been a significant factor in my award, but so had my work with Acción Puertorriqueña and the Third World Center, which Princeton recognized as a benefit not merely to the few dozen student members of those organizations but to the broader community as well. The dynamism of any diverse community depends not only on the diversity itself but on promoting a sense of belonging among those who formerly would have been considered and felt themselves outsiders. The greater purpose of these groups had not been self-exile or special pleading. It had been to foster a connection between the old Princeton and the new, a mutual acceptance without which the body as a whole could not thrive or evolve.

This was the work not of one person but of a community: y Amigos. And in my speech I wanted to acknowledge that collaboration, as well as bow to those among the newest alumni, like Margarita Rosa, who, walking in shoes very much like my own, had cleared a path for me to follow in.

"The people I represent are diverse in their opinions, cultures, and experiences. However, we are united by a common bond. We are attempting to exist distinctly within the rich Princeton tradition, without the tension of having our identities constantly challenged and without the frustrations of isolation. In different ways and in different styles, some loudly and others quietly, Princeton's minorities have created a milieu in which I could act and see the efforts accepted. In this way, today's award belongs to those with whom I have worked to make Princeton realize that it contains groups which are distinct and honorable in their own traditions.

"However, Princeton's acceptance of our existence and thoughts is only a first step. The challenge to both myself and Princeton is to go beyond a simple recognition. I hope today marks the beginning of a new era for all of us: a new era in which Princeton's traditions can be further enriched by being broadened to accommodate and harmonize with the beat of those of us who march to different drummers."

Looking out at that crowd, I imagined those who had not yet arrived, minority students who, in years to come, would make this multitude of faces, the view from where I now stood, a little more various. If they could have heard me, I would have confided in them: As you discover what strength you can draw from your community in this world from which it stands apart, look outward as well as inward. Build bridges instead of walls.

SPRING EASED into summer, exams and final papers were wrapped up, my thesis review completed. Graduation brought one last unfamiliar laurel when Peter Winn called me into his office to tell me that I would graduate summa cum laude. Once again, facing the pleasure with which this news was delivered, I didn't have the heart to inquire what it meant; for now it was enough that I should act very glad and honored. When I'd finally looked up the translation of the Latin phrase, the irony of my needing to do so was not lost on me. It was perhaps then I made a measure of peace with my unease: the uncertainty I'd always felt at Princeton was something I'd never shake entirely. For all the As and honors that could be bestowed, there would still lurk such moments of estrangement to remind me that my being there was not typical but an exception.

I marched out of Nassau Gate with my classmates in a final ritual of return to the real world, knowing that I was headed back to the Ivy League for law school at Yale in the fall. Meanwhile, a summer job doing research in the Office of Social Responsibility at the Equitable Life Assurance Society in Manhattan would provide my first glimpse inside corporate America. It was, to say the least, a letdown: I was shocked at how much time presumably productive people were capable of wasting. It was similar to what I'd observed the summer before, working in New York City's Department of Consumer Affairs, only stranger perhaps, considering it was a business with the aim of making money.

Junior by then had graduated from Cardinal Spellman and completed the first year of a program at NYU that would lead to medical school. He hadn't grown up with dreams of becoming a doctor. His ambition at that stage of life was only to do something different from whatever I was doing, to find his own path out from under my shadow. Though our constant bickering had mellowed by then, and mutual respect prevailed, each of us was too involved in his or her own life to pay much attention to the other's. But in a bind we would always turn to each other first, and given the experience that we alone shared, not much would need to be said. Family was family.

The big event for ours that summer was the wedding. That Kevin and I would eventually marry had been a given ever since the day I introduced him to Abuelita. With hindsight I can see how unexamined that certainty was. I had long mapped out a hypothetical route to marriage at the age of twenty-eight, which had less to do with the reality of my relationship with Kevin than with a desire to avoid the mistakes of others. My aunts had married at fourteen or fifteen, my cousins at eighteen. I was going to do things in the right order and finish my education first. But with the prospect of my beginning law school at Yale, and Kevin's own plans for grad school still up in the air, it seemed sensible that he should move to New Haven with me. In our world that couldn't have happened without our getting married.

My mother and I had radically different views of what the wedding would be like. My vision was frugal, modest, and practical. Hers was extravagant. Her own wedding had consisted of a visit to city hall and dinner at Abuelita's. She had not walked down the aisle, and therefore I had to. We battled over every detail, and she wasn't above playing dirty. If I crossed someone's name off the list in an effort to trim the numbers, she'd find an opportunity for us to run into that person and mention, to my well-masked dismay, that the invitation was in the mail.

Once I recognized that this whole production had more to do with her needs than mine, I resigned myself to simply getting it done as painlessly as possible. I scoured the city for the cheapest ways to furnish the essential elements. The prices horrified me, each piece of the fairy tale seeming a bigger rip-off than the last.

"I'm not spending hundreds of dollars on a dress that I'll only wear once. I'm just not doing it!"

"So what are you going to wear, Sonia?"

How many times could we repeat that exchange? Elisa was my savior. She was an old friend and neighbor of my mother's from the Bronxdale Houses and also a seamstress. It had been a while since I'd gone back to the projects after our move to Co-op City, and I was stunned by how tiny and cramped the rooms seemed when we visited Elisa. I drew a diagram, a simple A-line dress. "That's all I want." I could see the horror rising in Mami's eyes like water in a sinking boat.

"It's too plain. You have to make it fancier!"

"It's my wedding! You've decided everything else!" I couldn't believe we were fighting so shamelessly in front of Elisa, but she handled it with a skill that hinted at plenty of prior mother-daughter experience.

"Sonia, we can keep it simple and still make it elegant with a little beadwork here and here . . ."

And so, with help from friends and family, gradually the plans came together. Junior was still working as a sacristan at St. Patrick's, and it was one of the privileges allowed employees that they could arrange to have wedding masses for family celebrated at the cathedral. Through his job selling insurance, Alfred had a client with a limousine rental service who gave him a spectacular discount on three antique Rolls-Royces.

Marguerite, who had remained a close friend since high school, was my maid of honor. She graciously volunteered to host the bridal shower, but it was not such a simple proposition given that we were all New Yorkers, among whom assumptions and traditions run deep and are as varied as the places we come from. Would it be tea sandwiches and punch for ladies only on a Sunday afternoon? Or rum and real food and dancing on a Saturday night, with the men of course invited too. Somewhere equidistant from Poland, Germany, Ireland, and Puerto Rico we negotiated a path.

"Sonia, what are we going to do about *los regalos*?" Mami looked seriously worried. The gifts she was concerned about were those rather risqué items traditionally given a bride, who is assumed to be innocent and in need of instruction about the wedding night. Along with these oddities, there are of course practical gifts: the toaster, the vacuum cleaner, and other household necessities. Typically, the women arrive early for the giving of the gifts; the men don't need to know about such things. Asking my aunts and cousins to abandon this custom was not an option. It would have been seen as disrespectful, and anyway they wouldn't have listened. The best we could do was contain the danger of Irish sensibilities being scandalized by Nuyorican humor: we would deploy a strategic seating arrangement and various other diversionary tactics as the boxes were passed around for inspection.

The Puerto Rican idea of a registry was for the bride's aunts to check in with her mother to see whether they could help to furnish anything needed for the wedding itself. Titi Gloria, for example, took me shopping for a gorgeous pair of silver shoes to match my dress. The traditions in a modest Irish family like Kevin's were not so different. At the wedding, people gave cash in substantial amounts. That was how a young couple could be expected to pay for the party, as it was their obligation to do, and also start a new life.

ON THE BIG DAY, I was woken and dragged out of bed by a gang of women bent on getting an early start at the beautification effort. They were yakking nonstop, also running my mother through her own preparations, just one step ahead of mine.

"Celina, get out of the shower now!"

"You want the hair first or the makeup first?"

"Ay! Who took the iron?"

I felt like a mannequin passed from hand to hand, until at the very end, when, with the cars already downstairs, their engines idling, I finally got a word in edgewise. We had forgotten one very important thing: I needed to eat something and have a shot of insulin. My mother froze in panic: whatever she had in the kitchen had disappeared in the comings and goings. So my cousin Tony ran to the diner across the street to get a turkey sandwich. I gave myself the shot and devoured the sandwich with a towel for a bib as the roomful of women screamed at me not to get mustard on the dress. With that, we were off.

At the church, Kevin was waiting, dressed in a rented but very fashionable beige tuxedo, beaming proudly. Marguerite showed me the sugar cubes she'd tucked into her bouquet, assuring me that the maid of honor would be sticking very close by in case the bride suffered any drops in blood glucose. I was especially thrilled to see my cousin Milly arriving with her husband, Jim, and her mother, Elena. They were yet another family of Mami's brother Mayo, and when they had first arrived from Puerto Rico, before I was born, they had come to live with Mami and Papi. I rarely saw them anymore, because they lived upstate, but they were very dear to me. It was Milly, a champion at dominoes, who finally taught me to play. With them beside me, my wedding felt like one of those parties from my childhood that I missed so much.

And so it would be: after the ceremony in the Lady Chapel, we danced into the wee hours at a wedding hall in Queens, along with a dozen other nuptial parties in neighboring rooms. We ended the night by tossing frugality to the wind and splurging on a room at the Hotel St. Moritz overlooking Central Park. I was happy to sign the register as Sonia Sotomayor de Noonan. Room service was closed by the time we checked in, and I was starving; the banquet fare had left much to be desired. Kevin walked several blocks in the rain on a chivalrous quest for a greasy hamburger with cold fries.

Inside the room, Kevin opened the last of the wedding gift envelopes. It was a handful of quaaludes, compliments of his buddies at Stony Brook. I gave him a look of horror and insisted he flush them down the toilet.

"I should just give them back to the guys," he demurred. "They're worth a lot of money."

But I wasn't having it. I watched as he shook the pills into the bowl, muttering, "Man, they would kill me if they could see this."

All told, having a real wedding wasn't as bad as I'd feared, although it didn't increase my taste for such extravagance. I still tell all my cousins—and every bride-to-be I know—skip the pageant and take the money instead. Nobody listens.

Nineteen

I F OUR DECISION to get married was essentially unexamined—it was what couples like us were expected to do—we were hardly more reflective about the marriage once inside it. We simply set about playing house, which seemed a natural enough extension of our companionable coexistence before exchanging vows. Like me, Kevin was young when he'd lost his father. Neither of us had observed particularly inspiring models of married life, TV sitcoms providing what baseline we had. If we'd thought about it, we might have imagined ourselves among the more progressive of those exemplars, this season's new series, in which the couple share the housework and the financial burdens, taking turns supporting each other through grad school.

Kevin's own plans were still uncertain. He was applying to medical schools while also contemplating a research track in science. Law appealed to him too; we had taken the LSAT together, he getting the higher score. He was intellectually equipped for any path he might have chosen, but the gears hadn't yet meshed to drive him forward. So in the meantime, he took a job as a laboratory assistant in the biology department, and I picked up one in the mimeograph room of the law school. A full scholarship covered my tuition, so all we needed was money to live on.

We scoured New Haven for something affordable in an unthreatening neighborhood, finally finding a small apartment in what was once a boardinghouse on Whitney Avenue, a mile from campus. Our landlord betrayed a not very high opinion of lawyers, so I let Kevin do the talking. Home was a living room with a built-in storage chest that doubled as a couch; there was a real bedroom, separate from the living room, and a tiny cubbyhole of a kitchen. We loved that place and would keep it for the three years I was at Yale. Though furnished entirely with hand-me-downs, it never lost the glow of a first home, the sweet mix of nesting and independence.

Kevin decided that we needed a dog to complete our nuclear family, and Star was the much-loved addition. He was a tiny, camel-colored greyhound mutt with steel springs for legs and a passion for chewing. The very first sacrifice to his toothy enthusiasm was my wedding shoes, that pair of gorgeous silver sandals that Titi Gloria had spent an unthinkable fortune on. Well, they were wretchedly uncomfortable the one night I wore them, anyway.

The housework, as I said, was a team effort. I handed Kevin my paychecks, and he paid the bills. I dusted and made the bed; Kevin mopped the floors. He washed the clothes; I ironed them. I did most of the shopping and cooking; he did the dishes. I learned how to boil an egg, and much more, from the *Joy of Cooking*. When in doubt, I phoned Mrs. Gudewicz, Marguerite's mother. One time I found turkey drumsticks on sale for pennies a pound, and she helped me wrangle them long-distance. Every few months, Marguerite and her boyfriend and future husband, Tom, would come for a weekend visit, always with a care package of quality meat we couldn't have afforded. Marguerite's mother was a second mother to me, and nothing says "we believe in you" like a New York sirloin.

YALE LAW SCHOOL WAS and is uniquely small among the top law schools in the country. There were only about 180 in our class. The numbers reflect not only highly selective admissions but also a commitment to fostering a supportive environment on a human scale. Not surprisingly, I found myself surrounded by the most brilliant, dazzlingly articulate, and hard-charging people I'd ever met. Many were entering the field having already established stellar reputations doing something else. There were PhDs in philosophy, economics, math, and physics. We had writers, a doctor, a film critic, an opera singer, not to mention several Rhodes scholars in our class. It would have been even more daunting if we could have known at the time that the class of 1979 would go on to extraordinary success even by the school's extraordinary standards: so many members are now deans and professors at top law schools, federal and state judges, or otherwise in the highest echelons of government or practice. I'm told that this rarefied company made everyone feel as insecure as I did, but that would be difficult to verify.

To take a bit of the edge off this ultimate clash of academic all-stars, grading was elided into something resembling a pass-fail system. Students were not ranked. One friend believed there would have been a significant homicide rate otherwise. No one wanted to be seen trying too hard, and all affected a coolly casual demeanor. But behind closed doors they were working like maniacs, and I was no exception. I read the cases scrupulously and would never have dreamed of walking into class unprepared. But that wasn't enough to banish the threat of being humiliated at any time. Instruction proceeded by a process of interrogation, an only somewhat less terrifying version of the Socratic method at Harvard that had recently been dramatized in *The Paper Chase*. If I faced no one as sadistic as John Houseman's character, professors still sometimes relished eliciting an inadequate answer as an opportunity to dig deeper and lay fully bare the flawed understanding that had produced it. Even a correct answer could lead to further probing that might leave you looking for a hole to crawl into.

I could see there was a method to this torment. We were being conditioned to think on our feet and immunized against the emotional rough-and-tumble of an adversarial profession. Professors at Yale did not look down on us: they assumed that everyone there was smart and in many ways related to us as peers. But often I felt as if I were floundering. It wasn't merely the intense circumstantial pressure. Listening to class discussions, I could follow the reasoning, but I couldn't anticipate where it was headed. For all Princeton had taught me about academic argumentation, law school seemed to operate on a plane of its own. If history involved more than memorizing names and dates, the practice of law was even more removed from merely learning a body of rules and statutes, as I had naively assumed it would be. Instead, becoming a lawyer required mastery of a new way of thinking, and not one that followed obviously from other disciplines. What's more, there was often recourse to distinct and not necessarily concurrent frameworks of jurisprudence, theories of law that our professors had devoted whole careers to exploring and elaborating. In retrospect, it occasionally made for a rather chaotic and perhaps overly theoretical approach to the basic aim of preparing new lawyers for practice. But there is no doubt that the jurisprudential systems to which I was exposed would be put into service much later when I came to the bench.

What systems particularly? I know some readers will be inclined to sift this chapter for clues to my own jurisprudence. I regret to disappoint them, but that's not the purpose of this book. Suffice it to say, during my years there, from 1976 to 1979, Yale was on the cusp of some radical changes in the way that law was taught and understood.

But let me not overstate the influence of those innovations, which seem in hindsight more dramatic than they did at the time and which sometimes were more methodological than theoretical (Guido Calabresi's torts class, for instance, which I took in my first semester, incorporated quantitative methods from economics, an approach that appealed to me given the computer work I'd done at Princeton and that heralded further melding of law with the social sciences at Yale). For the most part, however, of necessity, we were learning the law as it had traditionally been taught. In constitutional law and other areas, the theories presented were primarily those enshrined in the particulars of Supreme Court cases, as articulated in the opinions, concurrences, and dissents of the justices. Many of my courses were taught by established giants in their field; I had Grant Gilmore for Contracts, Charles Black for Admiralty, Elias Clark for Trusts and Estates, Geoffrey Hazard for Procedure, Ralph Winter for Antitrust Law. They followed the time-honored approach to common-law development: analyzing particular cases to extract principles and then considering whether those principles applied in subsequent cases, and if not, what exceptions they created.

In fact, most of the theoretical ferment that would come

to dominate the study of law, particularly constitutional law, with professors' commentaries coming to overshadow the opinions of justices, was as yet on the horizon. I did take a course on Speech, Press, and the First Amendment with Robert Bork, but arguments about judicial restraint, original intent, and strict construction had not yet entered our conversations as students, let alone the focus of our training. The Federalist Society, with its commitment to originalism, would not be founded until three years after I'd left Yale, and its liberal responders were still further in the offing. My own awareness of these debates would not gel until I'd become a judge, when, by happy coincidence, I joined three of my colleagues on the Second Circuit Court of Appeals—Guido Calabresi, Ralph Winter, and José Cabranes, former professors of mine at Yale. It was then I'd have the conversations I was not remotely equipped to have as a student.

IT MAY SEEM UNLIKELY, but even among my ultra-high-wattage classmates, and with minimal time to spare for social life or extracurriculars, I did not feel isolated at Yale. Partly, this was because "1Ls" were divided into small groups for some classes. In this way, the intense pressure we all felt became a bonding experience, with competitive animus channeled outside the group while within it we made some friends for life.

There was also something of a sisterhood in my class. Although the law school had been admitting women since 1918, they were still a minority. In our class of 180, there were only 41 of us, and that was a significant increase over previous years. Naturally, we felt connected and especially supportive of one another. There was Martha Minow, now dean at

Harvard; the future professors Susan Sturm and Ellen Wright Clayton; the journalist-lawyer Carol Green; and Susan Hoffman, now a leader in the California state bar. The obvious brilliance of these women often frightened me, but I realized quickly that it didn't make them any less human or companionable. And once we became friends, I learned that some of them, in their own way, felt just as insecure at Yale as I did.

My very closest friends, however, were of a different stripe.

Felix Lopez, a Puerto Rican orphan from the tenements and projects of East Harlem, was a high school dropout who'd been clever enough to let himself get caught in a minor act of controlled arson so that he could enter the safe haven of a home for juvenile delinquents. From there, via Vietnam and the GI Bill, he would graduate at the top of his class at the University of Michigan. Early struggles wouldn't prevent Felix, a teddy bear with a huge heart, from committing himself to alleviating the suffering of others. If he hasn't yet saved the world, he's not done trying.

Born a member of the Mohawk nation, Drew Ryce, with his streety Spanish, could have passed for Latino, especially after he'd cut off his braids. He recounted tales of surviving a childhood on the streets of Chicago so close to hell that its fires burnished his accounts of that time with a sometimes unbelievable glow, or of how Yale had poached him from Harvard. He had a mind like an IBM mainframe, only much less predictable. He and Kevin would become very close, spending long hours talking music and old movies.

A Chicano from small-town New Mexico, Rudy Aragon spent six years in the air force as an intelligence officer, after which he had a very clear objective for his career in law: he was aiming for the top of a major law firm. George Keys, who had known Rudy since their U.S. Air Force Academy days, was similarly hell-bent on corporate success, determined to attain what had been denied his father as a black man living in the segregated southern town that was this nation's capital.

These compadres, whose concern and intelligence I could always count on, were the four older brothers I'd never had. Each remained acutely aware of the parallel universe, the other America, from which he had been beamed into New Haven. Each was worldly-wise beyond any experience of mine. They all called me "kid." And that's how I felt around them. When Kevin and I played host to them, the menu consisted of stretchable specialties I had recently mastered—soups, stews, spaghetti. But when it was Felix's turn, he pulled out the stops with exotic offerings he'd picked up during his tour in Vietnam—summer rolls with peanut sauce, and a lemongrass-caramel chicken dish—and finished with a French apple galette. These guys even knew how to choose a bottle of wine and couldn't have been nicer the one time I got drunk trying to keep up with them.

They became the center of my extracurricular life, what time for it we could spare. With Rudy, I co-chaired LANA, Yale's Latino, Asian, and Native American student association. The focus was on recruitment and other issues like those I'd dealt with at Princeton. It was sometimes surprising how the support of their own kind, which had been so essential to my survival at Princeton and which in a smaller way I'd re-created among my law school friends, was not such a priority among some of the minority students at Yale. Here I found more Latinos and members of other groups who seemed determined to assimilate as quickly and thoroughly as possible, bearing any attendant challenges and psychic costs in private. I could understand the impulse, but it was never a choice I could have made myself.

Drew got me into more mainstream activity at the Graduate and Professional Student Center, better known as the GPSC—or "Gypsy." Essentially, it was a bar for grad students—the cheapest drinks in New Haven—and as vice president of operations, he hired me to work the door, taking tickets and checking IDs. I would have preferred to work behind the bar, which paid better, but I was a more than adequate bouncer. Nobody could talk their way past me, and I ejected many a townie trying to climb in through the window to avoid the cover charge. My instincts only failed me once: A group of girls wanted to have a look around inside before paying the cover, to see if they really wanted to stay. Not having been born yesterday, I told them nice try and was about to send them on their way, when Drew appeared. Getting worked up when he caught wind of the situation, he wound up apologizing to the ladies and insisting I let them in for free. The bar, he told me, was full of desperate guys with no one to dance with—a very bad situation for liquor sales.

"It's not right, Drew, the guys are paying, why should the women get in free? Can't you see that's sex discrimination?"

"Not everything is a civil rights case, Sonia!" he yelled. "I've got a band to pay and nobody's drinking." We argued some more, until finally he solved the problem by promoting me to bartender and putting someone else on the door.

With such a colorful crew, alliances could shift and tensions flare from time to time, but the gravitational pull of adoptive family always held. I invited my compadres to Co-op City to meet my mother and then for many a holiday dinner. They felt comfortable enough to critique Mami's taste in art. The Three Graces that hung in the living room, a metal bas-relief on velvet, they dubbed "a tit and three asses." But behind their bravado I could sense that they were slightly in awe of my mother's steadiness and her unassuming concern for so many people around her; it was something they in their wanderings had missed out on and would sometimes struggle to find.

IT WAS at Yale that I met the first person I can describe as a true mentor. I had long known the good of seeking out the guidance of teachers, from Miss Katz to Nancy Weiss and Peter Winn at Princeton. And I had an even older understanding of how much friends and classmates could teach me. But I had not yet discovered the benefit of sustained dialogue with someone who epitomized the kind of achievement I aspired to, and much beyond that. It was not the comfort of hand-holding; rather, it was a style of learning by means of engaging a living example. Some of us are natural autodidacts; others learn best by visual representation; others still by auditory cues. For me the most agreeable and effective instruction has come from observing the nuances and complexity of live action, the complete package of knowledge, experience, and judgment that is another human being. Whenever I make a new friend, my mind goes naturally to the question, what can I learn from this person? There are very few people in the world whom you can't learn something from, but even rarer are those souls who can reveal whole worlds to you if you observe them carefully.

I first met José Cabranes through a Princeton friend who'd worked with me in Acción Puertorriqueña. Charlie Hey-Maestre had been a year behind me, and when I was in my first year at Yale, he was writing his senior thesis, which dealt with issues around U.S. citizenship for Puerto Ricans. He had come to Yale to consult José Cabranes, who was an expert on the topic. I had offered Charlie our couch for the night, and we stayed up late talking. "So who is this Cabranes guy?" I asked. Charlie explained: José Cabranes had served as special counsel to the governor of Puerto Rico and head of the commonwealth's Washington office, and he was now Yale's general counsel, the first ever named to that position. Earlier, he had been a founder of the Puerto Rican Legal Defense and Education Fund and a professor at Rutgers. He was a trailblazer and a hero to many for his work promoting civil rights for Hispanics.

Charlie insisted that I come along to the lunch meeting he had arranged. José Cabranes was gracious, warm, and brilliant. He spent the first half hour addressing Charlie's questions and then gradually drew me into the conversation. We talked about the relationship between the mainland and the island and how it affected Puerto Ricans' view of the world, our self-image, and the scope of our future. I was surprised at the way he used the term "colonial" so neutrally, as if it were a statement of fact rather than a moral condemnation, a description of present economic and political circumstances rather than a judgment on history. Our discussion turned on the tensions inherent in a circumscribed statutory citizenship, a status with more limited rights than were enjoyed by citizens on the mainland, and the consequences of living under those limitations for the better part of a century and perhaps indefinitely.

It had been three hours when José looked at his watch and said he needed to get back to work. Charlie and I thanked him and said our good-byes. As we were about to leave, José turned to me and said, "What are you doing this summer?

Come work for me." I had just arrived at Yale and certainly hadn't thought that far ahead. But I didn't hesitate a moment before accepting, nor did I wait for summer before starting work for him.

My job involved research for the book he was writing on the legislative history of U.S. citizenship for Puerto Ricans, as well as minor assistance with the day-to-day legal work of the university. But what I learned came from having a front-row seat, observing his conduct of meetings or simply the traffic of people, issues, and ideas through his office. In the hothouse of very bright people that Yale was, he was one of the brightest, with an intimate knowledge of the law, a passion for history, and the skill to engage with warmth and depth whomever he encountered.

Until I met José Cabranes, I could not have imagined him. I had glimpsed Congressmen Herman Badillo and Bobby Garcia at work when I interned on Badillo's mayoral campaign. But they were dealing with their constituents, people like those I knew. José maintained similar community relations in his pro bono work as the very model of a citizen-lawyer, but he could maneuver with equal skill and self-assurance, a kind of courtly grace, in the most rarefied corridors of power. And yet he remained infinitely generous with his knowledge, time, and influence, especially with young people. He would take Felix under his wing, too, and offer Drew guidance on the confusing thickets of Indian tribal law, a different manifestation of the American empire. We tried mightily to impress him. If he doubted some of the ideas we presented to him, like so many dead mice offered up by eager kittens, he always tempered his skepticism with good humor.

When a young person, even a gifted one, grows up without proximate living examples of what she may aspire to become—whether lawyer, scientist, artist, or leader in any realm—her goal remains abstract. Such models as appear in books or on the news, however inspiring or revered, are ultimately too remote to be real, let alone influential. But a role model in the flesh provides more than an inspiration; his or her very existence is confirmation of possibilities one may have every reason to doubt, saying, "Yes, someone like me can do this." By the time I got to Yale, I had met a few successful lawyers, usually in their role as professors. José, the first I had the chance to observe up close, not only transcended the academic role but also managed to uphold his identity as a Puerto Rican, serving vigorously in both worlds.

I knew better than to try to imitate José. I had enough self-awareness to understand that the best I could do was derive what lessons I could from his success as they might relate to my own capacities. I still consider his advice carefully— indeed, I've sought it at every crossroads in my career—though I'm more likely to translate it into my own terms than to take it up directly. José has often spoken of what an unusual protégée I've been: how I often confer with him, only then to do exactly as I please. He's only half joking.

IN THE ABSENCE of grades and class rank, the only clear mark of standing at Yale Law School is to get on *The Yale Law Journal*. The most straightforward way to do that is to write a piece and have it accepted for publication. It's called a "note," but it's really a very thorough paper.

"Bring me a proposal," said Bill Eskridge, who was the note and topics editor. Bill has since returned to Yale as a respected professor specializing in statutory interpretation, though in my memory his lanky form, forever in plaid shirt and jeans, is of a piece with the journal's stifling, dust-caked offices at the top of the Sterling building. He laid out the criteria: the note had to be original, significant, and logically cogent. I had to find some unresolved legal problem—one tightly focused but of real consequence—and then solve it. It sounds straightforward until you consider that countless students have ascended this temple to propose a topic and been rebuffed.

At Princeton, I had pondered the question of Puerto Rican citizenship historically, politically, and economically, but in doing research for José Cabranes's book, I had started to see it in legal terms, a different lens and perhaps a more powerful one for some purposes. But if you look too closely at what the islanders had been granted as against what other U.S. citizens enjoy by birth or naturalization, issues emerge that no one wants to grapple with. Could, for instance, the U.S. citizenship of Puerto Ricans living on the mainland be revoked were they to return to the island in the case of independence? Such unresolved questions constitute the legal morass underlying decades of political stalemate and still sway small but decisive percentages of the commonwealth's electorate. If I could find one legal knot to untangle, it might avail not only a good topic for a note but something useful for Puerto Rico.

The island couldn't afford statehood or independence, many people reasoned at the time. But having studied seabed rights, treaties, and offshore territorial sovereignty in Admiralty class, I could see a wealth of potential for the island underwater. Might the unexploited mineral and oil resources be tapped to fund development? After all, the island's poverty had always been ascribed to the dearth of natural resources.

Control of those neglected rights would be vital to local prosperity, whatever the island's future, be it commonwealth, statehood, or independence. Many have since argued, however, that the economic impact of the seabed rights would be negligible, and in fact thirty years later little of their promise has been realized.

I was in the ballpark. Now I had only to narrow the topic to a single legal question I could answer. I focused on statehood for purposes of the note because that was where precedent was clearest. I combed the old case law cases relating to the so-called equal footing doctrine, which gives new states joining the Union the same constitutional rights enjoyed by existing states, even while ceding to the federal government other powers enumerated in the Constitution. There were among the precedents a variety of obstacles, strange particulars of what some states had been permitted or denied. In the end, I couldn't establish affirmatively that Puerto Rico was entitled to its seabed rights in all circumstances, but I could prove that retaining them would not violate the doctrine of equal footing in the event of statehood. It was one small step, a tiny clearing in the jungle that has grown around the status question, but I thought it unassailable.

Bill Eskridge liked the idea. Fortunately, the other members of the journal did too, despite their preference that notes address themselves to current case law. After seemingly endless rounds of drafts and revision, "Statehood and the Equal Footing Doctrine: The Case for Puerto Rican Seabed Rights" was published.

ONE DAY, we were having a perfectly civil exchange when out of the blue Rudy interrupted me: "You know what I love about you, Sonia? You argue just like a guy." Kevin, stretched out on the couch, snorted a gulpful of his soda, choking down a laugh.

"What is that supposed to mean, Rudy?"

Suddenly I was seething, and they knew it. Felix asserted his calming influence: "It's a good thing, Sonia, he means it as a compliment." I had heard compliments like that before.

Rudy forged on, explaining: I didn't hedge every statement with disclaimers, apologies, and self-doubts. He did his impression of how women raised their hands in class. " 'Excuse me, Professor, I'm sorry, this might not be important, but you may want to consider the possibility . . .' Not you, Sonia," he said. "When you ask to be called on, you just state your case plain and defy anyone to prove you wrong."

Rudy was right in that sense: I have always argued like a man, more noticeably in the context of those days, when an apologetic and tentative manner of speech was the norm among women. I don't know where I learned this style, but it has served me well, especially in the years when most of the people I was arguing with were men.

Where Rudy was wrong, however, was in suggesting that I had ever volunteered to speak in class. Having suffered the repetitive trauma of getting grilled, I was well into my third year before I'd ever raised my hand. But when I did, Rudy would be there to see it. It happened in Clark's class on Trusts and Estates; he was teaching the common-law rule against perpetuities, which limits how far into the future a will can control a line of inheritance. Professor Clark was charting a hypothetical family tree on the blackboard, a sequence of births and deaths, when it occurred to me that the fate of this inheritance was essentially a math problem. Moreover, I could see a mistake in his calculation. I raised my hand, he called on me, and I pointed out the error. He turned and stared at the blackboard for several very long, silent minutes. Finally, he turned around. "She's absolutely right," he said. "I've made a mistake." He explained to the class what I'd caught and put up another example, only to make a similar mistake. When I raised my hand this time, he paused more briefly before turning around and saying, "Why don't you come up and teach this part?"

I got a slap on the back from Rudy after class. But an even bigger confidence breakthrough was shortly to come, with my participation in the mock trials for the Barristers' Union competition. Perhaps the courtroom playacting somehow liberated my inner Perry Mason. Or maybe Forensics Club experience had come to the rescue again, or a buried memory of Abuelita mesmerizing her audience. Somehow or other, in this setting I felt for the first time I could actually be a lawyer.

As it happened, in one trial, Drew was my client, the defendant in a he-said/she-said rape case. We rehearsed the argument in great detail, but in the moment when I stood before the jury, people recruited from the community through an ad in the local paper, the analytic preparation receded into the background, and some other instinct came forward. I found my eyes automatically scanning their faces, trying to read them: Are they following me? Do I need to push harder or to pull back? There was a sweet spot where I was able to meet them halfway. Most of them, anyway.

In the jury box, one middle-aged man kept shaking his head ever so slightly and pursing his lips, again and again. But the subtle signals of antipathy didn't track my remarks; they were out of sync, as if he were responding to some other stimulus rather than what I was saying. We were encouraged to approach the jury members afterward for feedback on our performance. As people were milling around at the end of the session, I approached him and said, "I have a feeling I rubbed you the wrong way. Can you tell me why?"

He seemed startled, then shook his head. "It's nothing you did."

I told him that I was trying to learn. That was the purpose of the exercise. Whether it was something I was doing or not doing, I wished he would let me know so that I could adjust my approach in the future.

He shut down. "It's my own thing," he said. "I can't help you." But I continued to press him politely. Finally, he blurted it out. "Look, nothing personal. I just don't like brassy Jewish women." That took me by surprise. I froze as my mind raced through the things I could possibly say to this man, when the right response occurred to me.

I looked at him. "You're right," I said. "I can't do anything about that." And I walked away.

MY SECOND SUMMER at Yale, I landed a job as a summer associate at Paul, Weiss, Rifkind, Wharton & Garrison, one of the very top law firms in Manhattan. I was working under men known as giants in litigation, and I was given a variety of assignments, the most challenging of which was a contribution to a brief being prepared for a huge antitrust case—an auspicious opportunity if ever there was one. But when I sat down to write, my arguments seemed continually wide of the mark. True, antitrust was not an area of the law I'd studied, and I had no background in business to speak of. But considering the difficulty of proving a violation of the Sherman Act, I couldn't figure out why I was failing to articulate a persuasive argument on the client's behalf, despite racking my brains on the long daily commute between New Haven and New York. I finally handed in my effort to a young associate one notch up the totem pole. Only when I saw what he eventually wrote himself and passed up to the next level did I fully realize how poor a job I had done. I obviously wasn't thinking like a lawyer yet. If this was what it meant to work in a prestigious law firm, I clearly was not ready.

The sense of failure was confirmed when I concluded my stint as a summer associate without receiving a job offer. I had never heard of such a thing happening at Yale Law School, and though I've learned since it was not so uncommon, of course no one advertised it. But anyway, in my own eyes I had officially blown it. I had worked hard—I always had and still do—but somehow that wasn't enough. And it was difficult not to conclude that I was simply not in the same league as my classmates who were pulling in job offers from firms just like this one. There were some around me encouraging me to view the rejection as an expression of bias or personal animus, but I had seen no evidence of that, while my sense of having underperformed seemed to me well enough substantiated. For this pain of failure—the first real failure since having enrolled in law school—I had only myself to blame, and knowing that, I was profoundly shaken.

The way forward was daunting if obvious. I needed to figure out what I was doing wrong and fix it. At the very least I had to learn this area of law, and so I signed up for Professor Ralph Winter's class on antitrust as well as one called Commercial Transactions. The trickier part would be mastering the skill that was at the heart of being a lawyer, my deficiency in which had been exposed: how to write a brief, not as some classroom exercise aspiring to an objective analysis of the case law, but as a piece of persuasive advocacy, advancing the interests of my client. In both kinds of remedial efforts, I would do what I'd always done: break the challenge down into smaller challenges, which I could get on with in my methodical fashion. And certainly I would need to prove myself at another kind of work in the legal profession before I could even consider joining a large commercial firm. In the meantime, the unfamiliar taste of utter failure from that summer would stay in my mouth. The memory of this trauma, which I was determined not to repeat, while not suffocating my ambitions, would overhang my every career choice until I became a judge.

ONE OBVIOUS GOOD did come of my ordeal at Paul, Weiss: I made more money that summer than I had ever seen before. Now Kevin and I could actually afford a honeymoon, and a change of scene seemed in order as I licked my wounds and considered the way forward. Soon dreams of America were unfolding across our living room floor as we planned to cross the continent and head west.

Carol Green, a close friend from my study group, was a journalist from Denver visiting Yale for a yearlong program on law and journalism. She invited us on a camping tour down into New Mexico, Four Corners, the Grand Canyon . . . She and her husband were old hands at this, equipped with all the right gear and experienced at roughing it. The appeal of sleeping under the stars, protected by nothing but a tarpaulin and far from the safety of civilization, eluded me then and still does. But Kevin, no less a city kid than I, was eager to try it, and so we did. There was so much that I had wanted to see for so long, so many sights that would inspire a pilgrim's awe, that I wasn't going to complain about the want of a few urban comforts.

For years I had studied American history, law, and society, but I had barely scratched the surface of the great geographical reality. What I knew of this land was a library's worth of cases, treaties, the shifting tides of politics, human migrations, and technologies. The natural wonders I recognized only from childhood picture books and the plates of our *Britannica,* but it was something else altogether to watch the vast stretches of forest and plain unfurl for hours along the highway, or to feel dwarfed by the immensity of the sky. As we headed south out of Denver, the Rocky Mountains lay to the west like bones of the continent exposed to the afternoon light. As the road ran straight and flat, my mind rambled along its own bumpy, winding course. Two-thirds of the way through law school, and everyone around me was considering job offers. I needed to figure something out.

Most of my classmates were aiming in the direction of prestigious midtown law firms, including Rudy, whose objective couldn't have been more unvarnished: make big bucks. If the shortest path to that goal was to defend corporations in massive tort cases and antitrust litigation, then so be it. He could always pursue labors of love by doing pro bono work on the side. My own ambitions were not as susceptible to the same inducements, but I did recognize a greater good in Rudy's approach. Until minorities learned how to navigate at those altitudes of the legal system, their communities would lag the rest of the country. If our experience as a group was ever to advance beyond disadvantage and grievance, we needed to move with ease where money and power move.

The splat of raindrops on the windshield interrupted my reverie. Surely we now had to find a motel. No way was I

sleeping out in the rain, pitching a tent in a puddle. "Let's see
if it passes," said Carol. She's got to be kidding, I thought,
as a bolt of lightning cracked the sky open and electrocuted
the mountains.

My ruminations continued through the days of driving,
as if the white line in the road were an arrow pointing toward
the future. José Cabranes had advised me to keep my sights
on a major law firm in the long term, saying it was a good
platform from which to launch into government or any other
direction, but that first of all I should clerk. I had heard
classmates mention clerking and I knew it was prestigious,
but José had to explain to me that it meant working, essentially as a researcher, for a judge. Though I knew he wanted
the best for me, clerking sounded tediously academic. How
much longer could I live in the library? If I was wary of going
to a big firm, I still felt the need to get out in the real world
and earn some money.

Much later I would realize my naïveté. Especially working with my own clerks, I've come to appreciate how clerking for a judge can be the most vital mentoring relationship
open to a young lawyer. It has become even more prestigious over the years since I left law school and the most
direct stepping-stone to higher levels of legal practice. Many
minority students and others who struggle under financial
pressure sacrifice the long-term benefits of clerking for better
pay in the near term. I advise them to resist that temptation
and aim for the necessary grades, journal experience, and
mentoring relationships with professors that can open the
door to a clerkship. Part of me still regrets not having taken
José's advice at face value.

When we rolled to a crunchy graveled stop and cut the
engine, the silence of the desert was complete. The ruins of

a Pueblo village were visible halfway up a cliff, nooks and crannies revealing themselves as we walked. You could see traces of daily life in the contours carved into the mountain, the footholds for climbing out of enemies' reach, the cistern to capture precious rainwater. I tried to populate the village in my mind and imagined myself looking out from a window of that cliff-side aerie to the desert expanse. The only moving feature in the landscape was the light itself and the slow shadow of clouds piled in the distance. The wind was a constant, and when you paid attention, it seemed like the earth's own breathing.

One possibility I'd long had in mind was the State Department. I was fascinated by Professor Michael Reisman's course Public Order of the World Community, as well as my glimpse of international law working with José on his book about the Puerto Rican status problem and citizenship, and also exploring the narrower question of maritime rights in my journal note. As tiny as Puerto Rico is, studying maritime issues had given me a taste of what it might be like to work on the exceptionally complex intellectual puzzles of international law, whose solutions have very real consequences for millions of people. And the idea of public service on a big stage appealed to me deeply.

Of course, such thoughts might all be moot: Kevin was applying to medical schools and graduate programs, and when I finished at Yale, it would be his turn to decide where we would live among the places where he was accepted. At least Washington was on his list of possibilities.

I had not forgotten my childhood dream of becoming a judge, but if law school had taught me anything, it was what pure fantasy that dream would have to remain. Even at Yale, there was no such thing as a "judge track" to prepare you specifically for the rigors of those heights of the legal profession. I could see that it was a matter of accumulating a broad range of legal experience in positions that are challenging and respected and, eventually, being visible to those who could offer a nomination. And still, luck and timing would play their inscrutable roles. The relative scarcity of women on the bench and the practical nonexistence of Latinas also gave me reason to keep this idea in the drawer with other idle wishes, any expression of which would have marked me as delusional.

Kevin and I made a detour to Albuquerque to visit Dolores, whom I hadn't seen since Princeton. She was so much more at ease on home turf. Her family's modest house reminded me of Puerto Rico, with her father, mother, and three sisters filling the small rooms with their laughter and chatter. And I discovered that Dolores hadn't been the only one their father had taught to sing and play guitar; all Mr. Chavez's daughters made music together. As half-familiar smells drifted in from the kitchen—roasting peppers and cumin, caramelizing onions, the earthy steam of beans—as well as others I couldn't identify, the guitars got passed around. For me, the most precious memory of the evening was hearing Dolores and her father's duet of "Cucurrucucú Paloma." In that gentle exchange, the handing of the melody back and forth between them, I recognized again how very far from home she had felt at Princeton.

We flew on to San Francisco for the final leg of the trip, a visit with Ken Moy, who was living in Berkeley with Patricia Kristof, with whom he'd been a couple since Princeton. There was a sense of completion in seeing a sunset on the Pacific Coast, and it felt equally fitting to close out the trip with the touchstone of very old friendship. Celebration was in order. I accompanied Ken to the market, where he chose things I'd never seen before: passion fruit and butternut and spaghetti squash. He cooked up a feast, and I marveled to see him so happy in a home, and a family, of his own creation, a long way from East Harlem.

AT THE ALL-STAR BREAK in 1978, the Yankees lagged a dozen or so games behind the Red Sox, and yet there was no question but that I'd be betting on them to win the American League East. My hometown loyalties run deeper than any season's ups and downs, and while I'll root for the underdog in many other arenas, when it comes to baseball, the Yankees' knack for setting aside the day's personal dramas to get out there and win always impresses me. Felix, as a New Yorker, was with me of course, and Drew was shrewdly calculating the odds. But Rudy and George were backing the Red Sox out of sheer contrariness, and so I arranged that when the Yankees won the pennant, those guys would buy me dinner at the best restaurant in New Haven.

It was the top of the seventh in the final, tie-breaking game. The Yankees had two men on when Bucky Dent, a shortstop with no hitting power in his history, came up to bat. The bat cracks, like a sign from heaven. He takes a new bat, and when it kisses the ball, a hand reaches down from the sky and lifts it out of the park. There's an eerie silence over Boston as Bucky Dent crosses home plate. All hell broke loose. Rudy and George were screaming in agony, Felix was crowing like the sun just rose, I was sitting there shaking my head, saying over and over, "They did it! They pulled it out again!"

My winner's dinner would have to wait till another night,

however, even if we hadn't already felt stuffed to bursting on Felix's feast of *picadillo* with rice and black beans—the best I'd had since Papi died. Though nothing would have made me happier than to stay right there, basking in the glow of victory and friendship, I had to pull myself together for a recruiting dinner that same night. The host was Shaw, Pittman, Potts & Trowbridge, a well-respected, small Washington firm that did varied corporate and international work. Scott Rafferty, who had graduated summa cum laude alongside me at Princeton before also coming to Yale, had worked there as a summer associate and loved the experience. He enthusiastically encouraged me to attend the dinner.

There were eight or ten of us at a large table, and I happened to be seated facing the partner who was steering the event. Scott made introductions, circling the table with a few words about each of us. "Sonia's Puerto Rican and from the South Bronx in New York. She was at Princeton before she came to Yale." Very few words, as it happened, but as students we didn't have long résumés.

As soon as the introductions were over, and before another word was spoken, the partner facing me asked whether I believed in affirmative action. "Yes," I said, somewhat guarded but hardly imagining what my answer would unleash.

"Do Princeton and Yale have affirmative action programs?" Yes, of course they do, I told him, at which the challenge only escalated: "Do you believe law firms should practice affirmative action? Don't you think it's a disservice to minorities, hiring them without the necessary credentials, knowing you'll have to fire them a few years later?"

I was stunned, as much by the bald rudeness of the interrogation as by its implications. I'd heard nothing of the kind so blatant since the school nurse caught me off guard at Cardinal Spellman. "I think that even someone who got into an institution through affirmative action could prove they were qualified by what they accomplished there."

He looked at me skeptically. "But that's the problem with affirmative action. You have to wait to see if people are qualified or not. Do you think you would have been admitted to Yale Law School if you were not Puerto Rican?"

"It probably didn't hurt," I said. "But I imagine that graduating summa cum laude and Phi Beta Kappa from Princeton had something to do with it too."

"Well, do you consider yourself culturally deprived?"

Gee, Officer Krupke, I thought, how do I explain? Shall I talk about my ancestors, the heritage of Spain? About having two languages, two ways of seeing the world? Is there only one culture that counts? I didn't even know where to begin answering that one. And an awkward silence descended upon us, before spreading like a stain to the other end of the table, where Scott was seated. Sensing the discomfort, he deftly jumped in with a new topic. My adrenaline ebbed slowly, and I did what I could to get through the rest of the dinner without making others more uncomfortable. Afterward, Scott came to me to express outrage and apologize.

"It was horrible," I admitted. "So insulting."

"It was completely out-of-bounds," he said, adding he intended to complain about it the next day. But I asked him to wait. I needed to figure out what to do.

In the cafeteria the next morning, Scott had already found Rudy, Felix, and George. The forces were marshaled, the coffee flowing.

"I would have punched him out," Rudy announced, rarely one not to verbalize a thought.

"This guy was a lot bigger than me; I don't think I could have taken him," I said.

But when we got more serious about considering a proper response, I decided to go ahead with the formal recruiting interview scheduled later that same day, at which I could engage the partner from Shaw, Pittman in a more private setting.

With my résumé in front of him, he seemed to think that we were on a cordial footing. Before I knew it, he was encouraging me to come to Washington for the next step in the hiring process. That's when I called him on what he had said at the dinner.

"That was really insulting. You presumed that I was unqualified before you had seen my résumé or taken the trouble to learn anything about me."

He seemed to be waving it off as just a conversational gambit, albeit on a sensitive topic, and he expressed admiration at how I had stood my ground.

"You didn't seem terribly upset. You didn't make a scene. You were perfectly civil."

Now I really couldn't believe my ears. What was he expecting, Hysterical Puerto Rican Syndrome?

"That was the Latina in me," I said. "We're taught to be polite." If we were going to rely on stereotypes, at least they should be accurate. I further explained that it wasn't in my nature to cause everyone at the table discomfort because of how I felt about his behavior. But neither was I simply going to accept being treated so unfairly. I've long known how to control my anger, but that doesn't mean I don't feel it.

After the interview I talked through my options with the gang. I decided to address a formal complaint to the firm through the university's career office and challenge Shaw, Pittman's right to recruit on campus in light of that partner's disregard for Yale's antidiscrimination policy.

"You're going to need counsel, Sonia," Rudy said. "You're going to need one tough lawyer."

"You're hired," I said. "Pro bono, I assume."

"I think 'jailhouse lawyer' is the correct term," said Felix. Bluster aside, Rudy was the one who came to meetings with the dean and to the ensuing formal hearings of a student-faculty tribunal.

News of the incident flared across campus and divided the school into camps—those who thought I had made too much of some offhand comments, jeopardizing Yale's relationship with an important employer of its graduates, and those who were solidly in support of my action. The latter view spread far beyond New Haven as word reached one minority student group after another across the country. Letters and news clippings describing similar affronts elsewhere started to arrive. Clearly, I had opened a bigger can of worms than I'd intended. For while I was pleased that this type of offensive behavior was being brought to light, I had no wish for personal notoriety, as a symbol or anything else. I still wanted a career in law, not a place on every firm's blacklist.

The university, clearly uncomfortable with the attention the complaint was drawing, was eager to reach a settlement. The student-faculty tribunal impaneled to investigate the complaint negotiated a full apology from Shaw, Pittman. They were not barred from recruiting, but the firm and the offending partner did voluntarily keep a low profile at Yale for a time.

Throughout, I marveled at the courage that Scott Rafferty had shown in taking my side without hesitation. It meant giving up a plum job that he had been looking forward to. He had been very happy at Shaw, Pittman as a summer associate, but he was not eager to join a firm where a partner would behave in that way. That disillusionment did nothing to advance the start of his career, but it signaled a measure of integrity that would remain evident over a distinguished professional life in public service.

WHEN THE ANGER, the upset, and the agitation had passed, a certainty remained: I had no need to apologize that the look-wider, search-more affirmative action that Princeton and Yale practiced had opened doors for me. That was its purpose: to create the conditions whereby students from dis-advantaged backgrounds could be brought to the starting line of a race many were unaware was even being run. I had been admitted to the Ivy League through a special door, and I had more ground than most to make up before I was com-peting with my classmates on an equal footing. But I worked relentlessly to reach that point, and distinctions such as the Pyne Prize, Phi Beta Kappa, summa cum laude, and a spot on *The Yale Law Journal* were not given out like so many pats on the back to encourage mediocre students. These were achievements as real as those of anyone around me.

My brother's story was similar. Junior stumbled into a program that put minority kids on a fast track to medical school, essentially free of cost. He wasn't inspired by child-hood dreams of becoming a doctor; he had never considered the possibility. But once he started, he found that he loved what he was doing, loved the process of learning itself, and had excellent study habits compared with most kids in the program, 45 percent of whom would drop out. Affirmative action may have gotten him into medical school, but it was his own self-discipline, intelligence, and hard work that saw him through, where others like him had failed.

Much has changed in the thinking about affirmative action since those early days when it opened doors in my life and Junior's. But one thing has not changed: to doubt the worth of minority students' achievement when they succeed is really only to present another face of the prejudice that would deny them a chance even to try. It is the same prejudice that insists all those destined for success must be cast from the same mold as those who have succeeded before them, a view that experience has already proven a fallacy.

WHEN MY NOTE for *The Yale Law Journal* was finally laid out and pasted up, typeset, proofed, printed, collated, and bound—in short, when it was a physical reality ready to go forth into the world—the editors took the unusual step of sending out a press release announcing it. It was an indication of their belief that my work had practical import beyond the limits of academia: that my argument might even have some influence on the outcome of the status question.

Meanwhile, acceptance of the note had come with an obligation to work on the journal in other capacities, such as checking citations. The teamwork of the job was wonderfully rewarding, and out of that camaraderie, as from my small group, would come some lifelong friendships. I so enjoyed the work that I volunteered to serve also as managing editor of another student-run journal, *Yale Studies in World Public Order*, which specialized in a rigorous quantitative policy-oriented approach to international law, as developed and taught by Professor Reisman. After editing a couple of lengthy articles by alumni working in the field, I noticed myself feeling intellectually comfortable in a way that I could not imagine when I first arrived at Yale. That, together with the enthusiastic reception of my note among those working on Puerto Rican status issues, provided a feeling of real-world validation that was moving and meaningful in ways student honors could not rival.

Maybe, I thought, I am ready to go out there.

Me, age one, between Papi and Mami

First birthday. The photo was given to Abuelita as a memento years later when it was inscribed "For Grandma, from your granddaughter who never forgets you. Sonia."

Celina *(right)* with her "adoptive" family by marriage: Mercedes *(center)* and her daughter Gloria *(left)*

Abuelita and her second husband, Gallego, in Puerto Rico

Juli as a young man, soon after first arriving in New York

Celina in the Women's Army Corps, age nineteen

"To my beloved grandmother, I dedicate this humble remembrance in proof of my love for you. Your little grandson, Juan Luis Sotomayor" (translated from the Spanish inscription)

Juan Luis (Juli) Sotomayor, age two, in a photograph he gave to Celina early in their courtship, with an earlier dedication to his grandmother written on the back

With Junior on his first birthday: Papi's handwritten notes on the backing paper were discovered for the first time fifty-four years later while writing this book.

10 p.m.
October 29, 1958
Tomorrow is the birthday of my beloved Julyto, alias "Little Bull." May God give him many years of life and the same for my adored Sonia, the light of my eyes. To my beloved wife Celina, "Cucarocha," "Michaela," "Barcelo," and to all of my family, and that of my wife, may God bless you all. "July," Juan Luis Sotomayor (translated from Spanish inscription)

Juli *(above, at left)* at the radiator factory

Juli's playful spirit would later recede.

I preferred boys' toys, like guns, to dolls. With Papi, Junior, and Mami, beside the Christmas tree decorated by Papi

Birthday girl with *(left to right)* my godmother, Carmin; Mom, Celina; and maternal aunt Aurora

Celina *(center)* was the Jackie O. of Bronxdale, but Carmen *(right)* was a beauty, too. Abuelita is second from top left, flanked by her sisters. Gloria is behind Carmen, and in the front-row peanut gallery, from left, are Junior, Nelson, me, Eddie, and Miriam.

With cousins: *(from left)* Eddie, Miriam, Nelson, and Lillian. Miriam and I often dressed like twins.

¡Vámonos de parranda!: Abuelita loved a picnic.

Trying very hard at age four to match Mami's glamour, both of us dressed in new hats for Easter

Senior year at Cardinal Spellman High
School

At Blessed Sacrament, I first discovered
a love of learning and a lust for gold
stars.

SONIA MARIA SOTOMAYOR

I am not a champion of lost causes, but of causes
not yet won.
— Norman Thomas

My Princeton experience has been the people I've met.
To them, for their lessons of life, I remain
eternally indebted and appreciative.
To them and to that extra-special person in my life

Thank You — For all that I am and am not.
The sum total of my life here, has been made-up
of little parts from all of you.

In the Princeton yearbook, class of 1976

The Bronx comes to Princeton for the weekend: Kevin on the left, standing next to me; Mami on far right, followed by Ken Moy and Junior. Kneeling, front left, is Felice Shea.

Beside one of the bronze tigers
outside Nassau Hall

In the kitchen with Titi Aurora and Mami on a visit home from Yale

I whip up some homemade Chinese food for the gang at Yale.

High school sweethearts just after the wedding in the Lady Chapel at St. Patrick's Cathedral. Mami's friend Elisa helped design the dress, and Kevin rented the tuxedo.

The wedding shower, with maid of honor Marguerite Butler *(right)* and college roommate Mary Cadette *(left)*

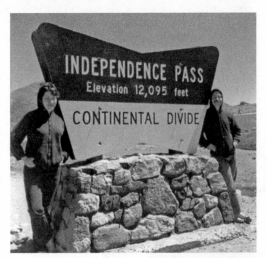

With Kevin in the Rocky Mountains on our road trip out West, second summer at Yale

Discovering the grandeur of America's wide-open spaces for the first time, while struggling to figure out a career plan

Visiting with Dolores Chavez at her parents' home in Albuquerque. She and her father did a beautiful rendition of the ballad "Cucurrucucú Paloma."

Sonia Sotomayor, Assistant District Attorney,
representing the people of the County of
New York

. . . and the badge to prove it

Partners and associates of Pavia & Harcourt gathered to celebrate a wedding of one of their own soon after I became a judge. David Botwinik is at bottom left and George Pavia is beside him.

With Alessandro Saracino-Fendi, the client who became like a brother

The annual courthouse follies: After much rehearsal, I make a serviceable singing hobo alongside U.S. District Court Judges Charles S. Haight, Jr., and Jed S. Rakoff

Three generations of Sotomayor
women: my niece Kiley, Mami, and me

With Robert M. Morgenthau
("The Boss") on the day I was sworn in

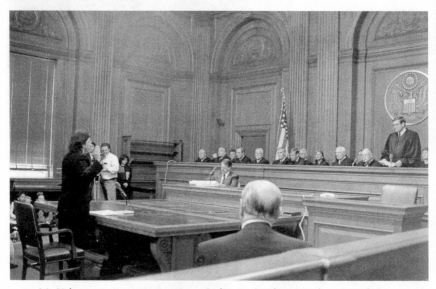

My Yale mentor, now Circuit Court Judge, José Cabranes, administered the
oath of office at my induction to the U.S. District Court for the Southern
District of New York.

The bride Celina and her groom Omar, with Junior, now Dr. Sotomayor. As my first official act, I performed the marriage of the couple on the night of my induction to the Second Circuit Court of Appeals.

At the White House: Mami, Kiley, Conner, and Corey as President Obama announces my nomination to the Supreme Court

Justices of the Supreme Court of the United States are required to take multiple oaths. Here I take the Judicial Oath, administered by Chief Justice Roberts in the Justices' conference room, with my mother holding the Bible and Junior looking on.

Twenty

Y ALE WAS ONE of the very first law schools in the country to admit women, and yet every point in the building seemed to be separated by miles of corridor from the nearest women's restroom. On a typical trek, of an early evening, taking a break from the library and a treatise on tax law, I passed the open door of a conference room. At the back, I spotted a bonanza—a table of cheese and crackers and cheap wine, the kind of arrangement that passes for hospitality in university budgets and a free meal in the straitened lives of graduate students. The makeshift sign on the door read, "Public Service Career Paths." A panel of public-interest lawyers were pitching alternatives to private practice to a thin scattering of third-years. Just then, the moderator was introducing the final speaker, a district attorney from New York whose name I didn't recognize. He seemed none too comfortable at the podium and promised to be brief. I decided it was worth sticking around until he finished so I could make for the cheddar cubes.

My ears perked up when I heard him say that he had a couple hundred assistants who all tried cases. "Within your first year on the job," he said, "you'll be going to trial, with full responsibility for how you develop and present your own cases. You'll have more responsibility than you would have at any other job coming out of law school. At your age now, you'll be doing more in a courtroom than most lawyers do in a lifetime." I liked what I was hearing. At Paul, Weiss, I had watched an associate who was thoroughly steeped in the details and strategy of a case brief a senior partner who then did a star turn in the limelight before a judge. The associate was too diplomatic and well compensated to admit to any demoralized frustration, but clearly work in a big firm meant laboring in the shadows for years.

When the presentation was over and we descended on the food, I found myself in line next to the New York district attorney, Robert M. Morgenthau, a legend unbeknownst to me. His halting, raspy voice was no different talking face-to-face. This was not a man who relished chitchat. But being capable of talking up anybody, I proceeded to ask him to tell me a bit about his background, what he'd liked about each of his jobs. Maybe he was used to talking to ignorant students; he didn't betray any hint of annoyance. He asked me what my plans were—not sure, maybe a small firm, still exploring—and then he said, "Why don't you come by and see me? I have some openings in my schedule tomorrow."

Sure enough, the next morning at the Career Office, there were still interview slots open: among Yalies, the DA's Office was not the most sought-after place to work. But I was surprised to find my name already penciled in. In fact, Bob Morgenthau had come by, pulled my résumé, and already placed a call to José Cabranes, whom he knew well from their work together on the Puerto Rican Legal Defense and Education Fund. The interview was actually enjoyable and ran a half hour longer than scheduled. At the end he invited me to visit his office in New York.

"You're interviewing *where*?" said Rudy, aghast. Even José, who had given me a glowing recommendation, seemed disappointed that I found the DA's Office more interesting than a clerkship. "Do you have any idea what they pay?" Rudy demanded. I did, but I had never seen money as the definitive or absolute measure of success. Sure, I wouldn't make much compared with an associate at a major firm. But my starting salary would still be more than what my mother had ever made as a nurse, which to Titi Aurora, who worked as a seamstress, had always seemed lavish.

In the end, as I usually do, I trusted my instincts, although I was a bit surprised where they were leading me. I knew I wasn't ready for a big firm, but apart from applying for a job at the State Department, I had not devoted much thought or effort to public-interest options. Nor was I encouraged to: unlike today, there were few pro bono law clinics at Yale then; I knew of one on prison disciplinary hearings, one of the few settings in which students were allowed to practice, another on landlord-tenant disputes, and a third on denial of veterans' benefits. But they were not attracting many from our hyper-ambitious cohort. Perhaps Bob Morgenthau's job stirred a memory of what had first intrigued me about being a lawyer: the chance to seek justice in a courtroom. Despite my success in the trial advocacy program and in reaching the semifinals of the Barristers' Union mock trials, Perry Mason was a vision that had been eclipsed at Yale amid the immersion in case law and theory and self-doubt. Now, it seemed, that untutored fantasy was beckoning me again, conspiring with a bit of free cheddar to decide my fate.

Twenty-One

A T THE NEW YORK District Attorney's Office, "duckling" is the term of art for a rookie assistant DA,
and in the mouth of a senior prosecutor it expresses
gallows humor more than endearment. Forty of us tender,
fuzzy types were about to be crunched in the jaws of a huge,
complex, and fast-moving machine. Guidance of senior
colleagues would add seasoning over time, but meanwhile
we would need every scrap of what scant training would be
provided during our first few weeks. I wasn't the only one
among us with minimal background in criminal law—just
the required basic course at Yale and the mock trials. But
even if I had devoted all my studies to the finer points of
the field, there remained essential lessons inaccessible in the
classroom or from books and acquired only through the
fiery baptism of the courtroom. I was about to get that
baptism.

New York City in 1979 had been struck by a crime wave
of tsunamic proportions. Mayor Ed Koch had been elected
two years before on a promise to restore order after a summer of widespread looting, vandalism, and arson triggered
by a ten-day blackout. If the immediate threat to public

safety had lifted after the lights and air-conditioning came back on, New Yorkers still had reason to live in a state of diffuse chronic fear. The city's fiscal troubles summed a decade of economic doldrums nationwide, and severe budget cuts were preventing the DA's Office, as well as the police department, from adding enough staff to cope with an avalanche of criminal cases. To make matters worse, rising tensions brought a rising number of police brutality complaints.

Most of the new ADAs were assigned immediately to one of six trial bureaus, each with up to fifty prosecutors of varying levels of experience, along with support staff. We would cut our teeth on misdemeanors: petty thefts, minor assaults, prostitution, shoplifting, trespass, disorderly conduct, graffiti . . . Later we would be promoted to felonies, and we might move to one of the bureaus that investigate fraud, racketeering, public corruption, sex crimes, or other specialized crimes. There was no choice in the matter, we were told. Soldiers go where they're assigned. Ducklings, too, apparently.

First we had to get to know the procedural maze. If a defendant is arraigned on an unsworn complaint, how many days do you have to fix it? Failing that, how do you handle a preliminary probable cause hearing? We also went out on patrols to get a sense of how cops do their job, the routines and the issues we needed to be sensitive to. Every sixth day we were in the complaint room for a nine-hour shift, interviewing arresting officers and witnesses to draw up the initial charges on each case. Every street arrest in the city funneled into the system through this room, which was not unlike a hospital ER on a rough night. Decisions made quickly would have a long tail of repercussions. It looked like chaos, but there was order and discipline under the surface, and that

combination appealed to me. So did the pressure to improvise, the comfort of clear rules, and the inspiration of a
higher good.

The way Bob Morgenthau, the Boss, structured the office
to meet extraordinary challenges was a model of efficiency
and integrity for jurisdictions across the country. All of our
case work, for example, was organized horizontally, with
cases assigned the same prosecutor from beginning to end,
rather than handed off up the hierarchy. The Boss also pio-
neered collaborative efforts with counterparts in other boroughs, as when the Office of the Special Narcotics Prosecutor
was established to coordinate investigations citywide so that
prosecutions were not restricted by boundaries that the drug
rings crossed routinely. He set up units for sex crimes, Chinese gangs, consumer fraud—each a center of specialized
expertise and methods of investigation.

But great ideas couldn't shift the reality that the city was
strapped for cash. The physical plant creaked under the burden of incessant use, our headquarters a warren of small
rooms, the larger of which had three or four metal desks
squeezed into them. My first office was an anteroom, actually more of a doorway, into which a desk had somehow been
implanted. Eventually, turnover would deposit me in slightly
more commodious shared space, though my desk still blocked
the entrance, behind which door was wedged an old couch,
horsehair poking out of cracked leather. Papers were piled
everywhere, stacks of files, boxes of evidence, somebody's
lunch. In the summer the air-conditioning failed constantly
and sweat soaked through my suit, while in winter the same
rooms became drafty caverns in which I might need to keep
my coat and gloves on all day. The lights were dim, the electri-

cal cords were frayed, and the plumbing leaked—sometimes into the courtrooms.

Of all the resources in short supply, time was the shortest, and mine perhaps more than most. Kevin had been accepted into the graduate program in biochemistry at Princeton, so we had moved there from New Haven. After our cozy nest on Whitney Avenue, we found ourselves living near campus in graduate student housing that had been built during and after World War II to shelter the families of returning soldiers. I was commuting by train between Princeton and Manhattan, sometimes up to two hours each way. I left home at dawn and rarely got back before nine. Kevin cooked and we'd share a late dinner every night, though I was routinely dead on my feet until the weekend brought a brief respite. I made it through the workweek on cans of Tab and my own adrenaline.

If the long hours were straining our marriage, I was too preoccupied to notice. What I did see, in the small corner of my awareness not cluttered with cases, procedures, and the minutiae of criminal law, was Kevin finally doing work that excited him and earning recognition for it. He was thrilled to be at Princeton again, this time on his own account, and he was making new friends. He was thriving at his own thing, just as I was at mine.

IN THE PRACTICE HEARINGS that were part of our training, I was cast in the role of the defense attorney. Somehow by pure instinct I realized a witness implied vaguely that she had seen something, though she avoided stating it outright. On cross-examination, I asked an apparently tangential question that led her to describe the precise conditions that would have made a direct line of sight impossible for her. The senior assistant DA leading the exercise came up to me afterward. "I've been doing this training for years. You're the first person who ever spotted a hole like that in a witness's story and then pried it open." It was fortunate that thinking on my feet in such a situation came naturally to me, because I was the first of the ducklings to have a case assignment come to trial. It happened faster than I thought possible, just weeks after I'd started in August. None of us had expected to enter a real courtroom before the new year.

The defendant was a young black man who'd been charged with disorderly conduct for getting involved in a street fight. He was a college student, a pretty good one too, and from a solid family; at arraignment he pleaded not guilty. His counsel was Carole Abramowitz, a seasoned Legal Aid attorney, who had defended felony cases for years. I don't know why she was handling a misdemeanor that day, but she was determined to get the case thrown out, knowing full well that any plea to the least of charges could destroy a black kid's future. That was all I knew about the case, and I was learning it on the spot as the defense attorney and I stood before Judge Joan Carey in the first conference. Normally, I would have written up the complaint myself and interviewed the arresting officer, but this case had been reassigned after the departure of my predecessor, one file in a big stack of them that had been dumped on my desk and that I hadn't so much as opened yet.

"We're ready to go to trial," said Carole Abramowitz.

"We'll start Monday," said Judge Carey.

"But, but, but, but . . . ," I stammered. It was then Friday.

I needed some time to prepare. I needed to find the witnesses. This was a real trial!

Judge Carey looked at me without pity. She complained that we weren't getting dispositions fast enough. "You'll start the wah-deer on Monday or I'll dismiss the case."

At least that's what I heard. I ran upstairs to Katie Law, adviser for the ducklings in our trial bureau. Katie was a Harvard graduate who had returned to law school after raising three daughters and getting a divorce. A southern belle from a wealthy family, she certainly didn't need to be in the trenches at the DA's Office, but she was passionate about community service. And she was infinitely patient with beginners.

"Katie, what does 'wah-deer' mean?"

She shook her head in despair. "They're sending babes into the wolves' den." It wasn't my fault, she assured me: not everything could be covered in our two-week training course. It was expected the rest would be learned by example and osmosis during the months new ADAs typically worked in the complaint room covering the pretrial motions before one of their cases went to trial. It was just my bad luck getting there so fast. Katie spent the remainder of the afternoon explaining the voir dire process and jury selection, the strategies for making the most of this chance not just to disqualify unfavorable jurors but to establish a rapport with those selected. Public awareness of voir dire is much greater these days thanks to media coverage of high-profile trials, to say nothing of television court dramas, and the science of juror selection that has spawned an industry of consultants. But when I joined the DA's Office, it was all rather arcane stuff, especially since New York State is one of the few jurisdictions where lawyers can get involved in the process, which in many states, as in the federal system, is handled by judges.

I wish I could say that my first real trial was a triumph of spirit over experience, but in fact Carole Abramowitz mopped the floor with me, and then bad luck wrung me out. The courtroom was a repurposed office with a few rows of rickety wooden folding chairs serving as a jury box and gallery, and the bench was of painted plywood. In the middle of my summation, everyone's attention suddenly turned elsewhere: the defendant's grandfather clutching his chest in a sweat, the old man's daughter panicking beside him. The judge called a recess; the paramedics came trooping in. And by the time it was clear that the poor man was all right, an hour of confusion had intervened before I could continue my remarks. The jury took less time than that to find the boy not guilty.

Although the grandfather's cardiac crisis seemed at the time the ultimate fluke, soon I would discover that among trial lawyers it was a familiar variant in the canon of mishaps that occurred so frequently as to have been enshrined in the lore and legend of the courtroom. Some view these events as rites of passage for a young lawyer, although their recurrence is likely due to a predictable degree of coincidence in the ways people react to the stress of a trial. In any case, there could not have been a better lesson in the necessity of being ready for any contingency. If anything redeemed that day, it came in the swell of pride I felt when I first introduced myself to the jury—"I am Sonia Sotomayor de Noonan, and I represent the people of the County of New York"—a moment of grace that would repeat, and ground me, at the opening of every subsequent trial I prosecuted.

If my first trial was a cartoon of chaos, my second was a

mess of a very different kind. A man had got into an argument with his wife while riding the subway. He chased her screaming off the train, before beating her and then kicking her in the face when she fell to the station platform. A Good Samaritan rushed to intervene, striking the husband with an umbrella, whereupon the defendant punched the Good Samaritan in the face, leaving him with a black eye. As often happens in cases of domestic violence, the wife was unwilling to testify against her husband, but a righteous and determined young prosecutor was not going to let that stand in her way. I subpoenaed the defendant's wife.

But on the day of the trial, the wife didn't show. She had a fair excuse; she was in the hospital. But then it became clear that she had scheduled an elective procedure on that day to avoid coming to court. When I learned that she had had an abortion, I felt a terrible rush of sadness and guilt. What had I set in motion by pursuing her? My action could not have reasonably provoked the decision, but by the time violence enters a marriage, often reason has already receded.

Even without the wife's testimony, however, we got a conviction. The defense attorney was Dawn Cardi, a rookie from the Legal Aid Society in her very first trial. She fumbled as badly as I had in my own maiden voyage, and this time by comparison I seemed like an old hand—pity the poor judge and jury with the likes of us two presenting! There were moments during cross-examination when Dawn seemed to be working for the other side, as when she got the Good Samaritan to repeat his story. Fortunately, there were no heart attacks, but Dawn did suffer the distraction of admission to the bar: while the jury was out for deliberations, she had to run out to attend her swearing-in ceremony. When she had raced back, the jury returned the guilty verdict. But any pleasure I might have derived from my first conviction vanished when we reconvened for sentencing.

"Ms. Cardi, I'm disposed to send your client to jail for a year," the judge said. The color drained from Dawn's face, and she began to tremble. I too was thunderstruck in that moment, realizing the terrible thing I'd accomplished.

"You can't do that!" Dawn sputtered. "He has a job. His family depends on him for support. He's never had an arrest before in his life. This will destroy him. You can't put this man in jail!" As Dawn's nervous verbal torrent flowed on, I was thinking about the abortion and the length this man's wife had gone to not to be there. And a part of me would have preferred not to have been there either. I have always believed that individuals are ultimately responsible for their own actions, and I have no tolerance for spousal abuse. But I also understood that the defendant would not be the only one bearing the hardship of his punishment. Jail might be a justifiable punishment, and the only absolute insurance against his striking his wife, but it would exact a high price on his whole family.

Dawn trailed off, and the judge looked to me. "I think Ms. Cardi is right," I heard myself saying, without premeditation, and feigning a self-assurance I wasn't feeling inside. I acknowledged that putting him in jail would have significant negative consequences for his family. I said that I would be satisfied with probation if Dawn could get him into a treatment program for domestic abuse that required regular attendance and that also checked in on his wife regularly. For a man in his thirties with no prior arrests, I thought that treatment and the imminent threat of jail would be sufficient protection for his wife.

"Find the program," the judge said to Dawn. And we both breathed a sigh of relief.

Dawn thanked me afterward. She was stunned by my concession, which seemed especially strange for a beginner, given that a prosecutor's career is built on a reputation for toughness and winning stiff sentences. I was having my own doubts by the time I reported my actions to John Fried, my bureau chief. John heard me out and responded in his typically thoughtful and deliberate way. He noted that he might have done differently himself, since the assault on the Good Samaritan suggested a danger to society, but he acknowledged my reasoning: "You did what you thought was right." I can't know if he extended the same trust to everyone who worked under him, but the freedom to exercise my judgment without fear of being disciplined promoted a confidence that helped me grow into the job more quickly.

Dawn and I would cross paths often, as her section at the Legal Aid Society was assigned to my trial bureau. Despite the unofficial rule against fraternization between prosecutors and defense attorneys, we would chat sometimes over brown-bag lunches on a park bench. We'd talk shop: the ins and outs of our cases, the temperaments and tempers of the judges we dealt with, the routine sexism that was an occupational hazard. Eventually, we became friends, and as we did, our conversations often edged into bigger themes that were written between the lines of the daily procedures: the explosion of misdemeanors that seemed more symptomatic of social ills than evidence of criminal natures; the crudeness of the tools the system wielded against complicated problems. We often started at opposite poles of an argument, recognizing that our views were conditioned by personality differences. Dawn was a born public defender, her support of the underdog grounded in a native distrust of authority. I was by nature more the prosecutor, a creature of rules. If the system is broken, my inclination is to fix it rather than to fight it. I have faith in the process of the law, and if it is carried out fairly, I can live with the results, whatever they may be. And knowing that the poor and minorities are disproportionately the victims of crimes, I'm loath to view the adversarial process of the law as class warfare by another name.

By the same token, I don't view prosecutors and defense attorneys as natural enemies, however common that view is both within and without the legal profession. The two simply have different roles to play in pursuit of the larger purpose: realizing the rule of law. Though the roles are oppositional, their very existence depends on a shared acceptance of the law's judgment no matter the passion of either side for a desired outcome. This is not to deny that the will to win drives both efforts. Nor is it to claim some simplistic equivalence between prosecution and defense. Rather, it is simply to insist that ultimately neither the accused nor society is served unless the integrity of the system is set above the expedient purposes of either side. This may sound naively idealistic, but there is a place for idealism in the practice of the law. It is what makes many of us enter the profession in the first place; it is certainly what drives some of us lawyers to become judges.

Dawn came to me in distress over another case we shared. "You've got to help me," she pleaded. It was a sad story: Her client had lived his entire life in institutions, foster care followed by twenty years in prison for killing a man in a fight. Then, released on lifetime parole, he had been given no support but a bus token. Without life skills, unable to find a job, he survived by selling copper pipes that he stripped from a derelict building, not fully aware that this was theft. The terms of his parole were such that a single violation, even a plea to a reduced charge of disorderly conduct, would have sent him back to state prison. There was something about this man that made Dawn trust him. All things considered, he wasn't doing so badly. He hadn't been dealing drugs; he hadn't robbed anyone. He wouldn't have been stealing pipes if he'd had any help finding a job. He had even met a girl and was in love . . . Dawn talked me into accepting an ACD, an adjournment in contemplation of dismissal, and she got him into a job program. If he stayed out of trouble for six months, the charge would be dismissed.

One day, two years later, he would be waiting for me outside the courtroom. He introduced himself, shook my hand. "You don't remember me," he said. "I'm the guy who was stealing the pipes." He had found a job and been promoted to supervisor. He had also married his girlfriend. By now, they had one child and were expecting another.

The quality of mercy: "It blesseth him that gives and him that takes."

THE OCCASIONAL MERCIFUL IMPULSE notwithstanding, I was racking up convictions. Whatever my insecurities—and I had plenty (still do)—I was also fiercely competitive (still am). I became addicted to the thrill of verbal sparring at trial, the exhilaration of having to reinvent strategy on the spot, not knowing whether it would work, under the specter of a judge who at any moment might catch me out with a question. Fearing such humiliation, I prepared compulsively, the way I had in law school, and my reward was the chance to go out and risk it all again the next day. That I could never be sure of myself while doing it was a big reason I loved my work as a trial lawyer.

Notching up top-count prosecutions—convictions for the most serious charges—while giving up little ground in plea bargains became the adult equivalent of collecting gold stars in fifth grade. I liked the particular challenge of taking cases to trial with unsympathetic victims and unreliable witnesses, like the drug addict whose methadone was stolen by another addict, or the elderly couple with fifty felonies between them who were robbed by their young protégé, a grifter in training; or cases that were hopelessly circumstantial, like the jeweler whose half-million-dollar pouch of gems went missing after a family of Gypsies swept through his store—who could be sure the jewels even existed, until I managed to get them returned? I won quite a few of those.

Certainly, no one could accuse me of being a soft touch, but talking with Dawn always reminded me of the human costs of my success, the impact on an individual's life and his family. Her perspective allowed me to trust the voice in my own head that occasionally whispered: how about exercising a little discretion; having a little faith in human nature? It wasn't easy, with around a hundred cases on my desk at any time and constant pressure to dispose of them as quickly as possible. Cases with the same charge tended to blur together, especially since the DA's Office offered standard plea deals for certain crimes: Possession of a gun? Settle it today, and it's a class A misdemeanor. Make me wait, and tomorrow it becomes a felony. Forget about mitigating circumstances; I don't want to hear it.

Still, I wasn't willing to prosecute a case that I simply didn't believe in, my zeal as a prosecutor finally circumscribed by my impulse to always keep both sides in mind. The impulse had first developed in Forensics Club as a matter of strategy, but in this setting it sometimes produced the inescapable awareness that, though I might win, justice would not be served. I was especially lucky, therefore, to have a mentor in John Fried, who embodied just that kind of measured attitude. Under an impossible caseload, his commitment to fairness was fundamental. If I believed in a defendant's innocence or doubted a witness's story, I would knock on John's door. We'd sit down together and analyze the evidence for as long as it took. In the end he might suggest offering a very low plea bargain, but he always left me an out: "If you can't in good conscience try the case, then don't."

John's essential fairness was of a piece with the idealistic standards that Bob Morgenthau set for the DA's Office. Nevertheless, it often felt as if we were swimming upstream against muddy currents with the right answer not clearly in view. With each prosecutor handling around a hundred cases at a time, expediency and rough justice were the order of the day. We fudged, we made do with the tools at hand, we performed triage in the trenches, but we still made an effort to do it with integrity.

MAYBE MY PROSECUTING misdemeanors with a ferocity usually reserved for felonies looked to some like real fire in the belly. In reality, it was still more like butterflies and the unremitting fear of leaving anything to chance that made me prepare and argue so intensively. But for whatever reason, I was among the first in our duckling group to be moved up to more serious crimes. By the time I switched to felonies, John Fried had moved up too and was replaced as bureau chief by

Warren Murray. Warren had a very different style: extremely soft-spoken but a 100 percent hard-as-nails prosecutor. I worried about how I would fare under him.

I was given a handful of low-level felony cases and a few others that were being retried. One of those cases involved a purse snatching. The defense attorney alerted me that it was flimsy, and I was dismayed to see that the facts were indeed thin to the point of being nonexistent. The young defendant had a clean record. His teachers had described him as quiet, polite, well behaved, but developmentally slow. He'd never missed a day of school. I interviewed the victim, an elderly woman. She hadn't seen the thief's face as he ran up from behind her, heading in the general direction of the subway entrance. The police grabbed a confused kid they found sitting downstairs on the platform bench, waiting for his train home from school. The woman identified him by the dark jacket he was wearing, like that of the thief, though she couldn't say what color it was. The purse was never found.

I wrote up a description of the evidence and took it to Warren. "You're right," he said. "It's weak. But we have the indictment, and it's our job to prosecute. Let the jury do theirs; they'll acquit him." I went back to my desk and pondered how to argue this to a jury. I went home to Princeton that night and thought about it some more. But I could imagine no way of standing up in court and saying with a straight face that there was sufficient evidence to convict.

By the time I marched into Warren's office in the morning, I was full of righteous indignation, fiery but totally in control. "I'm not trying this case. I can't lie to a jury. If you think you can go into that courtroom and argue that this is grounds to convict, then you'll have to do it yourself." I threw the file on his desk and walked out.

He came running after me. "Look, I just needed to make sure that you were sure."

"Why didn't you just ask?"

"Sometimes I figure I have to play devil's advocate."

I could have done without the drama. The office declined to prosecute the case.

THE FIRST TIME I found myself before Judge Harold Rothwax, he was in a full-throttle tantrum over the many delays that had dragged out a case before I'd caught it on reassignment. "And now, obviously," he shouted, "you're going to tell me that you're new and need a month to prepare!" I promised him that if he gave me fifteen minutes to confirm the availability of the witness, I'd be ready for trial the following week. That endeared me to him permanently. With plenty of misdemeanor trials under my belt, I had enough confidence—or the bravado of ignorance—to trust my performance under pressure. If nothing else, I knew my own standards of preparation. And sure enough, I would never once suffer the shame of his sarcastic warnings about "avoiding the dangers of over-preparation" dished out to so many other attorneys. I would, however, one time get a compliment of sorts out of him when, reading one of my motion papers, he allowed, "Misspellings are supposed to be a sign of genius. You must have plenty of it."

Judge Rothwax dealt with all felony pretrial motions for my trial bureau. He was painfully exacting and infamously unforgiving of lawyers who wasted his time, on one occasion sending defense counsel to jail for ten days for preventing the start of a trial. He was known as the Prince of Darkness, Dr. Doom, and Yahweh, among other epithets, particularly for striking terror in the heart of defendants whenever one with a weak case would decline his offer of a plea. His notorious stock line to defense counsel: "Your client has the constitutional right to go to prison for the maximum time allowable."

But it wasn't just fire and brimstone. Behind the infernal humor, a formidable clarity of mind and a keen legal acumen kept the docket moving with astonishing efficiency. A good judge must possess management skills as well as a deep understanding of the law. And there is no overstating the value of being able to keep all the facts of a case in your head. He might spend two minutes at a conference on a routine case, more on especially complicated ones, but two months later he would remember every detail.

However caustic, Judge Rothwax was no cynic, though like many a cynic he had been disillusioned, having started his career as a Legal Aid attorney and civil rights advocate before becoming a prosecutor. That early experience led him to conclude that given all the elaborate protections of the rights of the accused, any defendant whose case eventually came to trial was almost certainly guilty. In a controversial book, the judge proposed abolishing the *Miranda* warning and other rules that he believed handicapped the police and prosecutors; he also argued that a 10–2 jury verdict was close enough to unanimous for conviction. I wasn't prepared to accept his presumption of guilt, although it is borne out statistically: policemen don't normally make arrests on sheer caprice; most defendants do turn out to be guilty. But a probability of guilt doesn't seem reason enough to revise our standards of due process. These are designed to protect everyone from the human frailties of those whom we entrust to enforce the state's tremendous powers. Even if the vast majority of the law's agents exercise these powers scrupulously, it is unconscionable that anyone should pay for a crime of which he was unjustly accused. Blackstone's famous ratio ("better that ten guilty persons escape than that one innocent suffer") still speaks to a deep-seated sense of what is just.

Though I differed with some of Judge Rothwax's views of procedure, and didn't have much use for his hammy Prince of Darkness persona, the integrity and rigor of his thinking, his passion for the law, and the efficiency of his courtroom won my admiration. And he, in turn, offered me kind encouragement, even inviting Kevin and me to his home. As with José Cabranes, the deepest respect could not make me into a good enough protégée to take all his advice. Nevertheless, during those years at the DA's Office, a long-nurtured dream finally found a living example in Harold Rothwax's black-robed presence, the first embodiment of an ideal I would be able to observe up close.

NOT LONG AFTER I moved to felonies, I prosecuted the same defendant in two trials back-to-back. It was two different crimes; hence the two trials: the accused had jumped bail on an older charge of burglary, the outstanding warrant discovered when he was caught for a subsequent robbery. My cases were solid, but matched against a very experienced defense attorney from Legal Aid, I lost them both. It was a hard blow to my ego, but what was even worse, I couldn't figure out where I had gone wrong.

"Okay. Tell me what you did," Warren said in his usual tones, still the quietest voice I've ever strained to hear. I walked him through my presentation of both cases. He identified the problem instantly: I was appealing to logic, not morality, and in effect letting the jury off the hook. Since it is painful to most jurors to vote "guilty" and send a human being to jail, you couldn't simply reason with them to do it; you had to make them feel the necessity. "They have to believe that they have a moral responsibility to convict," Warren said. Even the most perfectly logical argument, absent passion, would make the choice seem like one of personal discretion rather than solemn duty.

Communicating your own moral certainty didn't necessarily mean chewing the scenery. But as when I had described the Kitty Genovese murder in forensics competition, the difference between winning and losing came down to the appeal by emotion rather than fact alone. It was something Abuelita could have told me without ever having gone to law school. And it was something I apparently knew in high school, if only intuitively, before the awareness was pushed aside by years of learning to reason dispassionately at Princeton and Yale.

Granting myself permission to use my innate skills of the heart, accepting that emotion was perfectly valid in the art of persuasion, amounted to nothing less than a breakthrough. Warren would teach me much else in the way of trial skills, as had John Fried, Katie Law, and others at the DA's Office. But that was the single most powerful lesson I would learn. It changed my entire approach to jurors, from the voir dire to the structure of my summations, and the results spoke for themselves: I never lost a case again. I had hung juries a couple of times, and once or twice a conviction on fewer than all counts of the indictment, but never an acquittal.

Leveraging emotional intelligence in the courtroom, as in life, depends on being attentive; the key is always to watch and listen. You don't need to take notes with the court reporter getting down every word. Lower your eyes to your pad, and you're bound to miss that hint of a doubt that flits across the witness's face. Scribble instead of listening, and you won't notice the split second of hesitation in which a witness hedges a choice of words, avoiding the ones that would flow naturally in favor of the ones whose truth he or she is more certain of.

Such attentiveness also figures in upholding one of a litigator's paramount responsibilities: not to bore the jury. Again, the key is not rhetorical pyrotechnics. What holds a jury's attention, essentially, is the quality of one's own attention. If you are palpably present in the moment, continuously mindful of and responsive to your listeners, they will follow where you lead. If, however, you are reading from a script, droning on as though they weren't there, soon enough they won't be, irrespective of how unassailable your argument.

Often the difference is a matter of remembering what makes sense to a human being as opposed to another lawyer. For example, a prosecutor usually has no need to prove motive under the law, and yet the human mind naturally constructs its reality in terms of causes and effects, weighing any theory against the plausibility of these links and how they might operate in someone else's mind. "Why would she have done that?" is something we instinctively ask before we allow ourselves to conclude "she did it." The state's case is a narrative: the story of a crime. The defense has only to cast doubts on the coherence of that story. The "why" elements of the story must make sense—what would have motivated this person to hurt that person—before you can engage the jurors' empathy, put them in the shoes of the accused or the victim, as needed: make them feel the cold blade held against their necks, or the pang of unappreciated devotion that might drive someone to steal from a former employer.

It is the particulars that make a story real. In examining witnesses, I learned to ask general questions so as to elicit details with powerful sensory associations: the colors, the sounds, the smells, that lodge an image in the mind and put the listener in the burning house.

Of course, narratives can be slippery. A story might change midway through the telling or the retelling. It wasn't enough to prepare meticulously, to anticipate every contingency, every conceivable counterargument. Katie was the one who taught me what to do when, through no fault of your own, the story unfolding suddenly changes, throwing your case into unexpected chaos. In that eventuality, everything depends on the power to improvise, the dexterity to change tack as if doing so were part of your strategy all along. If a witness alters his testimony without warning, the savvy prosecutor simply de-emphasizes the testimony and stresses the cumulative weight of circumstantial evidence. Devising the case is always a two-step process: build the strategy out of reason and logic; then throw yourself into it, heart and soul. But if you have to revise the plan, suspend feeling and revert to logic until you can think of something you can sell with passion.

Other lessons I would figure out for myself, often contrary to conventional wisdom. Some prosecutors, for instance, would look for legitimate reasons to eliminate black and Hispanic juror candidates in the voir dire, the assumption being that minorities are biased in favor of defendants. But to me that made sense only if you saw all people of color as potential perpetrators and believed, even more implausibly, that they all saw one another that way, too. It was obvious to me that any black or Latino who held a job, or went to school, or stayed home to care for an elderly parent was likely as law-abiding as anyone in my own family and, if anything, far likelier to be the victim of a crime than to commit one. The notion that such a person would, on the basis of racial or ethnic solidarity, let anyone walk who might pose a danger to the community would have seemed laughable where I came from. And so I packed my juries with the kinds of people I'd grown up among; the results, again, spoke for themselves.

Few aspects of my work in the DA's Office were more rewarding than to see what I had learned in childhood among the Latinos of the Bronx prove to be as relevant to my success as Ivy League schooling was. It was in effect to see that mastery of the law's cold abstractions, which had taken such effort, was actually incomplete without an understanding of how they affected individual lives. Laws in this country, after all, are not handed down from on high but created by society for its own good. The nearer one was, in fact, to the realities that had inspired those laws, the more persuasively one could argue for the justice of upholding them. To be able to relate to jurors as their own sister or daughter might, with real appreciation of their concerns and the constraints upon their lives, often put me at an advantage facing an adversary from a more privileged background—a refreshing change after years of feeling the opposite. But even more important, that connection fed my sense of purpose. Each day I stood before a jury, I felt myself a part of the society I served.

It was, as I've said, not the job that most Yale Law School graduates dreamed of, but it did furnish me with the basis for an eventual judicial temperament in ways that Yale could not. It also gave me the confidence that came of recognizing my personal background as something better than a disadvantage to be overcome.

Twenty-Two

I N THE SPRING of 1980, seven months into my first year
at the DA's Office, Bob Morgenthau encouraged me to
join the board of an organization he had helped to found
and had served for the better part of a decade. "They're on a
campaign to recruit young talent, and I have given them your
name," he said. In those days, few ADAs gave much time to
pro bono work, or had much time to give. I already felt the
combination of the daily commute and my caseload was testing my limits, which should have activated my natural tendency to avoid taking on too much too soon. But it's always
hard to refuse the boss's invitations, and this was especially
true of the Boss, who would become such a patron of my
career. Besides, I was no stranger to the organization in question: the Puerto Rican Legal Defense and Education Fund
(now LatinoJustice). I had applied for a summer internship
there while I was at Yale. During the interview, they asked
about my career goals. I allowed that I hadn't settled on a
short-term plan, but I did know that in twenty years I wanted
to be a federal district court judge. The interviewer raised an
eyebrow, causing me to conclude that in the future it would

be better to keep my fantasies to myself. I didn't get the job, but I remained interested in the group's mission.

The Fund, otherwise known by the acronym PRLDEF ("Pearl-def"), was founded in 1972 by a group of young Puerto Rican lawyers who drew inspiration from the NAACP's Legal Defense and Educational Fund and wanted to use their legal skills to challenge systemic discrimination against the Hispanic community. By the time I joined, PRLDEF was solidly established and had won significant reforms, its landmark *ASPIRA* suit against New York City's Board of Education proving as vital to Hispanics as *Brown v. Board of Education* had been to blacks. Until the *ASPIRA* case, Puerto Rican kids coming from the island, where Spanish was used in public schools, or from families like mine that spoke little English entered the New York City public school system with no help at all making the language transition. These kids routinely floundered and, though otherwise perfectly capable, would often find themselves in classes for the intellectually disabled. They naturally dropped out in staggering numbers, turning an imagined handicap into a real one, a temporary need for remedial help into a lifetime of minimal employment and poverty. The *ASPIRA* consent decree won by PRLDEF in 1974 established the right of students with limited English to receive bilingual education in New York City's public schools. The very next year, my cousin Miriam would enter college, eventually to graduate as one among the first wave of young teachers to earn a degree in bilingual education.

If PRLDEF seemed a natural follow-up to my work at Acción Puertorriqueña, this was no ragtag band of student activists but a committed group of highly skilled professionals with far more experience and savvy than I had, their sights set far beyond trying to get one Ivy League college to hire one Hispanic administrator. Some of the victories won by PRLDEF—for voting rights, or against discriminatory hiring practices—would open doors for hundreds or thousands of individuals. These efforts would shift the boundaries of opportunity and civic engagement for people across the nation, far beyond Puerto Rican New York. At the same time, the group was decidedly of my community, and that moved me deeply. It was the same pride I'd felt observing José Cabranes, so committed to his people and yet maneuvering so effortlessly in the wider world. On our board sat the Brahmins of Nuyorican society—as well as Puerto Ricans from the island and across the mainland—but there were also figures prominent in mainstream media or businessmen wealthy beyond what I had imagined possible in our corner of society. I was awakening to how much broader the Latino community was than I had known growing up in the Bronx.

As the youngest member of the board—even the others recruited as "young blood" were older and more established professionally—I felt honored just to be included and given the chance to learn from individuals already so accomplished and destined to achieve even more. If I could have looked into the future, I would have seen friends I made there going on to become federal judges, ambassadors, a U.S. attorney, college presidents, professors of law, partners at major law firms—every one of them upholding a lifelong dedication to public service. The women were especially inspiring, and not only for offering one another constant camaraderie and moral support, rare in any organization. At the DA's Office, I had seen very few women in positions of genuine power; the bureau chiefs were all men. But here were

women—competent, authoritative, professional Hispanic
women—who were leaders in their own fields as well as
determined to give of themselves for the sake of others.

I worked on the litigation committee, which hired the
staff lawyers and set strategy for the types of cases we would
take on. I also served on the education committee, which
arranged internships and found mentors for minorities, as
well as developing LSAT preparation materials to help more
Latinos become law students. Beyond what I was learning
from all the potential role models around me, these activities gave me a grounding in the nature of organizations and
how competing interests within them had to be balanced:
in a word, politics. The staffing work in particular threw
me square into the problem of allocating limited resources.
There were those with visions of taking on ever bigger cases
and more areas of advocacy, my own preference as always
being for smaller, more careful steps. Sometimes personalities clashed, especially given the presence of so many lawyers
who had succeeded as aggressive litigators in large corporate
settings and who were now maneuvering in the close quar-
ters of a small nonprofit where everyone involved had a deep
emotional investment. Occasionally, such conflicts can tear
the very fabric of an institution if they aren't handled wisely,
and indeed that almost happened.

Problems at PRLDEF came to a head in a labor strike that
split the organization and proved traumatic for every single
member of the board and staff. The points of contention
were the familiar stuff of labor-management disputes, not
salaries so much—because no one signing up to work there
could have expected much of one—as benefits, the formulas
for calculating hours, and the compensation for extra work.
My natural sympathies were with the staff lawyers, being

myself employed as one in the DA's Office and never having
been a manager anywhere. But as a board member I had a
fiduciary obligation to the institution, a ponderous word but
a real responsibility that I took seriously, appreciating as I
did PRLDEF's value to the larger community.

Learning how to balance the needs of individuals with the
no-less-real needs of an institution was an important lesson.
It's fine to be on the side of the little guy, but he too will ultimately suffer if the health and concerns of the greater body he
belongs to are neglected. That point would be driven home
a year later, when my mother phoned in tears to tell me that
she had lost her job. She, along with the entire staff of Prospect Hospital, had been locked out when it closed without
warning. The sudden bankruptcy eliminated dozens of jobs,
shattered a close-knit family that had shared their workdays
for decades, put homes at risk, and destroyed an institution
that had revitalized an entire neighborhood. Once again, my
heart inclined to those who were locked out of their liveli-
hood, but my head was calculating: What concessions, what
better choices, might have preserved the institution and
avoided this sad loss for all sides? Seeing Prospect Hospital
disappear, I appreciated all the more the fine balance, the
hard reckoning, and the personal sacrifices that ultimately
kept PRLDEF intact through difficult times.

PRLDEF WAS my first real experience of pro bono work and
the honorable role of a "citizen lawyer." I would continue
serving there for twelve years, long after I'd left the DA's
Office and right up to becoming a judge. To use my education to help others was so gratifying that despite having no
time to call my own, I would get involved with other groups

as well over those years. There was, for instance, my work
with SONYMA, the State of New York Mortgage Agency,
which was establishing a program to make mortgages available to working-class families. We prided ourselves then on
the strict criteria for qualification and the fact that most of
the loans were repaid. Still, it gave me pause to realize that
someone with my own mother's earning power, for all her
years of hard work and spotless financial history, could not
have qualified even in the category designed to capture the
lowest-income applicants. It seemed wrong that there was no
way to reconcile the standards of secure underwriting, and
the imperative of protecting the institution, with the good of
helping the most marginal but still deserving, including those
like my mother who had never defaulted on any obligation
and never would.

I particularly welcomed any chance to work on issues
such as economic development and education that were crucial to the community in which I was raised. I not only cared
deeply about those people but also understood their needs
from firsthand experience. As I made my way in the world,
however, I was seeing more and more that no group is an
island. Even the most cohesive (or the most marginalized)
consists of overlapping circles of belonging, just as every
individual's identity is constituted of many elements. To do
good ultimately meant seeing any particular interests in a
larger civic context, a broader sense of community. The specific needs of people like those I grew up with would always
tug at my heart, but increasingly the call to serve was beckoning me beyond the confines of where I'd come from.

It was somewhat in that spirit that I joined New York City's
Campaign Finance Board. Unlike PRLDEF and SONYMA,
the Campaign Finance Board was a relatively new organiza-

tion, founded in the wake of scandals that shook New York State in the mid-1980s, when certain vast campaign contributions, undoubtedly corrupting but some perfectly legal, were exposed. The need for oversight in the financing of the electoral process was dramatic, not only to guard against graft, but to ensure access for candidates who would be excluded if money alone determined the race. But before the board's creation there were no regulations in place, no model for the disbursement of public moneys. New York was the first major American city to institute such reforms, the only other example being Tucson.

What appealed to me was the possibility of devising a structural solution to a long-entrenched problem simply by creating an appropriate set of rules. That's as elegant as ethics gets. It was also an exhilarating exercise in the art of crafting compromise between opposing interests, always my first response to political division. The fact that I had always registered independently, without a party affiliation, enhanced my credibility as a dispassionate mediator. But the board's greatest asset in laying claim to evenhandedness and procedural transparency was its chairman, Father Joseph A. O'Hare. A Jesuit priest and the president of Fordham University, Father O'Hare was a man of such unassailable integrity that fairness seemed assured, even as his irreverent sense of humor banished every trace of sanctimony. Under his leadership the board exemplified how a government agency could rise above partisanship to work for a general good.

The CFB was my introduction to the city and state political scenes. Many lawyers I met working there would go on to become power brokers whose awareness of me and eventual support would matter to my career in ways that I couldn't yet imagine. I had always thought my career would be devoted to principles that transcended politics, but the fact is there would have been no way to the federal bench except through such political channels. It would matter crucially that I was familiar to people of influence who, though recognizing I did not involve myself in partisan efforts, could see that I was at least an honest broker. The integrity I had cultivated so jealously out of personal pride would be my calling card when the time came. Or so I was later told.

Sometimes, idealistic people are put off the whole business of networking as something tainted by flattery and the pursuit of selfish advantage. But virtue in obscurity is rewarded only in heaven. To succeed in this world, you have to be known to people. Nevertheless, where politics is involved, associations and recognition can work both ways. Years after I left PRLDEF, my involvement with the organization would be raised as an issue when I was nominated to the Supreme Court. Critics charged that LatinoJustice PRLDEF (as it was known by then) was a radical organization that no acceptable candidate should ever have been associated with. To hear PRLDEF's activities so grossly distorted during the Senate hearings, with no regard for the good it had done the Hispanic community and the cause of civil rights generally, was painful to me and to everyone else who had served on the board generously and honorably. But PRLDEF did not cower from the attacks. The entire staff and board, led by Cesar Perales, a founding member who is now New York's secretary of state, worked tirelessly to rebut the charges and muster community support on my behalf, efforts for which I will be eternally grateful.

Twenty-Three

"THIS IS DIFFICULT for me," my mother said. "He is like my son, Sonia. I watched him grow up. This is not easy for me."

"Please, Mami. You think it's easy for me?"

I can't deny my portion of the blame. The vortex of the District Attorney's Office was all-consuming, and I felt driven to do my utmost on every single case. How many nights had I spent poring over briefs I'd brought home, barely aware of his presence? But Kevin was also finding a new life of his own at Princeton, of which I had no part. One way or another, we had outgrown the first innocent bloom of love and its loyal attachment without having evolved new terms for being together.

On vacation together at Cape Cod in the summer of 1981, our first time there, an unseasonable chill hung in the air between us as tensions kept flaring up over nothing. It was a prelude to Kevin's cautious mention of the changes that had come over us and of how he no longer felt connected to me. Talking about our relationship, about feelings, was not something we did naturally. Even in the early days in high school, when we could talk for hours on end, it was always about some shared interest, or nothing in particular, but never ourselves. How long had it been since we talked like that, like children? Even the memory of those days seemed increasingly distant.

It was late when we got home to the apartment in Princeton after a four-hour drive in uncomfortable silence. I tripped over the mail that had piled up. Tomorrow's business. I fell into bed.

In the morning, I opened an envelope from the DMV. It had taken the whole five years we'd been married for them to send me a new driver's license with my married name on it.

"You know, Kevin, if we break up, it will probably take another five years for them to change my name back again." I was joking, sort of.

"I'm sure they do it all the time."

There are things you may know in your heart for a long while without admitting them to conscious awareness, until, unexpectedly, something triggers an inescapable realization. In that unhesitating matter-of-fact reply was a truth that I could no longer shut out: our marriage was over. When Kevin left for work, I picked up the phone. I had never complained about him to Mami, never mentioned any problems between us. To me relationships are private. In my experience when a friend unloaded about a boyfriend or spouse, the listener soaked up the complaint and remembered it long after the speaker had forgiven the offense. Unless something was really serious, my mother didn't need to know. As this was the first she had heard of any trouble, I was especially grateful that she didn't argue.

"Can I come home?"

"*Siempre*, Sonia." Always.

Kevin and I talked through the details without rancor. We

agreed that I would assume our credit card debt, since I was the one bothered by it. In return I got custody of the Honda Civic. The only problem was that I didn't know how to drive a stick shift.

Never take driving lessons from someone while you're breaking up with him. Every time I popped the clutch, Kevin was apoplectic, and neither of us needed the added stress. But it was unavoidable, especially since I was running out of time. Marguerite and Tom would soon be coming to Princeton to help me move out. Though overwhelmed and sad and frustrated at still being unable to drive that stupid car, I was determined to get out of the apartment that same weekend, even if they had to tow me all the way to Co-op City. I packed late into the night before finally collapsing in a troubled sleep. I had an extraordinarily vivid dream: I'm in the car, engine idling. I put it in gear, lift my foot off the clutch very gently till it engages, a little more gas, the wheels are rolling. Nice . . .

The next morning, Marguerite and Tom arrived. It was clear from her sighs and the strained conversation that this was painful for them too. We loaded up their car as well as the Civic with boxes of books and precious little else. I hadn't accumulated much of a life if you measured it in stuff. Five years of marriage and barely two carloads. Marguerite, it turned out, knew how to drive a stick, and so she offered to take the wheel. But I insisted on doing it and asked her just to ride with me. As I started the car, the knowledge I possessed in the dream seemed to be real. My sleeping brain must have learned the lesson my waking mind couldn't master because of the tension between Kevin and me. In a hyperalert state, I made it onto the highway and into fourth gear. From there it was a long, clear glide with plenty of time to gather my wits before I had to face traffic in the Bronx.

Mami greeted us with grim cheer as we unloaded boxes from the elevator. The house felt strange in spite of the old familiarity, empty somehow without Junior. He had graduated from medical school and moved to Syracuse for his residency. Mami cooked us a welcome dinner of *chuletas,* and the smells from the kitchen were more comforting than I could have imagined. Soon enough she and I would start pushing each other's buttons, but that night it was a relief to be home.

AFTER I MOVED OUT, Kevin and I began to talk in earnest. We dated intermittently for a year or so and spent the occasional weekend together. It was, in part, an unspoken effort to rekindle a spark, though as such it never took. In the end, it amounted to more of an extended attempt at understanding what had gone wrong.

One night, Kevin really opened up. "I was always proud of you," he said, "but it was hard not being able to keep up. While you were acing Princeton, I was partying at Stony Brook. But I always figured that I was smart enough to make it up. I always had an excuse, always believed I could fix things later. Now I'm working as hard as I can. I love where I am, and I like what I'm doing. It's a struggle in a couple of classes; overall, though, I'm doing okay. But it's finally sinking in: even doing the best I can, I'm not going to catch up with you."

It was a painful admission, and I was touched by his generosity in putting it like that. Many men, feeling as he did, would have lashed out to soothe their egos. Certainly, the idea of a wife outshining her husband was something neither of us had been brought up to expect in marriage. But there was more, too. "I want to be needed," he said. "I knew you loved me, but I felt you didn't need me."

He wasn't wrong about that, but it wouldn't have occurred to me as a problem. I'd never seen need as an essential part of love. Weren't caring and affection, mutual respect, and sharing a life really more the point? If anything, need seemed to make the feeling contingent, less genuine, almost as if there were an ulterior motive to loving someone. In retrospect, maybe I was looking at it too rationally. The truth is that since childhood I had cultivated an existential independence. It came from perceiving the adults around me as unreliable, and without it I felt I wouldn't have survived. I cared deeply for everyone in my family, but in the end I depended on myself. That way of being was part of the person I would become, but where once it had represented salvation, now it was alienating me from the person I had vowed to spend my life with.

It might be that if I'd been in more relationships before getting married, I would have understood a bit more of what it takes to make one last. Being with someone never seems simpler than it does when you are very young. The ease of companionship, the familiarity of knowing each other for half our lives, had been a glue between us. But as a certain lopsidedness in our natures and our degrees of success became more pronounced, with neither of us paying much attention, that glue dissolved. I have feared, at times, that my self-reliance, even more than my prominence, might prove hard for any man to take. My friends and family are incredulous, sometimes annoyingly so, that I could be as content as

I appear to be without someone. But whatever security or comfort I find in being single, a happy relationship remains an alluring alternative, and I'm actually optimistic about the chances of having one.

In the spring, Kevin called to say that his thesis adviser was moving to Chicago. There was no one else at Princeton doing the work that interested Kevin, and so he had to follow. He knew there'd be no question but that I would stay behind. My work at the DA's Office mattered to me at least as much as his research did to him. Besides, at that point I couldn't see what I'd be giving it up for even if I'd been willing to. And with that, our efforts to work things out came to an unofficial end.

Kevin's mother, Jean, was heartbroken by our breakup. As rocky as my relations with her had been initially, her prejudice had been worn down by the fact of having a daughter-in-law, and a real friendship had grown up between us over the years. She would later tell me that she realized only after I'd gone how many gestures on Kevin's part—holiday gifts or a thoughtfully timed phone call—had been prompted by me.

In the end, I sold my wedding ring to pay the lawyer who handled our divorce. Saddened though I was at seeing Kevin leave, I was no more sentimental about the formal trappings of marriage than I had been on our wedding day. When I told Judge Rothwax that I was getting divorced and wanted to revert to my maiden name, he started using it instantly and made a point of correcting anyone who still referred to me as Ms. Sotomayor de Noonan. The DMV would take longer to straighten out.

Twenty-Four

MY ABILITY TO compartmentalize leaves my friends incredulous and sometimes even a little frightened. But it works for me. When I'm focused on a project, nothing else intrudes. It's only when I stop on an evening or a weekend that I look down to realize I've walked off a cliff. Fortunately, those same friends are usually down there waiting to catch me.

Every weekend for almost a year, Jason Dolan, with whom I shared cramped office space, and Ted Poretz, our pal from another bureau, made plans for us three: Sunday brunch, a movie, a party. We never talked about my divorce or what prompted our regular socializing. It was simply their kind impulse to stand by a friend and minimize the possibility of loneliness.

Girlfriends, of course, had a different approach.

Nancy Gold, now Nancy Gray, had been my friend ever since taking the seat next to mine during orientation on our very first day at the District Attorney's Office. By lunchtime we were racing over to the Citibank on Chambers Street together to take advantage of a great promotional offer she'd seen advertised. Later, when Nancy learned I was commuting from Princeton, she offered me the use of her fold-out couch whenever I had a jury sequestered overnight. And then, through the uncertain months when Kevin and I were coming apart, the haven she provided included not only that sofa but easy conversation and moral support. "It's perfectly obvious to everyone but you, Sonia," Nancy would say in her capacity as a natural practitioner of talk therapy. She drew me out, gave me the full Freudian breakdown, and even tried Kevin in absentia.

There was shopping therapy as well. "Sonia, you've got how many pairs of shoes under your desk? Every single one of them is frumpy. Buy yourself one nice pair, will you?" It was tough love, challenging my ingrained relentlessly negative physical self-image: "Who cares what your mom told you twenty years ago? What matters is how you look this Saturday night. Stop censoring yourself. You look great." No, I don't. Maybe not quite as bad as I did then, but great I don't look. Standing beside Nancy in front of the dressing room mirror, I would say to myself: She has such great style. This would really look good on her. I wish I had my own sense of style.

WHEN SUMMER CAME AROUND, I still hadn't figured out my next move, but I knew I needed a break from my mother. We would be at each other's throats if I couldn't get away at least for some weekends. Nancy had a summer share on Fire Island, a group house she wanted me to join, and so I went to check it out. It was quite a scene: more people than rooms, parties, and late nights.

"It's not my style, Nancy."

But she insisted it would be a great way to kick-start my

social life. "Never mind the crowd," she said. "I don't know most of them myself." I wasn't sure why she thought that made it more appealing.

"Just try it."

In the end, I refused to be convinced, saying I needed something more sedate. So Nancy introduced me to a college friend who was in another group house on the island, a very different scene, as she described it: shared meals, quiet evenings playing board games and reading. I threw caution to the wind and signed up for that one sight unseen.

My first trip out, the ferry abandoned me on the dock late at night in the middle of a storm that had knocked out the power and phone lines. I got hopelessly lost on the half-mile walk through the dunes from the ferry landing. Knocking on a random door for directions, I was embarrassed to discover I had disturbed somebody's illicit love nest. When I finally found the house and burst in, Mark Serlen, a housemate who'd been dozing, looked as if he'd just seen a sea monster come through the door. But from there on it was a lovely, exquisitely peaceful summer. Every other weekend would find Valerie, her fiancé, Jack, Mark, and assorted other friends playing Trivial Pursuit and Scrabble, reading the Sunday *Times* or a good mystery, sailing the weathered little skiff, cooking marvelous meals with clams gathered from the bay, and smoking endless cigarettes. I confess that the first night I spent alone there, many things went bump in the dark and I armed myself with a kitchen knife and broomsticks. But I would eventually come to feel there was no place safer.

We repeated the house share for a few summers, each of us eventually moving on to other arrangements, but the friendships that began at Fire Island continue. The kids have grown up and have their own kids. The summer rituals have given way to other traditions, like season tickets to the ballet year after year with Mark. But at least one weekend every summer I still find my way back to the beach with my Fire Island family.

"YOU'VE GOT TO find yourself a cop," Nancy said. "Cops are sexy, believe me." I began to open up to the possibility of dating again. It was tentative at first, I'll admit, but being outgoing and enjoying the process of getting to know a person in all his curious particularity, I grew to like dating. I wouldn't exactly fall hard for anyone, but I did meet some men who renewed my faith that I might be appealing and who even caused some of that nervousness of anticipation that I hadn't really felt since high school. Even a little romance can do wonders, if you are prepared to enjoy the moment and let the moments accumulate, whatever may come of it.

Probably nothing constrained my dating life as much as living at home with my mother. To hear her screaming from the bedroom "Sonia, it's midnight. You have to work tomorrow!" did not exactly make me feel like Mary Tyler Moore. If I was out late, she panicked. If she couldn't reach me by phone, she would call all my friends looking for me. We were making each other miserable.

Dawn Cardi told me her next-door neighbor in Carroll Gardens, Brooklyn, had an apartment for rent. By train it was twenty minutes from my office at 100 Centre Street, forty minutes on foot. The neighborhood was great, she said, a kind of Mayberry-on-the-Gowanus, only Italian. Many of the families on the block had been there for generations, and they watched out for one another, which sounded something like Abuelita's neighborhood when I was little. I went to see it that same evening. The building had real character, even an original tin ceiling, and the apartment was adorable. Naturally, the landlord wanted a security deposit. I said I could bring a check the next day, not yet knowing where I would get the money. But before I committed, I told him, my mother would have to see the place, not to make the decision, but for her own peace of mind, to be sure it was safe. The landlord liked that so much, he later told me, he called the real estate agent as soon as I left to delist the apartment.

Marguerite would lend me the money for the deposit and take the opportunity to tutor me in certain basic life skills, like handling personal finances, which I hadn't yet learned. To be fair, there hadn't been much occasion. On my mother's salary, plus what Junior and I brought home working part-time, we had always lived paycheck to paycheck. In that context, I had always feared debt as something that could easily snowball, a worry that arose whenever Kevin used our credit card for small luxuries. Though I often made loans to my aunts, I was never the borrower. As for saving, I had no acquaintance with that beyond collecting bottles as a child to buy Christmas presents. So Marguerite helped me set up a plan to pay her back in regular installments. When the debt was clear, she had me putting the same amount every week into a savings account. Marguerite knew this stuff. She'd done things in the right order: college, a job, saving money, and then getting married. Dispensing practical wisdom was her low-key expression of profound emotional support.

Moving into Carroll Gardens, I began to enjoy decorating the place, getting a bit of confidence that I could develop a personal sense of style. I realized, to my surprise, that I had an intuition for how space works, how scale and dimensions affect feeling. Architecture has always had a visceral effect on me. But the affective power of Carroll Gardens had more to do with the people there. When Dawn and I became neighbors, we developed a cozy routine. Getting off the train after a ridiculously long day, often after ten, I would stop at her place most nights before going home. Her husband, Ken, who got up very early for work, had usually gone to bed, but he always left a plate of dinner for me—he's still a great cook. Dawn would pour us a drink, and we'd talk over that day in the life of New York's criminal justice system.

Actually, by then we'd found much more than work to talk about, having discovered our backgrounds had plenty in common. She was the daughter of first-generation immigrants who had weathered the sorts of challenges that can break a family, causing her to cultivate a certain self-reliance early on. And like me, she had a mother with extraordinary strength of character, one whom I would come to know and love like an extra mother of mine, just as I had Marguerite's. Over the years and many holidays, I'd get to know Dawn's entire family: her parents, her kids—Vanessa, Zachary, and Kyle, who became my unofficial godchildren—her sisters, brothers-in-law, nieces and nephews, cousins, and in-laws.

I've always turned the families of friends into family of my own. The roots of this practice are buried deep in my childhood, in the broad patterns of Puerto Rican culture, in the particular warmth of Abuelita's embrace and her charged presence at the center of my world, the village of aunts, uncles, cousins, in-laws, and compadres scattered across the Bronx. I'd observed how the tribe extended its boundaries, with each marriage adding not just a new member but a whole new clan to ours. Still, in Abuelita's family, blood ultimately came first, and she strongly favored her own. My mother, being more or less an orphan, poor in kinfolk, approached the matter less dogmatically. She treated my father's family as her own, and when he died, it was to her sister, Titi Aurora, that Mami would bind herself with an almost metaphysical intensity, not to mention filling the available space in the household. But she continued to expand the family of friends among our neighbors, whether in the projects or in Co-op City: Ana and Moncho, Irma and Gilbert, Cristina, Dinora and Tony, Julia . . . they were all family to us.

I have followed my mother's approach to family, refusing to limit myself to accidents of birth, blood, and marriage. Like any family, mine has its rituals and traditions that sustain my tie to every member, no matter how far-flung. My friend Elaine Litwer, for instance, adopted me for Passover, and though I otherwise see her family only rarely, joining her Seder nurtured our connection. Thanksgiving is Mami's and Dawn's in perpetuity. Christmas belongs to Junior and to Junior's kids, Kiley, Corey, and Conner, when they came. Travel becomes another source of tradition; friendships that might have faded with distance are preserved because every trip to a friend's city, for whatever reason of business, becomes an occasion to visit. In this way I stay meaningfully connected to old friends, like Ken Moy and his family, and establish new relationships that have sustained me, like those with Bettie Baca and Alex Rodriguez, and Paul and Debbie Berger, whom I met while traveling. We may hardly talk in the intervening years, but we pick up right where we left off.

CHILDREN ELEVATE the art of found families to another level. I adore kids and have a special affinity with them, an ability to see the world through their eyes that most adults seem to lose. I can match any kid's stubbornness, hour for hour. I don't baby anyone; when we play games, I play to win. I treat kids as real people. Sometimes I think I love my friends' kids even more than I love my friends. Over the years, I have gathered more godchildren than anyone I know, and I take the role seriously. I was only thirteen when my cousin Adeline asked me to be godmother to her daughter. Erica was my first, and I was more than a little awed by the responsibility and the honor that the request implied. Alfred's son Michael was next, then Marguerite's Tommy. Tommy's brother John has adopted me as his surrogate godmother. I thought David, the son of my dentist and dear friend Martha Cortés, would be the last, but then Erica asked me to be her own son Dylan's godmother. Michael and his wife Lisandra have just had a baby girl, Alexia, and they have asked me to be her godmother.

Kiley is mine in a different way.

When I first set eyes on her, she was little more than a tangle of stick-thin limbs and tubes in the neonatal intensive care unit: one pound, eleven ounces. She was impossibly frail, and then very unlikely to survive, but I stood there awestruck at the sight of her drawing little breaths, a miracle of both life and science. I thought I knew everything about family before that ringing phone woke me up in the middle of the night: Junior, calling from Detroit to say that he had rushed Tracey to the hospital. I got on the next plane.

Junior had met Tracey during his residency at Syracuse, where she was a nurse. She'd followed him to Philadelphia for a fellowship, where they married before moving to Michigan. Now Junior stood beside me before the glass partition of the ICU, reciting the clinical details in his best doctor's voice. It was how he kept himself from going to pieces, but I could tell he was very scared. I felt closer to him in that moment than I ever had. It was not just the effect of seeing my little brother going through the worst experience of his life. It was also seeing what fatherly strength and devotion he had learned. Junior, who couldn't even remember Papi, had figured out for himself what it was to be a man.

Kiley's prognosis was not good, but she would be spared the seizures that can lead to complications. Tracey spent hours and hours every day sitting beside the incubator, watching, until the amazing day when she was first able to hold her daughter in her hands. Almost daily, it seemed, the doctors were intervening to solve some new problem. But slowly, very slowly, we allowed hope to take root. And then one day, sitting alone beside her, I somehow knew with absolute certainty that Kiley would make it.

It was almost a year before she first laughed, every milestone seeming to come at an excruciatingly slow pace. She'd remain a tiny child, my mother horrified at how little she ate. But I would be the one to get her to have mashed bananas laced with brown sugar and to introduce her to White Castle hamburgers, watching with delight as she actually finished her very first. But not until she was five could I persuade Junior to let her spend the day alone with me. Kiley needed no persuading. We explored the Children's Museum, ate ice cream at Serendipity, saw the Christmas show at Radio City Music Hall and the crèche at St. Patrick's—all on our first solo outing. After Junior moved the family from Michigan to Syracuse, Kiley never missed a chance to come stay with Titi Sonia.

SEEING MY ENTHUSIASM for being something of a crazy aunt—Titi Sonia might drive for hours to deliver on a promise to a child, or show up in an elf costume—many loved ones naturally asked whether I would one day have kids of my own. The question was never uncomplicated, even when my marriage seemed secure.

The prospects of my having a baby, or rather the potential for complications caused by diabetes, terrified my mother. She let Kevin know that if we had any intention of having children, she was counting on him to become a doctor first, not so as to be able to support a family, but to understand fully the risks involved. It wasn't my mother's decision, but I was not indifferent to her fears. In fact, a part of me felt them too. I knew of course that type 1 diabetics did have kids. It wasn't impossible, but the incidence of maternal complications was sobering, especially since I'd spent most of my life imagining I'd be lucky to live past forty. My projected longevity and the chance for a safe pregnancy had certainly improved alongside the methods of disease management since I'd been diagnosed, but I still feared that I wouldn't see old age. Even if that risk did not dictate my decision entirely, it seemed inarguable that having kids would be tempting fate.

Adoption was an attractive alternative. Eight years after Kiley's birth, Junior and Tracey adopted a pair of twins, Conner and Corey. Tracey likes to point out that they are Korean boys with Irish names, a Polish mother, and a Puerto Rican father—the perfect American family. My nephews are all the proof I could have needed of how emotionally satisfying adoption might have been. Still, there remained the fear that I might not be around long enough to raise a child to adulthood. Ultimately, the satisfaction of motherhood would be sacrificed, though I wouldn't say it was sacrificed to career.

It is interesting to me how, even after all the strides of the women's movement, the question of whether we can "have it all" remains such a controversy in the media, as if the ideal can be achieved. Most women of my generation who entered professional life did not forgo motherhood, and many did succeed at both. But they paid a price, one still paid by most women who work outside the home (and men too, I believe, if they parent wholeheartedly): a life of perpetual internal compromise that leaves you always feeling torn, neglectful by turns of one or the other. Mindful of this struggle and of how often Junior and I needed to interrupt Mami's work-day at Prospect Hospital with our phone calls, I have always made a point of running my chambers in such a way as to help mothers feel comfortable working there. And if in some corner of my heart I am still sulking about her absence dur-ing our childhood, I nevertheless credit the powerful example my mother set me as a working woman. But as for the possi-bility of "having it all," career and family, with no sacrifice to either, that is a myth we would do well to abandon, together with the pernicious notion that a woman who chooses one or the other is somehow deficient. To say that a stay-at-home mom has betrayed her potential is no less absurd than to sug-gest that a woman who puts career first is somehow less a woman.

During my time at the District Attorney's Office, women were only beginning to enter the legal profession in signifi-cant numbers. Fewer still were those practicing criminal law, either as prosecutors or as defense counsel. As Dawn would grimly observe, the only client happy to have a female defender was one accused of rape. Men and women got equal pay at the DA's Office, but promotions came far less easily for women, my own quick move from misdemeanors to felonies being unusual. I saw many women who were no less qualified wait much longer than men for the same advance. And they would have to work twice as hard as men to earn it, because so much of what they did was viewed in the light of casual sexism.

Nancy was doing arraignments one time, and the judge kept addressing her as "honey." She actually approached the bench and said, "Judge, I don't think it's appropriate; I'd prefer you didn't call me that." But he didn't even acknowledge her plea and went right on doing it. I've even heard a court security officer call a woman judge "sweetie" in her own courtroom.

And how many times would a defendant's lawyer enter the courtroom before a session and ask each of the male clerks and paralegals around me, "Are you the assistant in charge?" while I sat there invisible to him at the head of the table? My response was to say nothing, and my colleagues would follow suit. If it rattled him a bit when he eventually discovered his error, that didn't hurt our side, and perhaps he'd be less likely to repeat it.

Nancy and Dawn had no use for such patient strategies. They faulted my reluctance to rage vocally, just as my friends at Princeton had wanted me to be more of a firebrand. I credited their passion, and admired their brave readiness to jump into the fray of protest, but I continued to believe that such wasn't necessarily the best or the only way of changing an institution. As difficult an environment as the DA's Office could be, I saw no overarching conspiracy against women. The unequal treatment was usually more a matter of old habits dying hard. A male bureau chief who'd headed a predominantly male bureau for many years would naturally have a man as his image of an exemplary prosecutor.

But this is not to deny that the culture was decidedly and

often inhospitably male. I was lucky to be in Trial Part 50 under the unusually enlightened leadership of John Fried and then Warren Murray. Some of the other chiefs were disdainful of having women lawyers around, and in their bureaus a locker-room atmosphere prevailed. Sexual innuendo was used to explain everything, from the judge who was in a foul mood (obviously he wasn't "getting any") to the sensation of winning a guilty verdict. When they did win a case, they would celebrate at Forlini's, a restaurant of wood paneling and tufted red leather banquettes, where lawyers dined alongside judges in clubby conviviality. I never felt the sting of exclusion from such outings. Though I was always glad to have won my cases, somehow the idea of a person going to jail, with all the misery that entailed for a family, never quite seemed cause for celebration.

Otherwise, I could hold my own among my male colleagues, not losing my sense of humor in the face of their macho antics. It certainly helped that I could, as Rudy had observed, argue like a man and that I'd actually heard far lewder jokes in two languages than most of these guys could have dreamed up. But could I have managed to negotiate this culture as well as the crushing caseload with a child tugging at my awareness in the background of every moment? I thought not. The idea of another life utterly dependent on me, the way a child needs his mother, didn't seem compatible with the professional necessity of living at this punishing pace. As it was, I thought there was already too little time to accomplish the things I envisioned.

HAVING MADE a different choice from that of many women, I occasionally do feel a tug of regret. When her mother died,

Dawn's eulogy was an expression of such feeling and care that I was shaken beyond the grief of having lost the dear friend her mother had become. I spent the following days pondering the bond between parent and child and wondering whether anyone would miss me that much when I died. Ultimately, I accept that there is no perfect substitute for the claim that a parent and child have on each other's heart. But families can be made in other ways, and I marvel at the support and inspiration I've derived from the ones I've built of interlocking circles of friends. In their constant embrace I have never felt alone.

Twenty-Five

I N RETROSPECT, I've wondered how I could have devoted all my waking hours to a job without reflecting more on the kind of work I was doing. Joining the DA's Office had represented a chance to be a practicing lawyer right away and to play a tangible part in protecting the public. There was no denying the allure of the mission, or the thrill I derived from accomplishing it, but while I was working fifteen-hour days, I wasn't giving much thought to the daily experience of confronting humanity at its worst, any more than I was noticing the subtle signs of the rift developing at home. It was Kevin who had made me see what was happening between us, but eventually, when the divorce was behind me, I would have to discover for myself what my job was doing to me.

Law enforcement is a world unto itself: few outsiders can appreciate the psychic effects of inhabiting it. And so prosecutors and police socialize mainly among themselves. They do a lot of drinking together. And their divorce rates are well above average. During our many talks about what had gone wrong in the marriage, Kevin had never suggested that being a prosecutor had changed me, even though the long hours had undeniably contributed to the strain. But once I realized that my intense focus might have blinded me to certain cues at home, I couldn't help examining myself for unremarked changes as well.

There are those in law enforcement who manage to remain unaltered by the work in their private selves, but they stand out with the rarity of saints. All around me I saw personalities darkened by cynicism and despair. Trained in suspicion, skilled at cross-examining, you will look for the worst in people and you will find it. I'd felt from the beginning that these impulses were at odds with my essential optimism, my abiding faith in human nature and its enduring potential for redemption. But now I could see the signs that I too was hardening, and I didn't like what I saw. Even my sympathy for the victims, once such an inexhaustible driver of my efforts, was being depleted by the daily spectacle of misdeeds and misery. I began to ask myself whether there weren't other equally worthy jobs. Meanwhile, I would persevere at the DA's Office, convinced at least I was doing something valuable.

It was a relatively minor crime that caused me to doubt even that. I was working in the complaint room one day, my eyes, as usual, skipping over the names, when I picked up a new file, going straight to the facts of the case. Names don't appear in the arresting officer's narrative: it's always the defendant did this; the victim did that. But as I read to the bottom of the page, I said to myself, I've already seen this episode. We caught this guy. We tried him. We locked him up. I swear, it's Mr. Ortiz!

Sure enough, it was. He had served his time, but no sooner had he landed back on the street than he was caught in a carbon copy of the earlier crime. What had been a misdemeanor in the first instance became a felony now by virtue of repetition, but otherwise the cases were identical. He was, of course, not the first repeat offender I'd come across, but somehow his unremarkable case crystallized a certain sense of futility in my efforts. If this was the system, maybe I should be working to improve it rather than simply enforcing it on the front lines.

It was now that the old dream of becoming a judge seemed, if still not within reach, at least something that I might reasonably start working toward, and I was aiming for the federal bench. The federal bench was where matters of broad consequence, cases affecting far more lives than those of a victim and a defendant, were decided. I'd been aware of this since law school, when I studied with particular fascination how the landmark rulings of southern judges like the legendary Frank M. Johnson Jr. had done so much to advance civil rights and bring an end to Jim Crow. The idea that a single person could make such a difference in the cause of justice was nothing less than electrifying, and having more or less accepted the primacy of career in my life, I saw no reason to stint on ambition.

By now I had seen enough of the world to imagine what a path to such a goal might look like. Most federal judges come to the bench with one of two accomplishments behind them: partnership in a prominent law firm or an important stint, at some point in their careers, in government. There are exceptions, of course, and the only invariable requirement is a record of excellence—in academia or elsewhere—that rises to the attention of a senator's selection committee or the president's staff. Nowadays many federal judges have served first as federal prosecutors, and though this was a less likely path when I was at the DA's Office, I knew that I needed a rest from criminal law. Throughout my time there I had interviewed occasionally when I spotted an opening in public service, but it became clear that I would need more varied experience if I was going to aim higher than a line attorney in a government bureaucracy.

In any case, I wanted to gain experience in civil law, a challenge I welcomed, having certainly enjoyed my courses in business law at Yale (how many people got honors in Commercial Transactions or really took an interest in tax law, anyway?). Those courses had also taught me how much of legal work involved representing corporations and economic power. To be a judge, I'd need to learn to move comfortably in that world. And so I decided that my next job would be an immersion in civil law.

When I announced my intention to jump, Bob Morgenthau tried harder than I might have expected to dissuade me. He indicated I would likely become a bureau chief if I stayed and that post could lead to a state court judgeship, unaware that my gaze was set on the federal bench. He did manage to delay my departure for well over a year by assigning me to a handful of exceptionally challenging cases that were very much in the public eye.

It was very soon after that exchange that my bureau chief called me. "Sonia, this is a very sensitive situation. The Boss wants you to be the one to handle it." The office needed to investigate an accusation of police brutality made by a church leader in Harlem. Relations between police and the black community were already severely strained. A year before, a man picked up for graffiti vandalism had gone into a coma and died in custody. Now a Harlem reverend was claiming to have been beaten after being stopped for a traffic violation. The two officers countered that he had assaulted them. "I'm not going to tell you what the outcome should be," the

Boss said. "Just make sure the office doesn't look bad in the press." I would hear from him once again during the investigation, asking for a status report. Otherwise, he left me to it and kept his distance.

Vernon Mason, the well-known civil rights lawyer, was representing the minister. Visiting my alcove office, Mason lectured me at length on the alienation of the community, its anger at the police, its distrust of the prosecutor's intentions, and his own belief that justice could not and would not be done, and he declared his client's unwillingness to cooperate. I in turn lectured him back: assuming the corruption of everyone in law enforcement was a self-fulfilling prophecy, I said, whose effect was only to sabotage the system, ensuring that justice could not be done. I made an emotional plea for him to give me a chance. While I could not pledge in advance to prosecute the officers, I did promise a thorough investigation with an open mind. But he would give me neither the benefit of the doubt nor any help at all in the investigation.

Mason didn't understand where this prosecutor was coming from. As much as I respected the police and appreciated the difficulty of their job, I was never so naive as to believe that abuse didn't happen. As in any other population, some on the force had emotional problems that could dispose them to misconduct. I had seen for myself how the frustrations of a massive crime wave and a woefully underfunded response could change people who'd started out with the best of intentions. The streets had become dangerously unpredictable, a place where violence might escalate faster than anyone could reason. But if the community could have no faith in law enforcement, the job of policing would be infinitely harder, the mission ultimately doomed. If I found wrong had been done that day, I would prosecute it.

For three months I scoured the streets of Harlem daily for witnesses. I knocked on every door within blocks of where the encounter had taken place, plastering the neighborhood with my card, begging anyone who would listen to talk to me if they had seen what happened. I parked myself on a stool at Sylvia's famous soul food counter and chatted with anyone coming or going. But no one ever came forward. If anyone had seen something, no one was saying.

One thing was accomplished, however: a genuine effort was observed. Ultimately, there would be no indictment, but there would be no explosive headlines either. Tensions had been defused, at least this time. But the larger story would not end any day soon. The DA's Office would continue to make outreach a priority. It had to: activists like Mason would continue to light a fire whenever abuse was alleged. The only long-term answer was to cultivate better relations with the community, but that would take time and effort. The cops would need special training. The community would need to learn the value of helping the force recruit, instead of branding anyone of their own who joined a traitor. Looking back over decades since, you can see that those efforts have borne some fruit. Even New York's high-crime areas are nothing like they were, although suspicion still remains even when the community cooperates.

The second big assignment that Bob Morgenthau sent my way would be my first murder trial. It was a huge case, very complex, and real tabloid fodder. As a homicide novice, I couldn't have led the prosecution, but Hugh Mo, the senior assistant DA in charge, ensured that my second-seat role was far from pro forma. Hugh was a slightly built figure with a booming voice and a big personality to match; a hard-driving prosecutor, he was also a gentle family man—an all-around confounder of stereotypes. Our offices were side by side, and we developed an easy, seamless teamwork and camaraderie. He generously allowed my visible participation in the prosecution of Richard Maddicks, who was charged with being the Tarzan Murderer.

The press had so dubbed the perpetrator because his modus operandi included swinging through a victim's apartment window from a rope secured to the roof. In a marathon of armed burglaries over a few months, he had terrorized one small area of Harlem, shooting three people to death and seriously wounding seven others. He would shoot anyone he found at home, whether or not the person resisted or posed any threat. He even shot one victim's small dog. If anything prevented him from finishing a job, he might return to the same building on another day or just lurk on a nearby rooftop or in an air shaft for a few minutes until he could resume.

Maddicks's rap sheet told the tale: a twenty-five-year career in assault and robbery. He was on parole when he was arrested and supporting a two-hundred-dollar-a-day drug habit. His hauls as a thief suggested what sorts of people he preyed on: a pocketful of subway tokens, a wad of bills that had been stuffed in a shoe or a bra, the food in the kitchen. One of his big jackpots was a few thousand dollars one couple had kept at home, their life savings. His victims were barely hanging on to begin with, and their lives were usually destroyed by his visit, if they survived it.

Maddicks's signature was not perfectly consistent, but there was enough overlap in the incidents to suggest a single perpetrator. The gun was one common denominator and the acrobatics another, whether he swung from a rope, scaled an air shaft, or crawled over a ladder stretched between two buildings. There was the flowerpot, the paint can, or the bucket weighted with a rock that came crashing through a window before he did. There was the chilling absence of fear.

Hugh and I had discovered twenty-three separate incidents, eleven of which had strong enough evidence to bring to trial and which we consolidated into one indictment. We figured the only way a jury could see the big picture of Maddicks's villainy was to try all eleven together. Easier said than done: the law does not allow you to try unrelated crimes together, and it was no surprise that the defense filed a motion to sever the various counts.

When the law permits this or prohibits that, the first question to ask is why. The "why" is the essence of the principle, and once you understand it, you can structure an argument for not applying it in a particular case. Why is evidence from unrelated crimes inadmissible? Because suggesting that someone is prone to criminal activity would prejudice a jury trying to decide whether he has committed the one for which he is being tried. There are, of course, exceptions where a common element links the crimes and makes a joint trial both sensible and legally permissible, but they are carefully circumscribed and complicated by differences between state and federal law.

"It's not a conspiracy," said Hugh. "There's only one of him." I dug into the library looking for an appropriate way to frame the common elements that linked the crimes, and we requested a *Molineux* hearing, a New York State proceeding in which a judge decides whether the facts of the case justify allowing evidence that is normally inadmissible. We argued that our purpose was to show not criminal propensity but rather proof of identity: given the rare level of physical strength and agility required for the acrobatics common to all the incidents, we could reasonably claim that this element, not unlike a signature modus operandi, identified Maddicks as the perpetrator.

Judge Rothwax handled the pretrial motions. As usual, I made sure to be prepared, and he was perfectly reasonable. We would prosecute all eleven incidents in one trial. I felt the very real satisfaction of having devised an argument persuasive enough to show the facts of our case fell within the boundaries of this corner of the law. The critical faculty that had remained an abstraction to me at Yale, and eluded me at Paul, Weiss, and wasn't even necessary to prosecuting most cases was now in my sure possession: I was undeniably thinking like a lawyer.

WE LOCATED forty witnesses who were willing to testify, Hugh and I each taking twenty to interview and prepare for trial. This being my first murder, much of the legwork was new to me. So was the huge volume of records—autopsy, fingerprint, and ballistic reports, multiple witness statements given to different officers—to be assimilated. But with Hugh's guidance I learned how to sift them for the crucial details to fashion our case. He instructed me too in the preparation of charts and maps and diagrams by which the evidence could be visually represented to prevent the jury from being overwhelmed by the dizzying minutiae, always a danger in complex prosecutions.

The effort also required Hugh and me to become intimately familiar with those few blocks in Harlem where Maddicks had conducted his spree. It's essential for a prosecutor to visit the scene of the crime. You have to root yourself in the space, internalize it, and absorb details that you would invariably miss in a secondhand description. You have to make the scene come to life in the minds of the jurors, and so it has to live in your mind first.

One squalid apartment I visited had been used by addicts as a shooting gallery. There were used needles and spoons all over the floor. The power had been cut, and you could barely see anything in the light coming through the windows dark with grime. A mattress already reeking of ancient urine had soaked up blood like a blotter. What could a man lying here possess that would cost him his life?

Another household reminded me sadly of Abuelita's. An extended family—a mother, three grown children and their spouses, several grandchildren—all sharing two apartments in the same building. The kids were in school; the parents had jobs—restaurant work or maintenance. Their father, long deceased, had been a security guard, and it was his old nightstick that the brothers had grabbed when Maddicks appeared at the window. They chased him to the roof, from which he spidered down the gap between two buildings as they rained blows on him from above. He seemed to disappear. Back in the apartment, the family gathered in the commotion to phone the police. His sister, brother, mother, and young niece were standing beside Steve Robinson when a bullet came through the window from the opposite building and entered his forehead.

Was Maddicks a skilled sniper too, or was it just a lucky shot? Either way, Steve Robinson's death would devastate that family, scattering them to the winds. Only one brother, broken and with few words, remained to show me what had been their home, the bloodstain still visible on the floor.

Azilee Solomon had come home from work to find her door unlocked, her home ransacked, her longtime companion— her husband, really, by common law—dead in the blood-soaked chair where he had been napping. They had both worked at the Hilton hotel for twenty years, she as a chambermaid, he as a janitor. Every last penny that they had saved for retirement was stolen. The meat and coffee from their refrigerator were gone, along with the shopping cart that Mrs. Solomon used to wheel her groceries home.

At Maddicks's girlfriend's apartment, detectives found the same meat and coffee, but that proved nothing: anyone could have bought those brands. Outside the building, however, there were six shopping carts lined up by the trash, among which Mrs. Solomon instantly recognized her own. It was true that shopping carts were also mass-produced. But only one could have had the piece of yellow tape that Mrs. Solomon had used to mend a broken rung. "Take out those old clothes," she told the detectives. "And you'll find that yellow tape underneath." At trial we staged a dramatic shopping cart lineup in Judge James Leff's court to re-create the moment of discovery.

I spent a lot of time with Mrs. Solomon in the process of preparing for her testimony. I got to know her well. She was a deeply religious woman who radiated kindness. My gift of faith was not as great as hers, but I was deeply touched to see the solace it brought her. Though the murder of her partner was senseless and had turned her life upside down, she somehow accepted it as God's will. She wanted Maddicks removed from the proximity of anyone else he might harm, but she expressed no desire for vengeance. Her tears flowed but without self-pity as she told her story in a matter-of-fact tone, first to me and then to the jury. I could tell that she had been loved.

The Tarzan Murderer himself was, by disturbing contrast, my first real-life encounter with a human being beyond salvage. Throughout the trial, I watched him obsessively, searching his face for the least trace of feeling. Something in me badly needed to see even a glimmer of empathy or regret, as witness after witness told one more horrifying story of loss. I would be disappointed. He sat there, utterly impassive, hour after hour, and I couldn't help thinking: the devil is alive right here. I've always had a fundamental faith in rehabilitation, always believed that education and effort, if applied intelligently, could ultimately fix anything. Richard Maddicks taught me that there are exceptions, however few. What we do with them is a separate question, but after he was sentenced to sixty-seven and a half years in prison, I was glad to know that he was unlikely to be free in my lifetime.

Later, when we said good-bye after the trial, Mrs. Solomon turned back to me as she left my office and added, "Miss Sonia"—she couldn't manage my last name—"there's something very special about you. You've been blessed. I'm glad we met." She was gone before I could answer, but I thought: Mrs. Solomon, there's something very special about you too. I am humbled and honored to have known you. There are people who make me believe, in ways that I can't fully explain, that I have something important to accomplish in this life. Sometimes it's a seemingly random encounter. The inscrutable words of a stranger that somehow say to me: Sonia, you have work to do. Get on with it.

THE LAST OF the really tough cases that I perceived as Bob Morgenthau's challenge to me carried a different stench of evil. Nancy and Dawn were both concerned about how it would affect me. "Can you handle it?" they asked. I knew I could, though I would surprise even myself with the feroc-

ity of determination this one provoked, a steelier side of me
than I'd ever known.

I was working late one night when I reached my limit for
the day. I turned off the projector, flipped the lights on, took
a deep breath, and tried to will away the nausea. Could I
show these films to a jury? Of course they were prejudicial;
the defense attorneys would fight me over this. But until a
person has seen this stuff, it remains abstract. You can understand that child pornography is abominable, you can appreciate the harm that's done to the children used to make it and
to the morals of a society, but you can't begin to imagine the
depth of revulsion you'll feel. You can't anticipate pity will
be so overwhelming that you yourself feel violated. I had to
get the films admitted. But there remained the question of
strategy. I always remembered Warren Murray's advice about
persuading the jury of the moral necessity of a conviction.
Some crimes, however, are so heinous that they can't fail to
stir outrage. In such cases, hammering the point can even
prove counterproductive. So I decided I would let the films
themselves do the emotional work and put my own energy
into building the most crushing argument for guilt, a logical
structure that was impervious to denial.

There were two defendants. Scott Hyman was small-fry,
the retail front end who'd sold a few films to an undercover
cop and was supposed to connect him with the wholesaler
for the big purchase. He was young, even vulnerable looking, showing up for court every day with the same oversized
sweater hanging on his scrawny frame. When I learned that
his own parents had run an adult bookstore, I wondered
what kind of a childhood he'd had. His partner Clemente
D'Alessio cut a much less sympathetic figure, stocky with
slicked-back hair and a pockmarked face, a garish gold cru-

cifix hanging on his chest. If he wasn't the brains of a bigger operation, he was at least smart enough to stay out of sight. Everything we had on him was circumstantial and hinged on identifying his voice in a single recorded phone call. My plan was to implicate them both in the same transaction, focusing on the link between retail and wholesale.

The case had its weaknesses. The wholesale deal—selling up to three hundred films to the undercover agent—was never consummated, because the police couldn't come up with the cash fast enough. They tried to stall, but D'Alessio got spooked and backed off. Then it took them six months before they got around to arresting him. They hadn't made my job easy. In a case where police credibility was essential, where so much rested on the testimony of the undercover cop, a lot had actually been bungled. Even the crucial phone call—Hyman calling D'Alessio on tape—was arguably tainted, the call having been placed minutes after Hyman was in custody, before he'd had access to counsel. On the other hand, the sloppiness of the investigation didn't mean those guys weren't guilty, only that I would have to work that much harder. Fortunately, I got plenty of able help from my second seat, Karen Greve Milton, and it was a relief to share the emotional weight of the case as well as the workload.

The first day and opening arguments were more nerve-racking than any I had experienced in a while. I remembered how a bureau chief had advised another female ADA. "Handle it like a man," he told her. "Go to the bathroom and throw up." The laugh was sufficient to quell my stomach. I've since accepted that all trial lawyers get nervous, even some judges, and the day you find being in court routine enough that you feel relaxed will probably be a day you'll regret.

D'Alessio's attorney was a high-priced criminal defense

lawyer with more than twenty years of trial experience, often on high-profile cases. A large man with surprisingly quick reflexes and a nose for publicity, he was intimidating on many levels. He poured on his rhetoric liberally and dripped condescension. Condescending to the prosecutor might be a tactic, but he was sloppy with it, and it sloshed onto the jury sometimes, which can be very damaging. I made a mental note to be extra polite to the panel and acknowledge the inconvenience we were putting them through.

The defense might have argued entrapment, but they chose not to. Instead, Hyman's attorney went for "diminished capability." Apparently, Hyman was addicted to quaaludes, and in exchange for them he supplied a pharmacist with child pornography. It was the pharmacist who, after the police had picked him up for another crime, turned informant, initially setting up Hyman with the undercover cop. The defense contended that Hyman only supplied the porn to keep the drugs flowing, and the drugs had in turn impaired his judgment.

Diminished capability is always a flimsy argument at best. It has no legal standing, and I could see maybe five different ways to knock it down. But the attorney dragged it out into an endless distraction, ordering the federal prescription records and bringing the pharmacist in to testify. As it happened, the pharmacist was under federal indictment on so many other charges that he had trouble keeping track of what his immunity covered. He couldn't say much at all. Another witness the defense had lined up was arrested on a completely separate charge while waiting outside the courtroom. It was hard to imagine a sleazier bunch of characters.

D'Alessio's attorney decided on a mistaken-identity strategy: there was another Clem who worked in the same building, and he, the defense claimed, was obviously the one Hyman was speaking to in the incriminating phone call. So D'Alessio had found a way to remain invisible, even as he sat there at the defense table. I would have to find a way of using to our advantage that cloak of secrecy he'd wrapped around himself. That he'd evidently taken such pains to keep his hands clean despite a mountain of circumstantial evidence was entirely in keeping with our view that we had netted quite a big fish.

I presented my evidence over six long, methodical, painstaking days. There was so much stuff—piles of films, tapes, documents—that we had to wheel it into the courtroom on carts. I mapped the locations in detail, painting a scene of seedy storefronts with names like Peep-In, Show Palace, the Roxy Burlesque Theatre. This wasn't just atmosphere. I needed the territory laid out clearly so as to lead the jury along the disjointed trail of evidence that came from the surveillance teams: Hyman coming and going between D'Alessio's office and the vault where the films were kept; the brown paper bag seen here, seen there, seen going in and not coming out; the locations where conversations were caught on hidden mics . . .

Was I pushing the jurors too far by subjecting them to the tedium of listening to the undercover cops' recordings? They had to suffer through long silences, incongruous music from the car radio while the clock hand swept slowly, and wait for a few damning words. But the tapes left no doubt about the nature of what was happening. You could hear Hyman boasting about other sales he'd made, about the quality of the films he was offering, and explaining how films with younger kids, "kiddie porn," were easier to come by; older kids got wise to the business and wanted their cut. He also talked about the wholesaler's concern for secrecy. And then, finally, we get the link between Hyman and D'Alessio: "Just like the last time, yeah, same guy."

The films were the very last piece of the puzzle I was helping the jury put together before I could rest my case. They were scratchy and grainy, the colors having shifted from having been copied too many times. They were silent: no sound, no dialogue, no plot. A bare bedroom was the set. The children appeared to be as young as seven or eight, no older than ten or eleven. Their little limbs were scrawny, bruised, and grimy. The lens zoomed in ruthlessly on genitals, probing and thrusting. Though you never saw or heard an adult presence, the awkward unmotivated action left no doubt about the ghost that gave orders from behind the camera.

I had thirteen films screened in all, each around ten or fifteen minutes. As the previous one rewound, the police officer would recite the litany of identification for the next one, and we all braced ourselves. Midway through the screenings, I noticed the journalist who had been sitting in the gallery every day, following the case for a book she was writing. She had taken off her glasses in a quiet refusal to see more and was staring sadly into space. The members of the jury didn't have that choice.

My summation didn't need rhetoric. The facts were damning enough. All I needed to do was to show how they were connected with relentless logic, step-by-step, leaving no piece out. I tried to put myself in the jurors' shoes and anticipate any possible misgiving or misunderstanding. Would they balk at the circumstantial nature of the evidence against D'Alessio? Words like "circumstantial" carry an exaggerated load when you consider the degree to which most of us live our lives by inference. Keep it simple, straightforward,

I reminded myself. This was a panel of citizens, not legal scholars. Having exposed them to enough horror, I addressed them with a bit of humor. How did your mother know it was you whenever you raided the cookie jar? I asked them. Only one of her kids was too short to reach it without the stepladder. And say you forgot to put the stepladder away, left it out there covered with cookie crumbs—it was a pretty safe bet the culprit was you and not one of your bigger siblings.

My closing ran two and a half hours. The judge took another two hours to charge the jury, reviewing all the elements of the law. It was early evening by the time they began their deliberations. But by the end of the next day, the jury forewoman was reading the verdict, pronouncing "guilty" eighty-six times—forty-three counts for each defendant. Hyman and D'Alessio had expected this; they had bail on hand.

But there remained the matter of the sentencing. I had seen cases in which defendants found guilty on all counts had evaded the full weight of justice because a single jurist was, for one reason or another, unwilling to impose it. In the conversations we had taped, when Hyman bragged about other crimes—drug deals and credit card scams—he said he never worried about getting caught. When it came time for sentencing, he said, you just had to keep postponing until you got the right judge. I could not let that happen. When we reconvened a month later, I pressed for the maximum. And when D'Alessio's attorney offered a profoundly offensive analogy—the maximum here, he said, would be like twenty years for possession of a single joint—my answer came with a fury so controlled that I doubt it registered as fury, but I felt it.

"In those films you see children about the age of seven

and eight engaged in activities which are normally reserved for an adult bedroom," I said, hoping now to make the moral case that I had the films make for me to the jury. "But it was more than that, Your Honor. There was an eight-year-old girl in one of the films, a small girl depersonalized to the extent that we don't even know her name or who she is, but she is a human being. An eight-year-old girl on a film was directed offstage to engage in acts which I am not sure she fully understood. That young girl was robbed and she was raped. She was raped of her virginity and her innocence by the individuals who produced those films. In a sense, her innocence was murdered . . . That is not the equivalent, when we request our sentence, of selling a stick of marijuana. When you sell a stick of marijuana, the buyer and the seller can make free choices. The children could not."

D'Alessio got three and a half to seven years; Hyman got two to six.

Earlier, Bob Morgenthau had offered me a promotion to head the Juvenile Office. My work on this trial had got him thinking that this might be a specialty area for me and asking himself whether the office needed a dedicated unit for child pornography. My refusal of his offer was instantaneous, an instinctive gesture of self-preservation. I knew I couldn't witness that much sorrow and depravity without drowning in it. It was time for me to move on.

WHEN THE CHILD PORNOGRAPHY CASE was wrapped up, I took a brief vacation in Puerto Rico, but my mind was back in New York, and in particular on my cousin Nelson, who had reentered my life. After disappearing for about eight years through the worst of his addiction, he had somehow managed to join the military and clean up. There would still be ups and downs, but he didn't lose touch with the family again, and so gradually we had been able to reestablish our connection. The worst had seemed long past when he married Pamela. She had a daughter that he cherished as his own. They had just learned that a second child was on the way when Nelson was diagnosed with AIDS. His was one of the very first cases linked to needle use, just before awareness of the disease exploded in the public consciousness.

Nelson, like me, had had a special connection with Abuelita, and it didn't end when she died. His old premonitions of an early death were haunting him now. He told me he could hear ghostly trumpets. "Abuelita is calling me, and I'm telling her I'm not ready. I want to live to see my child born." He would, but not much longer than that, the end coming before his thirtieth birthday. In his last weeks, we would have many talks for hours at a stretch, slipping into the transparent ease we'd had in childhood, as if making up for lost time. I hadn't understood until then that one could be addicted to drugs and yet function normally in the world, holding a job and supporting a family. Nelson wasn't robbing people to get his fix; he wasn't shooting up in stairwells. He managed his addiction like a chronic disease, not unlike my diabetes.

I told him how I had been dazzled by his brilliance and his limitless curiosity about how the world works. And how I despaired of ever matching up to him. He looked at me and shook his head. "You really don't understand, do you? I've always been in awe of you. There was nothing you couldn't learn if you set your mind to it. You would just study until you figured it out. I can't do that; I never could. That's why

I couldn't finish college, why I couldn't stick with a job. I didn't have the will. That determination that you have is special. It's a different kind of intelligence."

One day after little Nelson had arrived, we talked about his happiness at his son's birth and his sadness at the prospect of not being there for his children. We talked as well about the time a couple of months earlier, before his condition had gotten really bad, when he'd asked me to give him a ride to run an errand. He could no longer get around easily, and there was someone he needed to see, just for a little while. He asked me to wait, and so I sat in the car, parked outside the run-down tenement in Hunts Point, just a few blocks from where Abuelita used to live. I figured this was an old friend to whom he wanted to say his good-byes while he still could. But as he now confessed, inside he'd been scoring heroin. I wanted to kick myself—how could anyone, let alone an assistant district attorney who'd seen everything I'd seen, be so naive? I recited that essential lesson of Papi's, simplistic but also simply true: Good people can do bad things, make bad choices. It doesn't make them bad people.

As he begged me to forgive him, there was a hint of delirium fueling the shame and sadness in his voice. But I knew forgiveness was beside the point. I myself was carrying a load of survivor's guilt. Who was going to forgive me? Why was I not lying in that hospital bed? How was it I had escaped when my soul's twin, my smarter half, once joined to me at the hip, had not? His request only made the load heavier. My God, what a waste.

JULY 1983, I'm at the house on Fire Island. I wake very early from a deep sleep. It's still dark out, but I'm completely alert, even though I was up late last night. The clock says four thirty. I throw on jeans and a T-shirt and walk out to the bay. I sit on the dock and watch the deep blue draining from the sky in the early dawn. The sun is still hidden behind the island. It's probably just breaking the edge of the Atlantic. Nelson is here, I can feel him. He's come to say good-bye. Morning erases the last stars and dissolves the remaining night.

I walked back to the house to find the phone ringing: Nelson's dad. "Sonia, it's Benny," he started. I knew how difficult it was for him to make this call.

"*Yo ya sé*. I already know. I'll be on the first ferry home."

Twenty-Six

I F I TRY TO understand in my heart how it could happen that two children so closely matched could meet such different fates, I enter a subterranean world of nightmares—the sudden panic when Nelson's hand slips from mine in the press of the crowd, the monster I evade but he cannot.

Reason seems a better defense against the pain. Let me understand in my logical way what made the difference between two children who began almost as twins, inseparable and, in our own eyes, virtually identical. Almost but not quite: he was smarter; he had the father I wished for, though we shared Abuelita's special blessing. Why did I endure, even thrive, where he failed, consumed by the same dangers that had surrounded me?

Some of it can be laid at the door of machismo, the culture that pushes boys out onto the streets while protecting girls, but there's more. Nelson had mentioned it that day at the hospital: the one thing I had that he lacked. Call it what you like: discipline, determination, perseverance, the force of will. Even apart from his saying so, I knew that it had made all the difference in my life. If only I could bottle it, I'd share it with every kid in America. But where does it come from?

Good habits and hard work matter, but they are only the expressions of it, an effect rather than the cause. What is the source? I know that my competitive spirit—my drive to win, my fear of failure, my desire constantly to outdo myself—bubbles up from very deep within my personality. It's rarely directed at others; I compete with myself. But if ambition only feeds the ego and self-regard, what does it avail? The urge to win might serve to accumulate life's material pleasures, but those pleasures can be no less ephemeral and addictive than Nelson's high and often just another way of becoming the biggest and baddest on the block.

What Nelson saw driving me arises from a different kind of aspiration: the desire to do for others, to help make things right for them. Strange ambition for a child? Some might say so, but I've been aware of it for as long as I can remember. Self-aggrandizing? I've never felt such release from the awkward hold of ego as when helping others. Reaction to early years in a house of pain? Perhaps, but at some point I let go of my compulsion to please: it's my own standard of character that I need to meet. In any case, I'm sure of having learned it from others, my examples. And very good ones.

IF I TRY to imagine my most immediate examples of selfless love, instinct leads me first to those who were closest: Abuelita, healer and protector, with her overflowing generosity of spirit; and my mother, visiting nurse and confidante to the whole neighborhood.

My understanding of my survival was bound up in

every way with the fact of my grandmother's protection. It amounted to more than a refuge from the chaos at home: my sense of being under safekeeping, physically and metaphysically. It had given me the will to manage my illness, to overcome my insufficiencies at school, and ultimately to imagine the most improbable of possibilities for my life. And that feeling of Abuelita's protection would only grow after her death, made manifest in countless ways, from bizarrely fortuitous interventions that would save my life in diabetic crises to strange alignments of circumstances that have favored me unreasonably. Things that might easily have happened to me somehow did not; things that were not likely to happen for me somehow did. This seemed like luck with a purpose.

I was under no illusion of having been singled out, chosen for some particular destiny. But I did come to recognize in my good fortune the work of a blessing, a gift that made my life not entirely my own: I was not free to squander it if I chose. Gifts, Abuelita showed us, were for sharing with others. And though I was not given a mission, I had to find a worthy purpose, to earn this protection. The language of cause and effect would be misleading here, the implied exchange of one thing for another not relevant: suffice it to say, somehow a synergy of love and gratitude, protection and purpose, was implanted in me at a very young age. And it flowered in the determination to serve.

MY CHILDHOOD AMBITION to become a lawyer had nothing to do with middle-class respectability and comfort. I understood the lawyer's job as being to help people. I understood the law as a force for good, for protecting the community, for upholding order against the threat of chaos, and for resolving conflict. The law gives structure to most of our relationships, allowing us all to promote our interests at once, in the most harmonious way. And overseeing this noble purpose with dispassionate wisdom was the figure of the judge. All kids have action heroes: astronauts, firemen, commandos. My idea of heroism in action was a lawyer, the judge being a kind of superlawyer. The law for me was not a career but a vocation.

My earliest exposure to helping professions had been to those of medicine and teaching: Dr. Fisher, the staff at Prospect Hospital and the clinic at Jacobi, and the Sisters of Charity, who taught us at Blessed Sacrament. The law, I understood at a very young age, was different in scope. Doctors and nurses and teachers helped individuals, one by one. But through the law, you could change the very structure of society and the way communities functioned. In this way the law could help vast numbers of people at once. With so much hardship and suffering all around me, the need for change was glaring.

The spirit of the times inhabited this ideal of law as a noble purpose. The civil rights movement was the backdrop for my generation growing up. While Perry Mason's judge was an iconic glimpse of possibility to a child, the same small black-and-white screen framed the evening news stories about those courageous southern judges who unflinchingly defied mobs and the rule of the crowd. It was the same grandeur I perceived in Miss Katz's stories of nuns and priests working with the poor in Latin America, or in news reports about our own parish priest, Father Gigante, whose ministry took him into the blighted streets of the South Bronx. In those times, there seemed no higher purpose than to seek justice on behalf of those denied it.

Out of this tumultuous panorama came one heroic law-yer I would see in the flesh. Campaigning for the presidency, Robert F. Kennedy visited the Bronxdale projects in 1968. I remember pressing my face to the bars on our kitchen win-dow, which overlooked the entrance to the community cen-ter, waiting to catch a peek of him as he passed through the crowd. I was thirteen then. Soon I would be starting high school, getting involved in student government, swept up in our own elections, our poster parties and cafeteria stump speeches. Kennedy gave thrilling voice to the cause of justice for all and to a life lived in the service of that cause. And when, soon after my sighting, he was killed, the silencing of that voice, and the eloquence of those who mourned it, confirmed for me the nobility of his purpose, which I would make my own.

THERE ARE no bystanders in this life. That had been my point about Kitty Genovese's neighbors during my best showing in forensics competition. Our humanity makes us each a part of something greater than ourselves. And so my heroes were never solitaries. The figure of the lone visionary that enthralls so many young people in their own feelings of isolation never called to me. My heroes were all embedded in community. And the will to serve was first stirred by the wish to help my community.

When I got to Princeton, I saw right away that a sense of belonging would not come easily. The community was much bigger than any I had known, bound by its own traditions, some of them impenetrable to women and minorities. And so I found my place where I could, working with Acción Puer-torriqueña and the Third World Center. Through those associations came my efforts at the Trenton Psychiatric Hospital and my most formative experience of doing for others. Near as it was to Princeton, Trenton could not have been farther in human terms, a world apart from the certainties of privilege. But even by the standards of that afflicted city, the patients I served were vulnerable in the extreme: confused; distanced from whatever ties of family or friendship might have once sustained them; and, for want of a common language, cut off even from those looking after them. My outrage at their abandonment made palpable an emergent awareness that my community extended well beyond the place I came from, the people I knew.

While I was at Yale, the South Bronx was in the news again. President Carter paid a visit in 1977, the news cameras framing him against a moonscape of charred buildings, piled rubble, a neighborhood shattered by unemployment and other economic ills. The motorcade pulled up within sight of where Abuelita and my parents had lived when I was born, but until I had seen the place at the remove of the television cameras, I couldn't really see it. When you live in the midst of such decay, everyday life renders it almost invisible. Somehow communities continued to function amid their own ruins, and though this was perhaps America's worst urban catastrophe, it was hardly the only scene of desolation. Civil society, though carefully ordered by its laws, had nonetheless left a huge number of its members stranded. It was to the rescue of such communities that I first felt myself summoned, believing that the law must work for all or it works for none.

There were those at Princeton and Yale who, coming from such places as I had come from, resolved never to look back. I don't judge them. A degree from an Ivy League college or a top law school is assumed to guarantee entry to a world of plenty, and nothing obliges you to look back on what you've worked hard to escape. But I didn't see good fortune as a chance to write my own ticket; my sense of it remained as something entrusted to me, not given outright; and I would have enjoyed no peace of mind until I'd found some worthy use for it. My chance encounter with Bob Morgenthau over the cheese table would have led nowhere if I hadn't been deeply primed for what he offered. It was not what most of my classmates were looking for, but I could see that it fit into the scheme I imagined. Now, having completed that part of the journey, I was only more convinced that nothing had happened by chance.

All that remained to be seen was how far along the next step would take me.

Twenty-Seven

SHEA STADIUM, the 1986 World Series. The Mets and the still-cursed Red Sox are tied in a tense tenth inning of play that has the crowd on their feet cheering, first for one side, then the other, like kids on a wild seesaw ride.

The real drama, however, is happening in the parking lot, where I'm on the back of a motorcycle, wearing a bulletproof vest, a walkie-talkie screeching in my ear, in pursuit of a truck full of counterfeit goods. We're doing fifty, then sixty, circling the lot like a racetrack, when the truck dodges around a corner. It's a dead end, a concrete cul-de-sac, and in just a moment he's spun around and is barreling straight for us. My driver's about to bolt, but I tell him, "Stay put, he won't hit us. We'll stop him right here." This guy's not crazy, I'm thinking. But he could be, or maybe just panicked. Whatever the case, he's speeding up. Next thing I know, he's got half his wheels up on the concrete wall beside us, like a stuntman riding the wall of death—can you even do that in a truck? Before I know it, he's slipped past us, doing almost ninety in the opposite direction. Enough. Does someone have to die for a load of fake Mets caps, cheap shirts, and souvenirs?

What am I even doing here?

Good question. After I worked through the cases that Bob Morgenthau assigned me as inducement to remain at the DA's Office, it was finally time to leave. Believing that economic development was the only real cure for so many of the ills plaguing poor communities, I thought commercial law would prove useful. I was also open to something in international law, an interest since my days at Yale. One thing I knew for certain: I wanted to continue doing trial work, having learned to love my days in the courtroom.

I also knew very well what I didn't want: the life of a cubicle-encased cog in the machinery of a large firm. The practice that kept associates in the library for years, hoisting papers up the layers of organization to a partner at the apex of responsibility still appealed to me about as much as working in a coal mine. As I had when looking at opportunities after Yale, I would aim for a smaller firm where I might grow more quickly into a substantial role. But as I interviewed, I found that size was no guarantee of ethos. Small firms were often spin-offs that not only poached clients from but also reproduced the culture of the larger firms where their partners had started their careers.

One that stood out as an exception was Pavia & Harcourt, a tiny firm by New York standards, barely thirty lawyers when I was interviewing in 1984. Its founder, a Jewish refugee from Italy during World War II, had built its reputation on representing elite European business interests in the United States. Much of the firm's work related to finance and banking, to licensing of trademarks and distribution of products, and the diverse range of legal tasks attending international trade and business operations.

Arriving for my first interview, I was struck by the aura of the place—a midtown oasis of restrained elegance. George Pavia, the founder's son and now managing partner, was said to be fond of continuity, and the decorum of the offices befitted a roster of clients whose names were synonymous with European luxury and high style: Fendi, Ferrari, Bulgari . . . Conversations shifted constantly between English, Italian, and French. It was hard to imagine an atmosphere more remote from that of the DA's Office.

In spite of the old-world ambience, the firm was ahead of its time in welcoming women. There were two among the nine partners at a time when it was rare to find even one in the upper echelons of big Manhattan firms. This one was exceptional in its organization too: associates worked directly with partners in two-person teams that made mentoring natural. It was a situation where I could learn quickly and, I hoped, quickly advance.

I interviewed many times over, meeting with each of the nine partners and all of the litigation associates. The positive impressions I was forming seemed to be mutual. It was clear that my trial experience appealed greatly and would fill an immediate need. A degree from Yale didn't hurt. But at some point my progress seemed to lose momentum inexplicably, and I found myself waiting for a call that didn't come. Meanwhile, interviews with other firms only made it clearer where I really wanted to be. Pressing the headhunter who had connected us, I learned that George Pavia feared I would quickly get bored with the work of a first-year associate—the position they were hiring for—and move on.

Be diplomatic but direct, I told myself. I don't tend to bang people over the head, but some situations require a bit of boldness. I asked for another meeting and once again found myself ushered into that serene nest lined with Persian carpets and delicately etched views of old Genoa.

"Mr. Pavia, I understand that you have some hesitations about hiring me. Are you comfortable talking about it?"

"Yes, of course." He explained his concerns. They were valid, I acknowledged, and then laid out my own position: Never having practiced civil law, I had a lot to learn. As long as I was learning, there was no chance of boredom. As I became more familiar with the work, one of two things would happen. Either I'd still be struggling to keep up—still no chance of boredom, although I probably wouldn't last at the firm. Or else they would recognize what I was capable of and give me more responsibility. I didn't see how they could lose. I made clear that I had no reluctance about accepting the starting salary of a first-year associate—a fraction of what I could expect from a large firm—as long as he was willing to increase it when my work warranted it.

The bonus and raise that followed my first year-end review were huge, and by the second review my salary was up to standard.

MY FIRST CASES at Pavia & Harcourt involved customer warranty disputes and problems with real estate leases. The work of a beginning associate typically involved eclectic and sometimes marginal legal work for clients the firm represented in more crucial aspects of their business. It did, however, draw on skills that were second nature to a prosecutor. Within my first couple of days on the job, a colleague who sat within earshot of my phone calls let it be known to another litigation associate, who then spread the word, that

I was "one tough bitch" who could not be pushed around by an adversary.

I was shaken to hear myself so harshly categorized. Trying case after case by the seat of your pants at the DA's Office, you develop a bravado that can seem abrasive to lawyers who have no acquaintance with that world. It was a kind of culture shock in both directions. The great distance from the grimy halls of Centre Street to our genteel bower on Madison Avenue made itself known in other small ways, too. A gift from a grateful client, for instance, did not have to be returned in the presence of a witness—a nice perk I didn't expect.

"You're in private practice now, Sonia. There's no threat of corruption," counseled David Botwinik, the partner I turned to—indeed, we all turned to—for advice on any question of ethics. I called him the Rabbi. It was okay to accept a gift, he said, though allowing that "in the ten years I've had them as clients, they never gave *me* a gift."

The more I observed Dave in action, the more profoundly his sense of integrity, fairness, and professional honor impressed me. Just as I had done with John Fried at the District Attorney's Office, I turned to Dave instinctively as a guide. His presence was comforting, avuncular, and expansive in a way that suggested a hearty appetite, though his greatest interests were more of the mind than the body. Blinking owlishly behind his glasses, he stuttered slightly. The hesitation only made his words seem more thoughtfully considered.

In the practice of law, there are rules that establish a minimum standard of acceptable conduct: what the law permits. This is the floor, below which one can't go. There are other rules, not formally encoded, which set the higher bar that defines what's ethical behavior, consistent with respect for the dignity of others and fairness in one's dealings with them. There is no law, for example, saying you can't serve someone court papers at five o'clock on the Friday evening of a long holiday weekend. On the other hand, it's no way to deal honorably with an adversary, who is also a human being, with family, plans, and a personal life outside business. Some lawyers might argue that you owe your client any advantage you can squeeze out of a situation. But underhanded moves invite retaliation in kind, and then both sides end up grappling in the mud. Concerning the intersection of common decency and professional honor, Dave Botwinik's instincts were flawless.

It was through his instruction, too, that I became versed in a complex and little understood area of the law. Dave had specialized for thirty years in representing foreign commodity traders who bought in the American grain markets. He had worked hard to institute more evenhanded arbitration practices that tempered the influence of the big grain houses. Observing how I prepared witnesses and conducted cross-examinations, he asked me to assist him in grain arbitrations, which, though less formally structured than a trial, involved similar strategies.

"I'm too old for this now, you can do it," he said, but I could never have managed without his vast knowledge. He could read between the lines of any contract and see immediately why it was drafted as it was, what issues were important, respectively, to the parties involved. He knew all the players in the industry, which was a man's world entirely. Having begun as the scene of actual farmers bringing grain to market in the nineteenth-century Midwest, the game had evolved into an arcane trade of financial instruments conducted by roomfuls of traders working the phones. Even with my knowledge of admiralty law, I struggled at first to grasp the logic of the business. Finally, it clicked, though it took a late-night cry for help to cut through the Gordian knot of interwoven contracts: We were not actually tracking shipments of grain. The ephemeral exchange of contract rights that began with grain futures intersected with physical reality only at the end of a long chain of transactions.

Only once did I even see the grain. Our client had sent a sample for tests, and it was clear to me that the lab results had been falsified. I knew that a sealed plastic pouch from a private laboratory is no guarantee of a chain of custody when anybody can buy a heat-sealing kit for plastic bags at the supermarket. So I did. During arbitration, at the end of my cross-examination, I asked the witness to open the supposedly inviolate sample of grain. He tore the seal off the plastic bag and found inside it a note in my handwriting: "Bags can be tampered with."

I had learned over the years never to reveal that I could type. In the days before everyone had a personal computer, it was a sure way for a young lawyer to find herself informally demoted to secretary, and I stuck to that rule rigidly. Only once, in the wee hours approaching a morning deadline, did I ask Dave Botwinik to cover his eyes so I could type a final draft. Dave I could trust. He had a deft way of turning aside other lawyers' requests for the only woman in the room to get coffee.

Fran Bernstein, on the other hand, was far above this fray in the gender wars. She could sit for unbroken hours at her Smith-Corona while it rattled like a machine gun, as if her brain were plugged directly into the machine. I was astonished by her writing process, how the pages of elegant prose in no apparent need of polishing just rolled off the type-writer. But it was only one of her remarkable qualities. When she spoke, the flow of her ideas was just as irrepressible, as was the smile that lit up her dimpled face. As a law student, Fran was one of the first women to edit the law review at Columbia, where she later became a lecturer. She had also been among the first women to clerk for a judge on the Second Circuit. Having left work for several years to raise her children, she had returned only part-time. If that had put a crimp in her career, she didn't seem to mind. Though I was at first intimidated in her presence, she would become a true friend and another of my mentors at Pavia & Harcourt.

Fran's effortless eloquence so humbled me that when she first asked me to write a brief, I was paralyzed. For all my success in the courtroom, writing still terrified me. At the DA's Office, I had often volunteered for the overspill of appeals work that the trial bureaus were obliged to help with, just for the chance to work on my writing. Working on Fran's brief, I stayed up all night, my brain contorted in uncomfortable positions, suffering flashbacks to that traumatic summer at Paul, Weiss. The draft that I managed to finish past dawn was subpar. But when I confessed how utterly incompetent I felt, Fran was more than gracious. As a professor, she noted, she had been writing prolifically her whole career. The same role furnished her an instinctive sense of how to encourage someone trying to learn.

The one corner of my life in which I resisted Fran's influence was politics. She earnestly counseled me to join the Republican Party, though not so much for reasons of ideology. Reagan was running for president. Joining the party, she said, was a matter of affiliating oneself with where power in our society was headed, a necessary qualification for the kind of advancement I ultimately sought. I was historian enough to know that the GOP was the party of Lincoln, a connection that once held real meaning. And I was enough of a fiscal conservative to appreciate what Fran admired about Republican economic policy. But I couldn't see why those ideas had to be wed to the social views the party was now espousing. New York had produced some exceptionally progressive Republican leaders, Nelson Rockefeller having enacted some of the boldest social reforms the state had seen. At any rate, I felt no need to find a label that covered all my opinions, so I registered without any party affiliation. Contrary to Fran's careful calculations, that nonalignment served me well when I later joined the Campaign Finance Board, and in other political encounters since then too.

"WHAT DO YOU KNOW about handbags?" Fran asked me one day.

"Nothing. What's to know?" I was about to become an expert. To start with, Fran explained, a Fendi bag sold for eight hundred to several thousands of dollars. That deserved a double take. My cash, keys, and cigarettes were stashed in a bag that cost all of twenty dollars. She showed me one of the legendary pocketbooks, explained the finer points of stitching technique, how to recognize the quality of the fabric and the hardware—all the details that distinguished the real thing from a knockoff.

Fran had been tracking the development of intellectual property law for several years. It was a new field, as yet barely mentioned in law schools. Although patent and copyright laws were a well-established area of practice, trademarks drew less attention in those years. Meanwhile, fake Gucci and Fendi handbags, counterfeit Rolex and Cartier watches, and gallons of faux Chanel No. 5 were an exploding business on the sidewalks of Manhattan.

Fran presciently understood that the ultimate danger of not defending a trademark was loss of the precious rights to its exclusive use. She set about educating our clients, many of whom were in the business of fashion, creating luxury products whose worth was as tightly bound to the prestige of a name as to the quality of production. Fendi was the first to appreciate the importance of what Fran was trying to do. Cheap knockoffs of Fendi handbags were being sold not only in Chinatown and at flea markets all over the country but on the shelves of a reputable retail chain. Eventually, they showed up on the sidewalk right in front of Fendi's Fifth Avenue store.

Fran decided to educate me as well, because she wanted my help in taking that big retail chain to court. She was handing me books, and we discussed cases that we read together. When the Fendi case came to trial, we were excited to learn that it was assigned to Judge Leonard Sand, who was reputed to be brilliant. He had tried a very contentious case against the City of Yonkers over desegregation—a case that would eventually stretch over decades but was then fresh in the public awareness and especially familiar to me from my work at PRLDEF.

Leading up to the trial, I was in the conference room watching Fran prepare a witness when she was called away to the phone. She asked me to continue in her stead. The Fendi fashion house was very much a family business. Candido Speroni, our expert on the intricacies of Fendi's production processes, was married to one of the five Fendi sisters, each of whom was responsible for a different aspect of the business. Candido's nephew Alessandro Saracino, a young lawyer himself, was acting as interpreter.

Preparing witnesses is an art form. As a prosecutor, you learn that you can't tell witnesses what to say or not to say: they will blurt out the damnedest things when they're put on the spot in court. Instead, the purpose of coaching is to help them understand the reason behind each question so that you're working as a team to communicate their relevant knowledge to jurors. I was deep in the process with Candido, completely focused on the task at hand, when I looked at my watch and realized that Fran had been gone for a very long time indeed. I wondered aloud what had happened to her, and she answered from the corner by the door, "I'm here. I've been watching." After suggesting that we break for lunch, she said to Alessandro, "Please talk to your uncle and ask if he'll agree . . . Sonia should be the one to take this to trial, not me. It will cost you much less, but ultimately it's not the money. She's just that good at it!"

And so began my friendship with the Fendis, and the unlikely experience of going to court in front of the esteemed judge Leonard Sand as the only young associate calling the office at the end of each day to tell a senior partner what papers I needed prepared for the next morning.

Fran's handing me the Fendi case as my first crack at civil litigation was a tribute not only to her personal generosity but to the nature of Pavia & Harcourt, where freehanded collaboration was ingrained in the culture. The people I worked with were comfortable enough in their own skin to share clients and knowledge easily. That spirit of transparent teamwork was a joy to me, and I strove to be as open and helpful to others as Fran and Dave were to me. One young associate who struggled with dyslexia was as awed by my reading speed as I was by Fran's rapid-fire writing skills. "Sonia, you just inhaled that article as fast as you could turn the pages!" he moaned. But he had a reliable knack for spotting what was likely to be most useful, and so we often worked in tandem hacking through the dense undergrowth of required reading, swapping observations and ideas.

In this comradely environment, I learned to be more attentive to how I was perceived by colleagues. That initial impression of "one tough bitch" had mostly faded with experience but would resurface now and again when someone new joined us. Theresa Bartenope was hired as a secretary for a different department on the far side of the building, but I lured her into becoming my paralegal in the intellectual property practice. That meant I was often calling over the crackly intercom, "Theresa, I need you in my office." She would appear at my door a few minutes later, panting from the sprint, hands shaking, hives spreading up her neck. What's with her? I wondered. After she'd withdrawn to her side of the building, people in the hallway burst out laughing at the spectacle. Finally, someone clued me in, and I called Theresa in again, this time more gently: "Theresa, why are you so scared of me? I don't bite."

When I'm focused intensely on work, I become oblivious to social cues, or any cues for that matter. I block out the entire universe beyond the page in front of me or the issue at hand. Colleagues who knew me well didn't take it personally. In fact, they sometimes found it convenient. Hallway conversations could be carried on right outside my door, because I was the only person impervious to distraction, completely unaware. The same tendency as a prosecutor gave me a reputation—undeserved, I believe—for ruthlessness in cross-examinations. It's not how I mean to be; when I'm concentrating hard and processing information quickly, the questions just shoot out unceremoniously.

Theresa, thank heaven, overcame her fear, and she has since accompanied me on every step of my career. She remains my right hand and protector, the dearest of friends. When I miss something, she's the one who sees it. She's the one who holds a mirror up when she notices me getting intimidating or too abrupt, an effect only amplified by the trappings of my current office. When I am too wrapped up in something, she pulls me up for air and reminds me to be kind.

AS IT HAPPENED, the case I argued against the big retailer was settled mid-trial, but I would continue working closely with Fran Bernstein on intellectual property cases for the Fendis, as well as other clients. Litigation, however, was not an effective remedy to the problem of counterfeit goods sold on the street and in Chinatown; there was no point bringing petty vendors to trial. Instead, trademark owners decided to join forces in applying for a court order permitting us to confiscate the goods and the records related to their production and distribution. In building the case for a seizure order, we worked with private investigators to track down the suppliers funneling knockoffs into New York from several manufacturing points in Asia as well as moonlighting craftsmen in Italy. Investigators would purchase items from vendors at different locations, and we could map connections by matching hardware or fabrics from different lots. Keeping an area under surveillance, they could often identify a warehouse by spotting the runners who moved between that location and the vendors. If we could intercept the contraband at that distribution point, we might even find customs and shipping documents that would lead further up the supply chain.

I showed Fran how to work up an affidavit. She wrote most of the briefs. I loved the investigative work, the challenge of the puzzle, and the thrill ride of the seizure operations. Together we were Cagney and Lacey.

Dempster Leech, our private investigator, had a rumpled little absentminded-professor aspect and hesitant way of speaking that belied his own love of the chase. Through the pungent streets of Chinatown, he led a posse of burly sidekicks, most of them retired or off-duty police officers from beyond the five boroughs. They had to be armed: the street trade in knockoffs was controlled by gangs who, in addition to dealing drugs and whatever else, extorted protection money from the vendors. At a seizure, lawyers for each of the trademark holders were needed on hand to monitor the operation. It was our job to examine the goods and ensure that only counterfeits were taken, that papers were served properly, and that receipts were given for inventory seized. Normally, anyone involved vanished the instant our presence was detected. At the slightest hint of trouble, the glint of a weapon, Dempster would evacuate us quickly. No one wanted heroics. But a few times we brushed too close for comfort.

I was the lead lawyer one afternoon when I saw Dempster running toward me in the hubbub of Canal Street. His lookout had spotted someone leaving a building, pushing a hand truck loaded with boxes. One had fallen off the hand truck, spilling what looked like Fendis. Dempster's men were staking out the building. No windows, but he put his nose to the ground on a loading dock and peeked under the rolling gate that was left open a crack. In the shadows of the room, strewn all over, were hundreds and hundreds of counterfeit handbags. I phoned the judge, and minutes later we had a seizure order.

The place was so full of fake Fendis that after loading up all of Dempster's jeeps, we still had to bring in a trailer truck. Each time we thought we'd cleared the whole lot, another trail of stray bags would lead like bread crumbs to a further stash. The interior of the building, like that of many in Chinatown, was a labyrinthine warren of rooms that connected behind several separate storefronts. What had from the outside looked to be a small stand-alone structure actually stretched across most of the block.

Typically, a few days after a seizure, I would have been back at the courthouse to file an affidavit for the inventory. But on this occasion I had to be elsewhere, and so I sent a young associate who had been with us on the raid. When Tony walked out of the subway stop at Centre Street, a circle of young Asian guys with ominous tattoos closed in around him. "Where's the black-hair lady? Tell her we're looking for her. Tell her we know who she is." Tony wasn't the only one shaken that day. The entire litigation department at Pavia & Harcourt was called to a meeting, the partners aghast. The judge, when informed, was no less horrified, and marshals were dispatched to accompany me whenever I came to the courthouse . . .

The irony was not lost on me: I was now apparently in greater danger representing luxury brands at a genteel law firm than I had ever been prosecuting armed thieves and murderers. Dave Botwinik and some of the other partners argued that we should quit the seizures entirely, and right away. I, like Tony, understood that the risks were very well managed and that the value to our clients was huge. Perhaps we were also enthralled by the excitement: I wasn't ready to retire my bulletproof vest just yet. The debate within the firm was resolved with a lawyerly compromise that made explicit the full extent of risks on any specific operation and ensured there'd be no pressure to participate on anyone who might not care to take them.

WITHIN TWO YEARS of recruiting me to the work on intellectual property, Fran suffered a recurrence of the breast cancer that she had beaten into remission a few years before. The news weighed heavily: her mother, sister, grandmother—virtually every female in her family—had succumbed to the same disease. As her treatment, and the illness itself, progressed, she was less and less present. For a time, I depended on her guidance over the phone and tried to cheer her on through that same thin connection, but she was failing rapidly.

When I was up for partner in my fourth year at the end of 1988, she came into the office for the first time in months to cast her vote. She had lost a lot of weight and was very frail, but her spark was still there. That night, she and her husband, Bob, took me to dinner at La Côte Basque. It was my first time at a restaurant of such stellar opulence, and I was thrilled by the experience, though sad to see that Fran could barely eat. The outcome of the partnership vote was still under wraps, so it wasn't obvious yet that there was reason to party, but Fran couldn't wait. "You'll have to pretend that you don't know what I'm going to tell you, but tonight we celebrate!"

Later, as we stood at the curb while Bob was getting the

car, Fran looked me up and down. "If you're going to become a partner, you'll have to dress the part. Fendi is your client now. You should represent them appropriately. You need to buy a Fendi fur coat."

"Fran, I don't want a fur coat!" She sounded like my mother complaining about the way I dressed. I already had a wonderful relationship with the Fendi family, and it didn't depend on my wearing haute couture. Alessandro, the young lawyer who was apprenticing to the family business, had become a good friend over months of daily phone calls between New York and Rome, at all hours, irrespective of my time zone or his. Eventually, I helped to smooth the way for him and his wife, Fe, to move to the United States, and after some initial reluctance they would become confirmed New Yorkers, deeply in love with their adopted home and passionate in their support of its cultural life.

It was Alessandro's grandmother Adele who, with her husband, had established the Fendi name as the epitome of Italian luxury, quality, and design. It was she too who had groomed each of her five daughters to assume a different facet of the financial or creative management, their husbands in turn also drawn into the family business. Alessandro was therefore perfectly at ease working with assertive women, and I instinctively warmed to a business environment bound together by strong family ties. It was a natural collaboration.

Princeton and Yale had furnished me my first glimpses of how the extremely privileged lived. Working at Pavia & Harcourt would give me an even better look, with invitations to social events hosted by wealthy clients, where a kid from the Bronx would incredulously find herself rubbing shoulders with the likes of Raquel Welch and Luciano Pavarotti. Still, I felt much more like an observer than a participant in the splendor. The Fendis' friendship pulled back the curtain onto a more private world of luxury and exquisite taste. When I visited their place in Rome and vacationed with them across Europe, my eyes were opened not only to the finest of modern Italian design and a glorious classical legacy but to an entirely different sensibility. Spirited through celebrations of theatrical enchantment, I collected dreams to last a lifetime. Perhaps also a certain understanding, and with it the confidence that comes of having seen life from all sides.

What mattered most of all, though, was that they became family. Alessandro is a brother to me. He'll jump to my defense ferociously—I daresay he'd offer to meet you with pistols at dawn if my honor was at stake. I, in turn, wouldn't pause to draw breath before boarding the next flight to be by his side in a moment of need. Just as I never hesitated to invite his parents, Paola and Ciro, to Co-op City for Thanksgiving dinner at my mother's.

Twenty-Eight

A COUPLE OF WEEKS after my celebratory dinner with Fran and her husband, George Pavia called me into his office so he and Dave Botwinik could tell me, this time officially, that the firm's partners had elected me to membership. The good news came with a curious proviso, words that have stuck in my mind. "It's clear that you won't stay in private practice forever," George said. "We know you're destined for the bench someday. Dave is even convinced you'll go all the way to the Supreme Court. But with this offer, we ask only that you remain with us as long as you continue in private practice."

To offer a partnership to someone not planning to stick around was unusually generous, especially in a firm so small that each partner is an integral part of the team. I accepted with enormous gratitude but also obvious mortification at Dave's fantastical prophecy. If he could have known that I'd dreamed of becoming a judge since childhood, I might have taken it as an affectionate but overheated compliment. In fact, though, I had long refrained from verbalizing the ambition, understanding that any federal judgeship would require a rare alignment of political forces, as well as no small bit of luck. Dave may have intuited the direction of my dreams—as I would soon see, there was at least one other thing I kept mum about that was more obvious than I'd imagined—but even so, his talking about the Supreme Court like that made me wince, the way you might when an uncle exaggerates your accomplishments. It was awkward to hear such a naive thought from someone I respected so deeply, and I felt embarrassed for my Rabbi. I also felt strangely exposed standing there as colleagues alluded casually to my secret pipe dream in the same breath they were marking the professional milestone of my making partner, and even more so with the shadow of Fran's death looming.

When she finally lost her fight the following spring, the loss devastated everyone. Each death of someone close to me has come as a slap, reminding me again of my own mortality, compelling me to ask: What am I accomplishing? Is my life meaningful? When Abuelita died, I felt spurred to study even harder in college. When it was Nelson's time, I could no longer put off thinking about life beyond the DA's Office. Fran had entrusted me with the groundbreaking work in intellectual property that would become her legacy, and when she died, I threw myself into it with my best single-mindedness. Still, to see her go at fifty-seven, only one year younger than I am now, fired my habitual sense that I might not have enough time to make a real run at my ultimate goal.

I've lived most of my life inescapably aware that it is precious and finite. The reality of diabetes always lurked in the back of my mind, and early on I accepted the probability that I would die young. There was no point fretting about it; I have never worried about what I can't control. But nor could I waste what time I had; some inner metronome has continued to set a beat I am unable to refuse. Now diabetes has become more manageable, and I no longer fear falling short in the tally of years. But the habit of living as if in the shadow of death has remained with me, and I consider that, too, a gift.

ON A GLORIOUS DAY at the end of June, a group of friends were celebrating my thirty-seventh birthday with a barbecue in my backyard. I was lucky to have stumbled on the apartment right down the block from my old place and Dawn's, lucky to have grabbed it at a discount before the co-op conversion was even concluded, and luckier still that Dave Botwinik helped me find an unusually affordable loan for the down payment. Best of all, the backyard was perfect for parties.

Everyone was taken care of. All their glasses were filled. Let them dance, I thought. Exhausted, I needed to lie down for a few minutes. I didn't feel right, light-headed, but once supine I couldn't get my body to move. Eventually, I managed to drag myself off the bed, opening the screen door to the backyard. But that was as far as I could get. I needed to sit down right there. Fortunately, there was a step. And there was Theresa. She was talking to me, but I couldn't make out the words. She came closer, still talking gibberish. There was something in her hand that I wanted badly. I needed it. I grabbed for it, but my aim was shaky. I smashed the piece of birthday cake into my mouth. Theresa stood there with her own mouth open in shock. I must have looked pretty disconcerting with frosting smeared all over my face.

When I recovered and we talked about what had happened, Theresa told me that although she was vaguely aware that I was diabetic, she had no knowledge of what a sugar

low looked like. Friends who saw me lie down just assumed
that I'd had a few too many. But I was so busy playing host
that I hadn't had even one yet. The card I'd been given as a
child was still in my wallet, carried around for all these years.
I'd made it to my thirty-seventh birthday with no occasion
for someone to pull it out. It said:

I HAVE DIABETES
I AM NOT drunk. If I am unconscious or acting strangely,
I may have low blood sugar.

EMERGENCY TREATMENT
I need sugar immediately. If I am able to swallow, give
me candy, soda pop, fruit juice or table sugar. If I cannot
swallow or do not recover within 15 minutes, call a doctor
or the closest emergency medical help and tell them I have
diabetes.

Very few of my friends were aware of my being a type 1
diabetic and completely dependent on insulin shots. Not that
I was aware of hiding it. I would have said that I was being
politely discreet, but the truth is my secrecy was a deeply
ingrained habit. I was averse to any revelations that might
have seemed a play for pity. And managing this disease all my
life had been the hallmark of the self-reliance that had saved
me as a child, even if it may have partly cost me a marriage.
I didn't need anyone's help with it. But in truth, I was more
vulnerable than I was willing to admit.

The secrecy wasn't simply in my nature. When I was
young, disabilities and illnesses of all sorts were governed by
a code of silence. Such things were private matters, and you
didn't speak about them outside the family. I wouldn't have

dreamed of giving myself a shot in public, though I rarely had to worry about that because I was only taking one shot a day, first thing in the morning. If the situation somehow arose, traveling or spending a night away from home, my mother would tell me to go do it in the bathroom.

When I was a teenager, there was nothing to be gained by advertising that I was carrying around needles and syringes in a neighborhood where so many people were using heroin. Walking to work at Prospect Hospital one day, I tripped and spilled the contents of my bag at the feet of a police officer. There on the sidewalk lay my "works"; I happened to be carrying a syringe and needle, having planned to spend the night at Abuelita's. "Oh, no, no," said the cop incredulously as I explained, scooping everything up as fast as I could with trembling hands. My explanation carried no weight; neither did my bottle of insulin. What crazy story would a junkie come up with next? I had to persuade him to walk with me to the hospital so my supervisor could vouch for me. I was completely terrified: an arrest would have dimmed any hope of college, let alone law school.

By the time I was in college, the condition had seemed to become more of a nonissue, hardly rating a mention to anyone. I continued with the same regimen—one shot a day—no longer checking in at the clinic at Jacobi Medical Center, where I would have become aware of treatment advances. As it was, I still had no more accurate way of testing my blood glucose than those practically useless, delayed-report urine strips. But so long as I continued to eat carefully and mind how I was feeling, I was able to manage. That discipline was easier than the alternative: I hated the heavy lethargy that came with a blood sugar spike; and the effects of a dip—sweats, trembling, and disorientation—were unpleasant enough that I was quick to answer them with extra sugar.

It didn't occur to me, however, that my own body might be changing. Subtle hormonal shifts, long after the turbulence of puberty, can affect blood sugar levels. Exercise can make a difference too, speeding up the absorption of the insulin recently injected. Constantly on the move at Princeton, whether bicycling around campus or racing upstairs to class, I was oblivious to how, with these factors added, blood sugar levels could drop so fast that the usual telltale symptoms had no time to register before I was too disoriented to respond.

During my junior year, I started to have trouble waking up in the morning. Once I was so groggy that I managed to take an exam without being fully conscious and even make it back to bed, only to wake up later in a panic that I had missed the test. I still haven't figured out how I could have aced it. Another time I woke up and answered the phone with so little presence of mind that Kevin's mother finally figured out we were sleeping together. And then one morning I didn't wake up at all. If my roommate hadn't circled back to the dorm at an odd time, contrary to habit, she wouldn't have found me unconscious on the bed. After she was unable to rouse me, I ended up in the infirmary for several days.

All through college, law school, and my years at the DA's Office, I would stick with essentially the same regimen I'd had as a child. It wasn't until I reached thirty and settled in Brooklyn that I decided to seek out a specialist in type 1 diabetes. The advances in treatment that had passed me by were significant. I started to catch up, using improved forms of insulin and taking shots twice a day. When my first doctor moved, she referred me to Andrew Drexler, one of the foremost diabetic endocrinologists in the country. Under Andy, now a cherished friend and confidant, my treatment is as good as it gets.

I still use the tried-and-true approach of injecting insulin, though many diabetics today have switched to convenient insulin pens or pumps with computerized controls to adjust dosages continuously during the day. Urine strips are ancient history. In the mid-1980s, I bought my first portable blood glucose meter, which cost what seemed like a fortune at the time. It was four times the size of today's versions, which provide a reading in five seconds. I test my blood sugar and give myself shots five or six times a day now. When deciding what I'm going to eat, I calculate the carbohydrate, fat, and protein contents. I ask myself a litany of questions: How much insulin do I need? When is it going to kick in? When was my last shot? Will I walk farther than usual or exert myself in a way that might accelerate the absorption rate? If I weren't good at math, this would be difficult.

This regimen certainly takes a lot more attention than I gave to the disease when I was young, but it also allows for a much more fine-tuned regulation of my blood sugar levels. The benefit adds up, since the dire complications of diabetes—heart disease, blindness, neuropathy that can lead to amputation of limbs—are mostly the effects of long-term damage caused by chronically high levels. Meticulously keeping mine within normal range gives me an excellent chance of a normal life span. No matter how careful I am, though, a fever or infection can send my sugars soaring. Trauma or extreme stress has the same effect.

Even with the most conscientious monitoring, blood sugar can swing suddenly in a way that is a threat to one's life not in the future but in the immediate present. That's what happened the day I grabbed that hunk of birthday cake from Theresa. Surprises can insinuate themselves insidiously. I knew, for instance, how much carbohydrate was in a meal at a typical Chinese restaurant, but one time my calculations were thrown perilously off by a very different style of cooking at a Szechuan place of great refinement. Jet lag or losing track of shifts in time zone probably figured in another crisis. I'd flown to Venice for the wedding of a friend, an Italian lawyer who had worked for a time at Pavia & Harcourt. Somehow, after I checked into my hotel room, my blood sugar dropped precipitously, and I passed out.

Fortunately, Alessandro and his wife, Fe, had come to Venice for the wedding too. They realized something was wrong when I didn't show up on time. After trekking across the city to my hotel, Alessandro threatened to break down my door if the concierge didn't put aside hotel policy and unlock it. Orange juice was administered, an ambulance was called, which was in fact a boat and too big to squeeze into our back-alley canal. So a Venetian stretcher, which is to say a chair on poles, was provided, and I was conveyed, variously in and out of consciousness, to a hospital that was really a nursing home in an ancient convent, with facilities to match. I tried to show the doctor how to use my fancy glucose meter, but he was having none of it. "I am the doctor; you are the patient," he insisted, as Alessandro translated with chagrin.

We laughed at the story afterward, especially as recounted with Alessandro's gloriously expressive Italian gestures, conjuring images of Fe in a stunning blue evening gown and himself in black tie preparing to batter my door down, or the ultimate indignity of having the Italian hospital staff refer to the two of them as "the Americans."

Although they stick out in my memory, such episodes didn't happen very often and have been rare in the last decade, as technology has improved and my body has settled into middle age. Still, each time I found myself in a blood sugar crisis, I couldn't help but notice that some unlikely intervention had saved my life, whether a friend just happening by or phoning out of the blue, or, one time, Dawn's little Rocky, who, finding me unconscious, barked furiously, refusing to be calmed, until he drew attention where it was needed. Contemplating such good fortune reinforced my sense that Abuelita was still watching over me. But I decided that was no basis to push my luck. Though the Fendis and I would, for years to come, dine out mirthfully on the story of the Venetian affair, the bald truth is that if Alessandro had not been aware of my diabetes, I'd be dead. It was the final confirmation I needed that for safety's sake I had to be open about my condition. And since taking my present job these many years later, when the danger seems to have receded, I have another good reason to claim the disease publicly. I don't know whether they still give diabetic children a list of professions they can't aspire to, but I'm proud to offer living proof that big dreams are not out-of-bounds.

THERE IS ONE PERSON with whom I have deferred opening up as long as possible. The stories of those close calls suggestive of my nine lives have never been mentioned to my mother. I'll have to deal with the fallout when she reads this book. Her guilt, pity, sadness, and ultimately fear of my disease are still beyond all reason, and at times have driven me nuts. But then, any problem of mine she has discovered belatedly has resulted in the same hysteria. Junior reports she once called him to complain that I don't tell her what's happening. He answered her far better than I could have: "Sonia's never going to tell you anything, Mami, because you always over-react." Even more important, he told her, he didn't know a happier person than his sister. "Sonia lives her life fully. If she dies tomorrow, she'll die happy. If she lives the way you want her to live, she'll die miserable. So leave her alone, okay?"

I love my brother dearly. He knows me in ways the rest of the world never could. We've always watched out for each other. His kids still crack up whenever they hear me calling him Junior—he's Juan to everyone else now—but he'll always be Junior to me, even if he's no longer such a nuisance.

Mami hung up on him that time, he said. I could picture her sitting there in Co-op City, fuming in her jungle of house-plants, stems shooting up to the ceiling, the vines clinging to the corners, fringing the picture windows. That message would not go over easily, but eventually it would be received.

THE STORY OF my secrecy and the self-reliance that pro-duced it does not begin and end with my diabetes. But I've come to see that it does begin and end with my mother, who became my most constant emotional paradigm, informing my character for good and for ill, as well as the character of my relations with her.

Many times I felt there was a wide moat separating me from the rest of the world, in spite of my being, by all accounts, a great listener to all my friends. They felt free to tell me their troubles. Like my mother, I would suspend judgment, feel their pain, perhaps even point out a fact they might have overlooked: I have a knack for translating the mysteries of other people's minds and could open their eyes to what the world looked like to their husband, their boss, or their mother. The only trick I couldn't manage was to ask the same of them.

Sharing was not my style; my problems were mine to deal with. Ever since fifth grade, ever since putting behind me the misery and isolation visited upon an alcoholic's family, ever since that cute boy, Carmelo, convinced me that being smart could be cool, I'd surrounded myself with a crowd of friends. And yet inside I remained very much alone. Perhaps even within my marriage, which, for all our mutual regard and affection, had suffered from a certain self-sufficiency of mine that frustrated Kevin. It was not until these years after the DA's Office, as I started making more purposeful strides toward the person I wanted to be professionally, that I could begin to dream of reshaping the person I was emotionally, too. My faith in my potential for self-improvement, which had been the foundation for all my academic and professional success so far, would now be tested in more inaccessible regions of the self. But I was optimistic: if I could help fix your problems, surely I can fix my own.

I'd always believed people can change; very few are carved in stone or beyond redemption. All my life I've looked around me and asked: What can I learn here? What qualities in this friend, this mentor, even this rival, are worth emulating? What in me needs to change? Even as a child, I could reflect that my anger was accomplishing nothing, hurting only myself, and that I had to learn to stop in my tracks the instant I felt its surge. Learning to be open about my illness was a first step, and it taught me how admitting your vulnerabilities can bring people closer. Friends want to help, and it's important to know how to accept help graciously, just as it's better to accept a gift with "Thank you" than "You shouldn't have."

If there's a measure of how well I've succeeded in this self-transformation, it's that very few of my friends—even those who have known me the longest—can remember the person I was before undertaking the effort. Such is the nature of familiarity and memory. They also swear that they've always known about my diabetes and claim memories of seeing me give myself shots long before I ever did so openly. But there is no better indicator of progress, or cause for pride, than the thaw in relations with my mother.

Mami gone, checked out, the empty apartment. Her back to me, just a log in the bed beside me as a child. Mami, perfectly dressed and made up, like a movie star, the Jacqueline Kennedy of the Bronxdale Houses, refusing to pick me up and wrinkle her spotless outfit. This was the cold image I'd lived with and formed myself in response to, unhappily adopting the aloofness but none of the glamour. I could not free myself from its spell until I could appreciate what formed it and, in its likeness, me.

There was so much about my mother I simply hadn't known. When she was struggling through her nursing degree at Hostos Community College, terrified of failure, facing every written exam like a firing squad, she had told me a little about her school days in Lajas and San Germán. About her fear of being ridiculed by classmates, scolded by teachers, her certainty that she was stupid. Beyond that I knew practically nothing about her childhood. Her most telling stories would trickle out slowly, in dribs and drabs, but it was only when I had the strength and purpose to talk about the cold expanse between us that she confessed her emotional limitations in a way that called me to forgiveness.

"How should I know these things, Sonia? Who ever

showed me how to be warm when I was young? I was lonely; I was angry at Mayo. What else did I see?"

My anger at her would still surge from time to time, and when it did, I would call on this awareness: she had her own story, pieces that were missing in her own life. I called too on a talisman of memory, one I could grasp like the smooth beads of a rosary. I'd return to it like some childhood storybook I knew by heart but of which I never tired. It was the memory of those summer nights when I woke in a terrible sweat, and Mami would towel me down with a cool wet cloth, whispering softly, so as not to wake Junior, because this was for me, my time. The little fan whirring away; my neck turning cool as the moisture evaporated; my mother's hand on my back.

I wouldn't suffer the same lack of examples as my mother. Friends would show me how to be warm, and I would learn by allowing others a chance to do for me as they had let me do for them, until no one remembered a time when it was not that way. As I learned, I practiced on my mother—a real hug, a sincere compliment, an extra effort to let down my guard—and miraculously she softened in turn, out of instinct long dormant, even if she didn't quite know what was going on. Opening up, I came to recognize the value of vulnerability and to honor it, and soon I found that I wasn't alone even on this journey. My mother was taking every step alongside me, becoming more affectionate and demonstrative herself, the person who, given a chance, she might have been.

KILEY RUNS to greet me, jumps into my embrace. She throws her skinny little arms around my neck, squeezes her

tiny, birdlike three-year-old body to mine in crazy dispro-
portion. And without warning my heart bursts, tears well
in my eyes. A tenderness I have no name for rushes like a
drug through my veins, as I realize that the absence of human
touch has been, for so long, a burden carried unwittingly.

I wrote myself a prescription for hug therapy. I told each
of the children in my life that I wasn't getting enough hugs.
Tommy, Vanessa, Zachary . . . "Would you help me out by
giving me a hug whenever you see me?" Kiley didn't need telling, of course, but every one of the others got it instantly. In
this, the wisdom of toddlers is unassailable. The hugs came.
And feeling flowed that had never come so easily before.
Even as the kids grew into gangly teenagers, the hugs never
stopped. Younger siblings, John and Kyle, would join the
cause as the years went by.

What I've learned from children I've been able to give
back to adults. The stroke on the arm that says I understand,
the welcome hug, the good-bye kiss, the embrace that lingers
that much longer in a time of sorrow. I've discovered the palpable difference between such acts as mere gestures and as
sluices of true feeling between two people.

WE WERE IN the dressing room, and I was getting out of
my jeans, ready to attack the pile of possibilities that my
friend Elaine had gathered off the racks, when she dropped
the armful of clothes and doubled over, hooting hysterically.
I was afraid she would bring down the flimsy partition walls.

A client of Pavia & Harcourt's who'd become a very close
friend, Elaine Litwer was a gutsy and street-smart survivor
of extreme poverty and a colorful family from the Lower
East Side. She talked nonstop, was never wrong, and suffered

no fools in wielding her merciless wit. Many weekends we'd prowl the shops and hang out like a pair of teenage girls.

"Sonia! My God! Who buys your underwear? Your mother?"

"As a matter of fact, in this case, yes."

"We have to fix that right away!"

Any offense I might have taken at Elaine's uncensored mockery was offset by a discreet satisfaction at the thought of Mami's having, for once, been knocked off her pedestal as a fashion authority. I was happy to let Elaine help me choose some age-appropriate undergarments.

This was part of a much bigger project. Elaine was teaching me to shop, to recognize what looks good on me, how color works with skin tone, the drape of a fabric, how the eye follows a line. Alas, it was one subject in which I was not to prove a quick study. But little by little I developed confidence in my own judgment, and Elaine, bless her, found a way to make this process fun. Until she took me in hand, I'd hated shopping and confined myself to mail-order catalogs rather than suffer the smirks of salesgirls and the taunts of full-length mirrors. And even when I did something right, my mother's idea of encouragement was scarcely encouraging. Any compliment would be immediately qualified: "That looks nice, Sonia, but now you need to paint your nails."

But to be perfectly honest, it wasn't all my mother's fault. Dressing badly has been a refuge much of my life, a way of compelling others to engage with my mind, not my physical presence. I'm competitive enough that I'll eventually withdraw from any consistently losing battle. Elaine gave me the precious gift of showing me that it didn't need to be that way. I am a woman; I do have a feminine side. Learning to enjoy it would not diminish any other part of me.

She looked at me with her wide-eyed, wicked grin. "I would never in a million years have chosen that for you, Sonia, but it looks great on you. You see? You're becoming your own person."

NOT EVERY RELATIONSHIP ENDS with such mutual respect and dignity as Kevin and I somehow salvaged from our youthful mistakes. I would discover what it is to go down in flames romantically, disappointment that shakes your foundations. The despair would pass, but until it did, friends came to my rescue, just as they had after my divorce. Being left alone in my misery was never an option. Elaine's taking me shopping every weekend was part of a campaign undertaken in the aftermath of one ill-fated romance. Alessandro and Fe, too, have been known to jump into the breach of a breakup: "Mama says you must come to Ibiza with us for vacation."

One remedy for heartache I concocted on my own was learning how to dance. I scheduled the lessons, rolled up the carpet, and committed myself to learning salsa. No longer would I sit there like a potted plant watching others on the floor. The gawky, uncoordinated Sonia would make peace with herself in motion. I may never have a natural rhythm, but I know that the knees make the hips move, and I would learn to read a partner so well that I can now follow like an expert.

I still can't sing to save my life—a slight hearing impairment doesn't help matters—but after unnatural amounts of rehearsal to memorize where each syllable falls, I can now get up onstage at a holiday party and hold my own in a musical skit.

I finally learned how to swim, too. Okay, maybe not with

athletic grace, but I can swim twenty laps without stopping. I can jump off the boat with the best of them, and no one will ever need to rescue me. I never imagined that even later in life I would learn to throw a baseball, but really you never know. During my first term on the Supreme Court, I practiced twenty minutes every afternoon for weeks so I could be ready to throw the first pitch at Yankee Stadium. Not from the mound, of course, but I did send it straight down the middle. Exercise of all kinds has been a joyous discovery, and I've even biked a century tour. It would take years, but now when I look in the mirror, what I see is really not bad. It's true, I love food too much; my weight goes up and down. But when time permits, I actually enjoy the effort of keeping it off.

One reckoning with my physical self would prove harder than all the others. I had been a smoker since high school, burning through three and a half packs a day for much of my life. I made my first serious attempt at quitting in my final year at law school: every time I felt the urge, I ran around the block, often with Kevin and Star chugging alongside in solidarity. Going cold turkey during exams may sound like a needlessly brutal rigor, but in retrospect it seems less perversely self-punishing than lighting up again two years later when Kevin and I split. There would be further attempts, using various methods, including hypnosis, but nothing worked for good until I saw little Kiley holding a pencil between two fingers, blowing imaginary smoke rings. The guilt of endangering the health of a loved one is by far the best motivation I've discovered.

I checked into a five-day residential program and even wrote a long love letter, saying farewell to what had been my most constant companion for so many years. It was another heartbreak, but I comforted myself by imagining that if I were ever to become a judge someday, I couldn't very well be calling a recess every time I needed a cigarette. And it worked. I remain a nicotine addict, a fact that inspires a certain compassion for the addictions of others, but I haven't had a cigarette since. I no longer worry about slipping, but I do fantasize that I might indulge one last smoke on my deathbed, just as Abuelita did.

FERRARI WAS a client of mine, and I was invited to take one of the original Testarossas for a spin. The twelve-cylinder was a marvel of technology that Ferrari had developed for the racetrack, packed into the fastest street-legal car ever built: zero to sixty miles per hour in under five seconds, and a price tag of about a quarter of a million dollars.

Negotiating hills, winding through fields and scattered woods, I was fearless, even as I thrilled to the feeling of such vast power under perfect mechanical control. As the hills rose and fell and the woods blurred past, other scenes appeared to my mind's eye like so many glimpses in the rearview mirror. I remembered our useless car in the projects, my anger that Papi wouldn't drive . . . A dozen or more of us piled into Gallego's jalopy for a picnic, like a crazy *guagua* . . . Kevin lying on his back at the curb all summer long as I read aloud to him from the manual . . . The relief I'd felt that first time when, eerily, I got the clutch to engage, and I knew I'd be able to drive my things home to Mami's in Co-op City . . . Then Abuelita calling out to everyone, *¡Vámonos de parranda!*—a joyride at midnight! It was broad daylight, but for a long moment as the road rolled under the Testarossa, her smile didn't fade.

Twenty-Nine

SOMETIMES, no matter how long we've carried a dream or prepared its way, we meet the prospect of its fulfillment with disbelief, startled to see it in daylight. In part that may be because, refusing to tempt fate, we have never actually allowed ourselves to expect it.

In 1990, I flew to London with Alessandro, Fe, his parents, and his sister for a Boxing Day celebration. When I got back to work after the Christmas holiday, my office looked like the office of someone who had been let go. The towers of paper that normally obscured my desktop had vanished, exposing a dark polished wood grain I'd all but forgotten about. Upon it sat only one document for my attention: an application form for the position of a federal district court judge. This was obviously Dave Botwinik's doing. I grabbed the form and charged the short distance down the hallway to his office.

"Dave, come on."

"It's from Senator Moynihan's judicial selection committee. They vet the recommendation he makes to the president. Fill it out."

"Are you crazy? I'm thirty-six years old!"

"Humor me, Sonia. They're looking for qualified Hispanics. You're not only a qualified Hispanic but eminently qualified, period." He promised to give me back my files if I filled it out, which I promised to do before counting the pages: it was endless. But Dave would not be deterred: he volunteered his assistant as well as my own, plus the help of a paralegal, whatever I needed to get the job done. I had long suspected that Dave Botwinik's ambitions on my behalf were partly a displacement of ambitions he'd once had for himself. Until then, I'd just ignored it whenever he raised the topic. But this time he was showing a whole new level of determination, and he was not the only one on the case.

A few weeks earlier, I had shared a cab with Benito Romano after a PRLDEF board meeting. Having served as interim U.S. attorney when Rudy Giuliani quit the post to run for mayor, Benito had himself been approached by a colleague on Senator Moynihan's search committee. He had declined the offer, he said, but given them my name.

"Why not you?" I asked.

"I have a wife, Sonia. I have kids. How am I going to put them through college on a judge's salary?" It's a very real problem that has discouraged many a talented person from considering the bench. The pay cut I would suffer as a young partner wouldn't be as severe as a more experienced lawyer's, and having no children spared me the impossible choice. But this calculus didn't alter my feeling of reaching for too much too soon.

Even with help, the application took the better part of a week to complete. I had to account for every jot of my adult life, it seemed, as well as furnishing current addresses for each landlord, supervisor, judge, and legal adversary who had ever crossed my path. At least the financial information was easy; I still had little to report on that front. Beyond the summary of professional experience typical of job applications, this document would be the starting point for an investigation scouring my past for any ethical lapse. But I wasn't daunted by that. I soon realized that, perhaps more than I would ever have admitted, most of the choices I'd made over the years have anticipated this very moment.

I heard back from the senator's committee very quickly after submitting the application, the interview scheduled within a couple of weeks. If I still couldn't take the whole business quite seriously, I nevertheless prepared as if my life depended on it. When I had gone for recruiting interviews at Yale, it never occurred to me to do research in advance or rehearse the answers to likely questions. The entire culture of the law school was geared to the law firms that were the most sought-after recruiters, to answering the very sorts of questions most likely to come up in such an interview, and to knowing those one ought to ask. Years later, having waltzed into an interrogation for a very different sort of position at a federal agency in Washington, I would realize, only too late, that it was not the sort of cakewalk a Yale JD could expect interviewing with a big Manhattan firm. I would never make that mistake again.

So I prepared as thoroughly as I would have done for a criminal prosecution, reading whatever I could find and seeking out colleagues and any friends and family of theirs with the least experience of the judicial nomination process: What kinds of questions could I expect to be asked? What objections might I need to rebut? I was no longer afraid of the obvious one I myself first anticipated: "Aren't you too young to be applying for this position?" I'd certainly presumed so, but a bit of digging revealed I would not be the youngest to hold it. Becoming a judge in one's thirties was uncommon but not unheard of, and I would have the names of those exceptions at my fingertips. And also one ready truth: although wisdom is built on life experiences, the mere accumulation of years guarantees nothing.

Judah Gribetz, a childhood friend of David Botwinik's and long-time adviser to Senator Moynihan, chaired the committee, with whom I met in the conference room of a downtown law firm. I was facing some fifteen people around the table, most but not all of them men and lawyers. One of the few I recognized was Joel Motley, son of Constance Baker Motley, the first African-American woman to be appointed a U.S. district court judge. As questions flew at me from all sides, the answers were flowing easily, and I was pleased with how well I'd prepared. Then Joel asked one I'd never predicted. "Don't you think learning to be a judge will be hard for you?" I took a breath to gather my thoughts, and then the answer poured out: "I've spent my whole life learning how to do things that were hard for me. None of it has ever been easy. You have no idea how hard Princeton was for me at the beginning, but I figured out how to do well there and ended up being accepted to one of the best law schools in the country. At Yale, the DA's Office, Pavia & Harcourt—wherever I've gone, I've honestly never felt fully prepared at the outset. Yet each time I've survived, I've learned, and I've thrived. I'm not intimidated by challenges. My whole life has been one. I look forward to engaging the work and learning how to do it well."

When the discussion turned technical, my trial experience held up very well under scrutiny. As a state prosecutor, I'd tried many more cases than an attorney working in the federal system would have done. We talked at length about the child pornography and Tarzan Murderer cases, and I explained those investigations and the legal strategies employed. What about the areas where I lacked experience? There was much about criminal law at the federal level that I would need to learn, though my work at Pavia & Harcourt had included several hearings and a trial in federal court on trademark cases; I was at least familiar with the differences in the evidentiary rules. More important, I'd studied the resources that a novice judge would inevitably rely on—the readings, the seminars, the Federal Judicial Center. I might not know the procedural particulars as well as some, but I knew perfectly well where the issues lay. I cited the new Federal Sentencing Guidelines as an example. You can always look up answers to specific questions in specific situations, I said, so long as you have enough experience to know that a question exists. Learning the rules isn't hard when you're aware there's a rule to learn.

We talked about my community service, which I knew was especially important to Senator Moynihan. My work at PRLDEF was clearly a point in my favor, as was the Campaign Finance Board and my other pro bono activities. As I sat there fielding questions, I dared to believe that the interview was actually going very well. With each question, I could see the pitch coming toward me as if in slow motion. I was relaxed but also alert, centered but agile, ready to move in any direction. If I was not picked, I knew it wouldn't be because I had blown the interview. And that sense alone made the experience worth it.

But the whole process still seemed like make-believe, even when Senator Moynihan's office phoned soon after, inviting me to meet him in Washington. He turned out to be so forthright and gregarious that I warmed to him at once. We talked about Puerto Rico and the challenges facing the Puerto Rican community in New York, our conversation ranging widely from Eddie Torres (a judge who also wrote crime novels that the senator admired), to getting out the Latino vote, to the eternal question of the island's status. Here, clearly, was a scholar as well as a politician, someone who understood the sociology as well as the policy issues while also possessing the social skills of a master diplomat. I was enjoying our talk so much I would have forgotten entirely about being on the hot seat were it not for the continual interruptions of phone calls and questions from his aides. Each time, he filled me in afterward on the issue he was dealing with, and we would continue, weaving the new theme into the conversation. There was a gracious art to this seemingly effortless chat and to the way he exerted his prodigious intellect, never to intimidate, but rather to invite you to engage him at whatever level you found comfortable.

After more than an hour of this, I sensed that we were coming to an end and prepared to thank him before going off to wait out the predictably interminable period of deliberation I'd already girded myself for. But the senator had one more surprise in store, saying, "Sonia, if you accept, I would like to nominate you as a district court judge in New York." He warned me that the confirmation process would not be easy. The Bush administration was not in the habit of smiling on recommendations from a Democrat; on principle, it would fight any candidate he proposed. "It may take some time," he said, "but I'll make you a promise: If you stay with me, I'll get you through eventually. I won't give up."

Then he asked if I was willing to hold up my side of the bargain: Was I prepared to spend a good portion of my remaining professional life as a judge? I was stunned. Until that moment, I had still not allowed myself to believe lest I awaken from this daydream. But here was Senator Moynihan looking at me, waiting for an answer. "Yes!" With all my heart, yes.

I floated out of the Russell Senate Office Building and wandered down the street in a daze. After a couple of blocks I saw a monumental flight of stairs, familiar white columns: the Supreme Court Building glowing serenely, like a temple on a hill. There could not have been a more propitious omen. I felt blessed in that moment, blessed to be living this life, on the threshold of all I'd ever wanted. There would be plenty of time soon enough to deal with my insecurities and the hard work of learning this new job. For the moment, though, I just stood there, dazzled at the sight and glowing with gratitude—until reality intervened: Where could I find a cab to the airport?

All during the flight home my mind was racing through the practical considerations. How would all this change my life? Would I need to move to Manhattan? How much, exactly, does a judge make anyway? I was still immersed in such lofty considerations when I got off the plane and noticed all the people making a big fuss over some celebrity who had arrived on the same flight. I'd been too distracted to notice that I'd been sitting next to Spike Lee for over an hour.

MY MOTHER AND OMAR had been together for a few years at that point. At first she'd told me only that she was renting my old bedroom to this man. Then, meeting him a couple of times on visits home, I sensed that there was more to the story than they were saying. Arriving late one night, I surprised them kissing in the lobby. "Do you have something to tell me?" I asked. Mami was flustered, beaming, embarrassed, and clearly very happy.

"We were going to tell you, Sonia. I just didn't know how." As I got to know Omar over time, I fully approved of my mother's choice. Now they were sitting side by side on the couch in my living room in Brooklyn, and I was the one who had to figure out how to break the news.

"Mami, Omar, I'm going to tell you something, but you have to promise to keep it a secret. There won't be a public announcement for a couple of weeks, but I've been given permission to tell you." I asked if they knew who Senator Patrick Moynihan was. Tentative nods. "The senator is going to nominate me to become a U.S. district court judge in Manhattan."

"Sonia, how wonderful! That's terrific news!" As always, Mami's initial reaction was enthusiasm. She didn't always understand fully what my news meant, but as a matter of maternal principle she was a loyal cheerleader. Omar too congratulated me earnestly. Then the questions started.

"So, you're going to earn more money, right?" my mother said.

"Not exactly, Mami. A judge's salary is much less than I'm earning now."

She paused for a long moment. "Well, I guess you'll be traveling a lot, seeing the world?"

"Not really. The courthouse is in downtown Manhattan, and I can't imagine I'll be going anywhere else. Not the way I have at Pavia."

The pauses were growing a little longer. "I'm sure you'll meet interesting people and make friends as nice as the ones you've met at the firm."

I was determined not to laugh. "Actually, the people who

appear before a judge are mostly criminal defendants in serious trouble or people fighting with each other. There are ethical reasons too why I wouldn't be socializing with them."

Silence, and then: "Sonia, why on earth do you want this job?"

Omar, who knew me well by now, came to my rescue. "*Conoces tu hija*. You know your daughter, Celina. This must be very important work." The look on Mami's face carried me back to that moment under the rumbling El train when we shared our uncertainty about what lay ahead of me at Princeton: "What you got yourself into, daughter, I don't know . . ." In truth, I'd had no idea then that Princeton would be only the first stop on a magical ride that by now had already taken me farther than I could have ever foreseen.

Now all I had to do was wait for the political process to run its long and bumpy course. It's the president who appoints federal district court judges. In many states, however, including New York, the senators propose candidates, and the president accepts their suggestions as a courtesy. In a twist special to the Empire State, Senator Moynihan had long before hammered out a bipartisan agreement with his Republican counterpart, Jacob Javits, that would survive turnover in the Oval Office: for every three nominations from a senator of the president's party, a senator from the loyal opposition could offer one. There were several vacancies at the time, and it was Senator Moynihan's turn to submit names to President George H. W. Bush. But the existence of this entente between gentlemen of the Senate didn't oblige the administration to like it or even facilitate the process.

The eighteen months that it took my nomination to clear were an education in the arts of politics and patience. I knew that the delays had nothing to do with me personally. Two interviews with the Justice Department, investigations by various government agencies, and eventually the Senate confirmation hearings had all gone smoothly. No one had voiced doubt about my qualifications or otherwise objected to my appointment. But I was still just one piece on the board among many to be sacrificed or defended in the baroque, unknowable sport that was the biggest game in town and in which procedural delay was a cherished tactic. Through it all, Senator Moynihan was as good as his word, never flagging in his effort or allowing me to give up hope. I tried not to be overly disheartened, but the delay did put me in an awkward limbo at work. I was trying to make a graceful if protracted exit, wrapping up business with clients and making the appropriate handoffs to colleagues, but there was no clear end in sight. I can be patient but not idle, and I still needed to earn a living.

Meanwhile, I would become aware of a chorus of voices rising in my support. The Hispanic National Bar Association lobbied the White House steadily and rallied grassroots support from other Latino organizations. If confirmed, I would be the first Hispanic federal judge in the state's history, a milestone the community ardently wished to achieve (José Cabranes had very nearly claimed the honor in 1979 but was simultaneously nominated for a judgeship in Connecticut and chose to serve there instead, though much later he would take a New York seat on the Second Circuit Court of Appeals). Even before Senator Moynihan had settled on my name for the nomination, a veritable *This Is Your Life* cast of backers came forward: my fellow board members at PRLDEF, Bob Morgenthau and others at the DA's Office, Father O'Hare and colleagues on the Campaign Finance Board, lawyers I'd known through mutual clients. They wrote letters, made phone calls, and volunteered to make the sorts of informal appeals to colleagues that can be persuasive when echoing from many sides. I was astonished to see all the circles of my life telescoping on this one goal of mine, making it seem all the more as if everything until now had been a prelude to this moment.

Finally, on August 12, 1992, the U.S. Senate confirmed my nomination to the District Court for the Southern District of New York, the mother court, the oldest district court in the nation. The public induction ceremony followed in October. Though brief—perhaps all of five minutes—it was far from perfunctory. Every moment of it moved me deeply: donning the black robe, swearing solemnly to administer justice without respect to persons, equally to the poor and the rich, and to perform my duties under the Constitution faithfully and impartially. So help me God. I took, for that occasion only, the traditional newcomer's seat between the chief judge, Charles Brieant, and Judge Constance Baker Motley, the next most senior of the estimable colleagues I was joining. Such ritual was profoundly humbling, signaling as it did the paramount importance of the judiciary as an institution, above the significance of any individual, beyond the ups and downs of history. Whatever I had accomplished to arrive at this point, the role I was about to assume was vastly more important than I was.

The sense of having vaulted into an alternative reality was compounded by no less disorienting changes in my personal life. I moved to Manhattan, because I needed to live within the area of my jurisdiction. Dawn was appalled that I would shatter our neighborhood idyll on account of some minor rule, frequently bent. I feared she would never forgive me for abandoning her in Brooklyn, but for me there was a deep sense of honor at stake. I was becoming a judge! How could

I not follow the rules? I don't claim to be flawless. I'm a New Yorker, and I jaywalk with the best of them. On more than one occasion I may have broken the speed limit. But at that moment in my life, my deep and rational respect for the law as the structure upholding our civilized society was tinted with a rosy glow of irrational emotion. I felt a sense of awe for the responsibility I was assuming, and my determination to show it respect trumped even my loyalty to a wonderful neighborhood and the close company of dear friends.

My mother meanwhile had plans of her own. In what seemed a flight of wild impetuousness, more in keeping with the Celina who'd run off to join the army than the mother I'd known, she decided to move to Florida, leaving me to feel once more, perhaps irrationally for an adult and now a judge, the sting of her abandonment. She and Omar had gone there on vacation the Monday after my induction, and the next thing I knew, Mami was on the phone, telling me in a giddy voice that she'd rented an apartment.

Within days of their return to New York, the apartment in Co-op City was packed up. When the cartons were removed, I stood with Mami in the empty apartment, our voices bouncing off the scuffed walls, the hollowness echoing with so many years, amid a confluence of our tears and memories. We hugged, and then it was good-bye, Mami and Omar driving away.

Before they even reached Florida, I got a phone call from Puerto Rico: Titi Aurora had died. She had gone there to move her husband to a nursing home—the second husband, who was even crazier than the first and who'd entangled her already hard life into still further knots of sadness and exhausting labor. This was not news I could break to Mami over the phone. I needed to get on the next flight to Miami and be with her when she heard it. Titi had fought bitterly with Mami over the move to Florida. They squabbled often over all sorts of small things, but this had become a much deeper rift. To learn that death had cut off any possibility of reconciliation would, I well knew, cause Mami unbearable pain.

I marveled at how two such very different women could live so tightly bound to each other. Affection was not part of the recipe, nor was any emotional expression beyond their habit of snapping at each other. There was no confiding of secrets, no sharing of comfort visible to others. A lesson would emerge for me from their strange sisterhood: the persistence or failure of human relationships cannot be predicted by any set of objective or universal criteria. We are all limited, highly imperfect beings, worthy in some dimensions, deficient in others, and if we would understand how any of our connections survive, we would do well to look first to what is good in each of us. Titi could be disagreeable because her life had been harsh, but she lived it honorably, firmly grounded on a rock-solid foundation of personal ethics that I deeply admired. For her part, Mami, though more compassionate with strangers, brought to this relationship gratitude beyond measure for mercy shown in hardship a very long time ago. It was a gratitude time hadn't faded, and that too I deeply admired.

I rented a car at the airport and arrived at the unfamiliar apartment complex very late at night after getting lost, driving in tearful circles. My mother must have phoned Junior before I arrived; however it happened, when she opened the door, it was clear that the news had already reached her. She fell into my arms sobbing.

We traveled together to Puerto Rico to bury Titi Aurora.

I didn't break down until I was handed the envelope of cash that she had set aside with my name on it. We'd kept the old ritual: whenever she was going to Puerto Rico, I would lend her the money for the plane ticket. In recent years, I desperately wanted to give her the money, considering I could now afford it and she was living on Social Security. But she wouldn't have it: if she simply accepted the cash as a gift, she could never ask for it again, as, of course, she would surely need to.

Back in New York, I helped sort out the few wisps of a material life that Titi had left behind. There was precious little for someone known to us as a pack rat. Most of what remained was a closetful of gifts that she couldn't bear to part with or to use.

"WHAT ARE YOU so scared of?" Theresa asked. "What could possibly go wrong?" She had come with me from Pavia & Harcourt, her reassuring presence in chambers perhaps the only thing keeping me tethered to any semblance of sanity. My first month as a judge I was terrified, in keeping with the usual pattern of self-doubt and ferocious compensatory effort that has always attended any major transition in my life. I wasn't scared of the work. Twelve-hour days, seven-day weeks, were normal for me. It was my own courtroom that scared me. The very thought of taking my seat on the bench induced a metaphysical panic. I still couldn't believe this had worked out as dreamed, and I felt myself almost an impostor meeting my fate so brazenly.

At first, I worked around my anxiety by scheduling every single conference in my chambers. Until a case actually came to trial, I could skirt the problem. Finally, there came before me a case involving the forfeiture of the Hells Angels club-house in Alphabet City, and the marshals in charge of security drew the line. I could not meet with this bunch except in open court.

"All rise." The trembling would pass in a minute or two, I told myself, just as it always had since the first time I'd mounted the pulpit at Blessed Sacrament. But when I sat down, I noticed that my knees were still knocking together. I could hear the sound and wondered in complete mortification whether the microphone set in front of me on the table was picking it up. I was listening to the lawyers too, of course, as the telltale tapping under the table continued, a disembodied nuisance and reproach. Then a first question for the litigants occurred to me, and as I jumped in, I forgot about my knees, finding nothing in the world more interesting than the matter before me right then. The panic had passed; I had found my way into the moment, and I could now be sure I always would. Afterward, back in the robing room, I confessed my satisfaction: "Theresa, I think this fish has found her pond."

Epilogue

L OOKING BACK TODAY, it seems a lifetime ago that I first arrived at a place of belonging and purpose, the sense of having heard a call and answered it. When I placed my hand on the Bible, taking the oath of office to become a district court judge, the ceremony marked the culmination of one journey of growth and understanding but also the beginning of another. The second journey, made while I've been a judge, nevertheless continues in the same small, steady steps in which I'd taken the first one, those that I know to be still my own best way of moving forward. It continues, as well, in the same embrace of my many families, whose vital practical support has been bestowed as a token of something much deeper.

WITH EACH OF my own small, steady steps, I have seen myself grow stronger and equal to a challenge greater than the last. When, after six years on the district court, I was nominated to the Second Circuit Court of Appeals, and to the Supreme Court twelve years after that, the confirmation hearings would be, at each step, successively more difficult, the attacks more personal, the entire process faster, more brutally intense. But at each step, too, the numbers of family and community encircling me and coming to my defense would be exponentially greater.

Over a thousand people would attend my induction ceremony for the Second Circuit. A more intimate group of over three hundred friends and family stayed on to celebrate that occasion and to witness my very first official act as a judge of the Second Circuit, performed that very night: marrying Mami and Omar. Combining the festivities not only doubled the joy, making the party even livelier, but also permitted me to honor those closest to me and acknowledge a debt to them—to Mami especially—for their part in what I'd become. My awareness of that debt would not be felt so keenly again for years, until the moment when I unexpectedly saw Junior's face on the big television screen, crying his tears of joy at my nomination to the Supreme Court; the searing tears that image drew from my own eyes in turn would leave no doubt about how much the love of family has sustained me.

JUST AS I had to learn to think like a lawyer, I would have to teach myself to think like a judge. In my small, steady steps I have mastered the conceptual tools of a trial judge wrestling with fact and precedent and of an appellate judge dealing with the theory of law on a more abstract level. I have been a happy sponge, soaking up whatever lessons I could learn from mentors generous with time and spirit. I have been thrilled by the learning that came from the opportunities I've had to teach and the energy drawn from interaction with my law clerks and the freewheeling exchange of ideas I have nurtured in my chambers. Now my education continues on the Supreme Court as I reckon with the particular demands of its finality of review. Almost daily, people ask me what I hope my legacy will be, as if the story were winding down, when really it has just begun. I can only reply that if I were to determine in advance the character of my jurisprudence, mine would be a far more blinkered and unworthy legacy than I hope. My highest aspiration for my work on the Court is to grow in understanding beyond what I can foresee, beyond any borders visible from this vantage.

In this connection, one memory from high school days comes to mind. During my junior year, I was chosen to attend a conference of girls from Catholic schools all over the city. Over a weekend of discussions on religious and social issues, I found myself sparring again and again with one individual, a Hispanic girl who identified herself as a Marxist. I remember her wearing an impressive Afro of the sort I had seen before only on television; nothing so radical ever appeared in the halls of Cardinal Spellman High School.

The two of us were engaging with far more energy than anyone else at the table, a vigor that, for my part at least, derived not from the certainty of my convictions but from my love of the push and pull of ideas, the pleasure of flexing the rhetorical muscles I had been building in Forensics Club, and an eagerness to learn from the exchange. I argued, as I would so often with lawyers years later, not from a set position but by way of exploring ideas and testing them against whatever challenge might be offered. I love the heat of thoughtful conversation, and I don't judge a person's character by the outcome of a sporting verbal exchange, let alone his or her reasoned opinions. But in my opponent's responses I sensed an animosity that over the course of the weekend only grew.

After the final roundup session, at which we reflected on our experience of the meeting, I told her that I had very much enjoyed our conversation, and I asked her what had inspired the hostility that I sensed from her.

"It's because you can't just take a stand," she said, looking at me with such earnest disdain that it startled me. "Everything depends on context with you. If you are always open to persuasion, how can anybody predict your position? How can they tell if you're friend or foe? The problem with people like you is you have no principles."

Surely, I thought, what she described was preferable to its opposite. If you held to principle so passionately, so inflexibly, indifferent to the particulars of circumstance—the full range of what human beings, with all their flaws and foibles, might endure or create—if you enthroned principle above even reason, weren't you then abdicating the responsibilities of a thinking person? I said something like that.

Our conversation ended on that unsettled note, but I have spent the rest of my life grappling with her accusation. I have since learned how these considerations are addressed in the more complex language of moral philosophy, but our simple exchange that day raised a point that remains essential to me. There is indeed something deeply wrong with a person who lacks principles, who has no moral core. There are, likewise, certainly values that brook no compromise, and I would count among them integrity, fairness, and the avoidance of cruelty. But I have never accepted the argument that principle is compromised by judging each situation on its own merits, with due appreciation of the idiosyncrasy of human motivation and fallibility. Concern for individuals, the imperative of treating them with dignity and respect for their ideas and needs, regardless of one's own views—these too are surely

principles and as worthy as any of being deemed invio-
lable. To remain open to understandings—perhaps even to
principles—as yet not determined is the least that learning
requires, its barest threshold.

With every friend I've known, in every situation I've
encountered, I have found something to learn. From a task as
simple as boiling water, you can learn a worthwhile lesson.
There is no experience that can't avail something useful, be
it only the discipline to manage adversity. With luck, there
will be plenty of time ahead for me to continue growing and
learning, many more stories to tell before I can begin to say
definitively who I am as a judge.

Who I am as a human being will, I hope, continue to
evolve as well, but perhaps the essence is defined by now. The
moment when, in accordance with tradition, I sat in Chief
Justice John Marshall's chair and placed my hand on the
Bible to take the oath of office for the Supreme Court, I felt
as if an electric current were coursing through me, and my
whole life, collapsing upon that moment, could be read in
the faces of those most dear to me who filled that beautiful room. I looked out to see my mother with tears stream-
ing down her cheeks and felt a surge of admiration for this
remarkable woman who had instilled in me the values that
came naturally to her—compassion, hard work, and courage
to face the unknown—but who'd also grown with me as we
took our small steps together to close the distance that had
opened up between us in the early years. I might have been
little Mercedes as a child, but now I was equally my mother's
daughter. I saw Junior beaming proudly, and my family who
traveled from New York and Puerto Rico to be there, and so
many friends who have stood by me through the years. The
moment belonged as much to them as to me.

I sensed the presence too, almost visible, of those who had recently passed: my friend Elaine, who had suffered a series of strokes but to the very end managed to leaven both her own dying and the drama surrounding my nomination with her humor; Dave Botwinik, who had set this whole dream in motion toward reality.

Then I caught the eye of the president sitting in the first row and felt gratitude bursting inside me, an overwhelming gratitude unrelated to politics or position, a gratitude alive with Abuelita's joy and with a sudden memory, an image seen through the eyes of a child: I was running back to the house in Mayagüez with a melting ice cone we called a *piragua* running sweet and sticky down my face and arms, the sun in my eyes, breaking through clouds and glinting off the rain-soaked pavement and dripping leaves. I was running with joy, an overwhelming joy that arose simply from gratitude for the fact of being alive. Along with the image, memory carried these words from a child's mind through time: I am blessed. In this life I am truly blessed.

Acknowledgments

Before thanking the people who helped me with this book, I must thank the inordinately large number of friends and family, mentors and colleagues, who have made significant contributions to my life, without whom there might be no reason for a book. Even acquaintances and strangers have made lasting impressions. Just as I was unable to include in these pages many of my experiences and people who have played a part in my life, I cannot acknowledge all of you here by name. To those who have shared important parts of my life, know you are deeply valued even if you or those experiences are not mentioned.

There are many who helped me in the writing of this book by sharing memories or gathering information. If I do not acknowledge you here, it is because your importance in my life and my gratitude to you has already been made clear to the reader. Others who are vitally important to me today are not mentioned because you entered my life after I first became a judge, where this book ends.

I do want to give special thanks to a number of friends not included in the book who have been directly instrumental in the process of its creation and publication.

Given the demands of my day job, this book would not have been possible without the collaboration of Zara Houshmand. Zara, a most talented writer herself, listened to my endless stories and those of my families and friends, and helped choose those that in retelling would paint the most authentic picture of my life experiences. Zara, you are an incredible person with a special ability to help others understand and express themselves better; I am deeply indebted to your assistance. One of the most profound treasures of this process has been the gift of your friendship, which will last a lifetime.

I am truly grateful for the contributions of my editor at Alfred A. Knopf, George Andreou, in helping make my stories come alive. George's deft editorial touch added much, but he also expertly guided me through the publishing process. I am enormously grateful as well to Sonny Mehta, the publisher of Knopf, who has treated me with much kindness and attention. Everyone at Knopf with whom I have met and worked, and everyone at Random House, Inc., Knopf's parent, has extended assistance with professional skill and grace. I am appreciative of all of your efforts.

Research related to Puerto Rico, help in reviewing the manuscript, and translation of this book from English to Spanish were particularly important. I am especially indebted to three people for their tireless efforts in this part of the book's development. I can never catalogue all of the work they have volunteered in helping me with this book or the many gifts of love they have given me through the years. I can only say thank you to Xavier Romeu-Matta, a brilliant lawyer who was my law clerk during my first year as a federal district court judge; his wife, the accomplished writer Lyn Di Iorio, professor of English (and unofficial language and literature in Spanish expert) at the City College of New York and CUNY Graduate Center; and Emérida Rivera, who has traveled repeatedly throughout Puerto Rico to help in my research and proven by example that saintly hearts and souls still exist in the world. The Hunter College Center for Puerto Rican Studies also provided invaluable background materials. Thanks are due also to Ligia Pesquera and Ángel Rivera, whose kind hospitality supported our research in Puerto Rico; to Sylvia Gutiérrez, who assisted with travels; and to Lourdes Pérez, who provided background on Puerto Rican poetry.

I am grateful to Amanda Tong, Colin Wright, and Kate Beddall for their help in transcribing and translating interviews, and for the reflections they offered.

Another gift in the process of producing this book has been working with and befriending my book agent, Peter Bernstein, and his wife, Amy Bernstein, of the Bernstein Literary Agency. You both have shepherded this book with consummate professional skill, sage advice, and caring. I thank John S. Siffert of Lankler Siffert & Wohl LLP, and his wife, Goldie Alfasi, for introducing me to Peter and Amy and for being such supportive friends during this process. I also thank John for introducing me to Richard Hofstetter and Mark A. Merriman of Frankfurt Kurnit Klein & Selz, PC, and for their legal and professional advice. John, I am especially grateful for the wise legal counsel you gave me in drafting the book proposal, overseeing the contract negotiations, and reviewing this book. I have three brothers: my birth brother, you, and Robert A. Katzmann. All three of you have supported me through my recent life experiences in ways that cannot be acknowledged here but are inscribed in my heart.

Some friends who are not named in the text shared memories that appear in the book or reviewed the manuscript to offer advice. Each of you is special to me and I acknowledge you here in chronological order of your appearance in my life: Peter Kougasian, with whom I shared experiences at Princeton University, Yale Law School, and the New York County District Attorney's Office; Paula DiPerna, a journalist and author whose book *Juries on Trial: Faces of American Justice* provides an account of the child pornography trial; Cynthia Fischer, the second female partner at Pavia & Harcourt, and David Glasser, an associate then at the firm; Nicole Gordon, founding Executive Director of the New York City Campaign Finance Board; Mari Carmen Aponte, now United States ambassador to El Salvador and then member of the Puerto Rican Legal Defense and Education Fund (now LatinoJustice); Robert Sack, a former colleague on the United States Court of Appeals for the Second Circuit Court; and Jennifer Callahan, documentary film producer and writer.

Lee Llambelis and Ellis Cose, you encouraged me to write this book and guided me in the initial process of thinking about having it published. I give special thanks also to Sue Anderson and Kitty Reese: you pitched in each time I needed help to get things done while I worked on the book. You are all incredible friends. Thank you.

Finally, I thank Ricki Seidman, whom I worked with during my Supreme Court confirmation process and who has become a precious friend. Ricki tirelessly reviewed multiple revisions of this book and offered thoughtful suggestions that have improved it immeasurably.

A life filled with loving and caring family and friends such as mine is truly blessed.

Glossary

abuelita: grandma
aguinaldo: here, Christmas folk song
ají: pepper; hot pepper
arroz con gandules: rice and pigeon peas

Bendición, Abuelita: Bless me, Grandma; blessing
bisabuela: great-grandmother
brujería: witchcraft
burla: mockery

café con leche: coffee with milk
chiflado: literally, crazy, a looney, and used to translate for
    "stooge" in the title and show *The Three Stooges*
china: orange, as in the fruit
chuletas: pork chops
como una maldición: like a curse

Dame un cigarrillo: Give me a cigarette
despedida: farewell
Dios te salve, María, llena eres de gracia: El Señor es
contigo. Bendito tú eres entre todas las mujeres y bendito es

el fruto de tu vientre: Jesús. Santa María, Madre de Dios, ruega por nosotros pecadores, ahora y en la hora de nuestra muerte . . .

> Hail Mary, full of grace: The Lord is with thee. Blessed art thou among all women and blessed is the fruit of your womb: Jesus. Holy Mary, mother of God, pray for us sinners, now and in the hour of our death . . .
> (from the Roman Catholic "Hail Mary" prayer)

el jurutungo viejo: the boondocks; the end of the world
el luto: mourning
embusteros: liars
"En Mi Viejo San Juan": "In My Old San Juan." A bolero written by Puerto Rican composer Noel Estrada in 1943. It is considered by many Puerto Ricans to be a kind of unofficial anthem. It enshrines the narrator's desire to go back to his longed-for city by the sea, and the melancholy realization that this will never happen.
Es el precio de hacer negocios: It's the price of doing business
espera: wait
espiritismo: Spiritism
¡Estás loca!: You're crazy!

Feliz Navidad: Merry Christmas
fiambreras: lidded, stackable dinner pails made of iron or other metal; also, the food that is made elsewhere and delivered in these pails
ficha: a playing piece; usually refers to dominoes
flamboyán: flamboyant; also known in the anglophone Caribbean as the flame tree or the Royal Poinciana

grosella: a small acidic yellow or red berry that grows in backyards, or wild, in Puerto Rico; sometimes known as an Otaheite gooseberry

guagua: bus

güiro: musical instrument made from an elongated, hollowed-out gourd with notches on one side, played by rubbing a stick with tines along the notches

jíbaro: the straw-hatted peasant farmer or laborer who plays a significant role in Puerto Rican culture and identity; the values attributed to this almost mythical figure are being traditional, hardworking, plainspoken, and sagacious

la nata: cream; also, the skin on milk

la tetita: the tit; here, to denote the crunchy end of a loaf of Puerto Rican *criollo* bread

lechón asado: roasted pig

Mercedes chiquita: little Mercedes

merienda: midday meal; light lunch; snack

mi'jita: my dear; honey

Nacimiento: Nativity scene

nena: girl

¡No me molestes!: Don't bother me!

No tengas miedo: Don't be afraid

para: here, stop

picadillo: seasoned ground beef

Que Dios te bendiga, te favorezca, y te libre de todo mal y peligro: May God bless you, favor you, and deliver you from all evil and danger

¡Qué guapo!: He's so handsome!

¿Quieres una china?: Do you want an orange?

quinqué: country-style oil lamp

recao: an herb also known as *culantro,* or Thai parsley, which is one of the basic ingredients of the spice mixture known as *sofrito* used in so many Puerto Rican recipes

rosario: rosary

santos: saints; here, statues of saints

sebo de flande: mutton tallow used as a folk remedy for bruises and cuts

sofrito: seasoning sauce made of tomatoes, chopped peppers, onions, garlic, and *recao* or *culantro*

tamarindo: tamarind

¡Te vas a enfermar!: You'll get sick!

tío: uncle

titi: a term of endearment for *tía,* or aunt

tostones: fried green plantain

¿Tú estás ciego?: Are you blind?

¡Vámonos de parranda!: Let's go out caroling!; let's party!

velada: séance (although in Puerto Rico, the connotation is more often that of vigil, as for a corpse)

vendedor: salesman

vivero: livestock market

Yo soy Celina: I am Celina

A PUERTO RICO (REGRESO)
To Puerto Rico (I Return)

by José Gautier Benítez
Translated by Lyn Di Iorio

Por fin, corazón, por fin,	At last, my heart, at last,
alienta con la esperanza,	come alive with hope,
que entre nubes de carmín	for among crimson clouds
del horizonte al confín,	from the horizon end to end,
ya la tierra a ver se alcanza.	I can already see land.
Luce la aurora en Oriente	Dawn rises in the East
rompiendo pardas neblinas,	shattering dark mists,
y la luz, como un torrente,	and a torrent of light pours
se tiende por la ancha frente	on the wide swath
de verdísimas colinas.	of the deep green hills.
Ya se va diafanizando	The veil of thick fog lifts
de la mar la espesa bruma;	off the sea;
el buque sigue avanzando,	the ship advances,
y va la tierra brotando	and the land begins to rise
como Venus de la espuma.	like Venus from the foam.
Y allá sobre el fondo oscuro	And there on the dark ground
que sus montañas le dan,	of its mountains,
bajo un cielo hermoso y puro,	against a pure and lovely sky,

cerrada en su blanco muro,
mi bellísimo San Juan.

Y aunque esa ciudad amada,
mis afecciones encierra,
con el alma entusiasmada,
yo no me acuerdo de nada
sino de ver esa tierra.

Perdonadle al desterrado
ese dulce frenesí:
vuelvo a mi mundo adorado,
y yo estoy enamorado
de la tierra en que nací.

Para poder conocerla
es preciso compararla,
de lejos en sueños verla;
y para saber quererla
es necesario dejarla.

¡Oh! no envidie tu belleza,
de otra inmensa población
el poder y la riqueza,
que allí vive la cabeza,
y aquí vive el corazón.

enclosed by a white wall,
my beautiful San Juan.

And as a cherished city,
it holds all my loves,
and with an enthusiastic soul,
I don't recall
anything except seeing my
        homeland.

Forgive the exile
this sweet frenzy:
I return to my beloved world,
in love with the land where I
        was born.

To know her
you must compare her,
see her distant in your dreams;
and to love her
you need to leave her.

Ah! Do not let your beauty envy
the wealth and power
of another great nation,
because there is where the head
        lives,
and here is where the heart lives.

Y si vivir es sentir,
y si vivir es pensar,
yo puedo, patria, decir
que no he dejado vivir
al dejarte de mirar.

Que aunque es
templado y suave
no vive, no, en el ambiente
el pez de las ondas nave,
ni entre las ondas el ave,
ni yo, de mi patria ausente.

¡Patria! jardín del mar,
la perla de las Antillas,
¡tengo ganas de llorar!
¡tengo ganas de besar
la arena de tus orillas!

Si entre lágrimas te canto,
patria mía, no te asombres,
porque es de amor ese llanto,
y ese amor es el más santo
de los amores del hombre.

Tuya es la vida que aliento,
es tuya mi inspiración,
es tuyo mi pensamiento,
tuyo todo sentimiento
que brote en mi corazón.

And if to live is to feel,
and if to live is to think,
homeland, I can say
that I have not known how to live
since I stopped looking at you.

Though its climate be
    temperate and soft,
the seafaring fish cannot live in
    the air,
nor in waves can a bird soar,
nor can I thrive
away from my homeland.

Homeland! Garden of the sea,
pearl of the Antilles,
I feel like crying!
I feel like kissing
the sands of your shores!

If between tears I sing to you,
my land, do not be astonished,
because love is in these tears,
and this love is the holiest
of the loves of man.

Yours is the life that I breathe,
my inspiration is yours,
yours is my thought,
yours all feeling
that blooms in my heart.

Que haya en ti vida primero,
cuanto ha de fijarse en mí,
y en todo cuanto venero,
y en todo cuanto yo quiero,
hay algo, patria, de ti.

No, nada importa la suerte
si tengo que abandonarte,
que yo sólo aspiro a verte,
a la dicha de quererte
y a la gloria de cantarte.

My life flows from yours,
and in everything I deem
worthy,
and in everything I love,
there is something, my
homeland,
that belongs to you.

No, luck doesn't matter
if I have to leave you,
for I aspire only to see you,
to the good fortune of loving you
and the glory of singing to you.